Making Sense of Suburbia through Popular Culture

Making Sense of Suburbia through Popular Culture

Rupa Huq

B L O O M S B U R Y

LONDON • NEW DELHI • NEW YORK • SYDNEY

Bloomsbury Academic

An imprint of Bloomsbury Publishing Plc

50 Bedford Square
London
WC1B 3DP
UK

175 Fifth Avenue
New York
NY 10010
USA

www.bloomsbury.com

First published 2013

© Rupa Huq, 2013

British Library Cataloguing-in-Publication Data
A catalogue record for this book is available from the British Library.

ISBN: HB: 978-1-7809-3223-1
PB: 978-1-7809-3224-8
ePub: 978-1-7809-3258-3
ePDF: 978-1-7809-3259-0

Library of Congress Cataloging-in-Publication Data
A catalog record for this book is available from the Library of Congress.

Typeset by Newgen Imaging Systems Pvt Ltd, Chennai, India
Printed and bound in India

For Rafi

Contents

Acknowledgements

As no doubt all people who have authored books do, I have accumulated various debts of gratitude in the process of writing this one. I am grateful to individuals who have allowed me to rehearse some of my arguments prior to publication in speaking engagements on the subjects that have formed the content of these chapters. Andrew Harris of UCL and Christopher Daley at Westminster University invited me to address conferences that exposed me to various suburban cultural phenomena and also to make friends with other like-minded suburban theorists along the way including Clare Dwyer and David Gilbert who I spoke for as a result. Keith Negus invited me to speak on suburban pop at Goldsmiths, Mary-Jane Kehily and Sara Bragg got me involved in the Global Youth Cultures network and Sian Lincoln of Liverpool John Moores to speak on the ageing of subculture. Nazneen Ahmed, Caroline Rooney and Blake Brandes were also generous in their invitations to deliver a keynote at the Postcolonial Studies Youth Cultures conference at University of Canterbury at Kent and contribute to *Wasafiri*. My thanks also to Kira Kosnick and Harpreet Cholia for having me along to the Post-migrant Socialities workshop in Frankfurt.

At Kingston University conversations with Emma Casey, David Rodgers and others have been stimulating and informative. Julia Davidson has also been supportive in this project. A departmental grant enabled me to travel to Hostfra University in suburban Long Island which was my first ever visit to the USA in 2009; an eye-opener for me. Paul Watt and Gareth Millington of Birkbeck and York respectively were great colleagues to attend with both intellectually and as travel companions for the trip and our planned three-way writing project will still materialize at some point.

Further crucial lynchpins deserve special thanks for making this book happen. The Barrow Cadbury Trust was generous in affording me a grant towards teaching release, some of the ideas for this book germinated during that period of time. My editor Caroline Wintersgill was always enthusiastic about the notion of writing about suburbs through the prism of popular culture which others might have thought of as freakish. Once the copy was written, the process with Bloomsbury Academic was on the whole an efficient and enjoyable experience. Thanks must also go to Phil Bevin for his indexing skills.

The book is once more dedicated to Rafi who has put up with me throughout. To avoid this sounding like an Oscars speech it's probably best to end here. All it remains for me to do is to hope that every reader has as much fun reading the book as I did accessing all the material in the lead-up and in eventually writing it.

Rupa Huq
Ealing, January 2013

Seeking Culture in a Cultural Void?
The Relationship between Suburbia and Popular Culture

[Culture] . . . seeks . . . to make the best that has been taught and known in the world current everywhere, to make all men live in an atmosphere of sweetness and light, where they may use ideas, as it uses them itself, freely – nourished, and not bound by them.

(Mathew Arnold, *Culture and Anarchy*, 1869)

There is far too much of the suburban classes
Spiritually not geographically speaking. They're asses.
Menacing the greatness of our beloved England, they lie
Propagating their kind in an eightroomed style.

(Stevie Smith, 1949)

There are some concepts that lend themselves to watertight definition. We know that a recession is when an economy has experienced two quarters of negative growth and there is a clear formula for calculating gross domestic product (GDP) but by contrast we are not so clear on what exactly it is that unambiguously a 'suburb' may or may not be. Its derivative 'suburbia' also eludes easy definition notwithstanding that both are long established terms. The Compact Edition of the *Oxford English Dictionary* tells us that the origins and usage of the word 'suburb' go way back at least to Chaucer. Many of us have some sort of inklings about what this peculiarly Anglo-Saxon/Anglophone/Anglo-American notion is but there is no common agreement on what constitutes it. In the absence of any definitive definition of what we mean by suburbia, the concept has frequently formed in the popular imagination through representations of it in popular culture. Suburban imagery has changed over time: a rash of 1970s British tv sitcoms depicted suburban home furnishings in brown or even 50 shades of beige centring on couples like *George and Mildred, Terry and June* or Gerry and Margot (*The Good Life*). Age old US depictions feature white picket fences and manicured lawns of outward perfection, for example *Desperate Housewives* (2005–12). This book considers suburbia as a sociocultural category and examines its production and reproduction through representations in popular culture: onscreen, on the pages of popular fiction and musically. The angle taken of cultural depictions departs from the more familiar focus of academic suburban studies which have more commonly been grounded in urban planning approaches or concerned with building design and density of houses per hectare. The cultural significance of suburbia it will be argued is of critical importance. After all both narratives and practices contribute to our understanding of the meaning of place and of broader socio-spatial categories such as 'city', 'country' and a third lying somewhere in between the two 'suburbs'. The book builds on the valiant few academic examples that have taken this approach which inevitably have become dated particularly given the unfolding of new ways in which to read popular culture in the Web2 era (Silverstone 1997; Spigel 2001a; Webster 2001; Bueka 2004). In some senses this book then sets out to determine whether there is a separate cultural category of 'suburban' that characterizes the media texts to be described.

The social sciences tend to consider topics of enquiry in problem-solving terms. Accordingly in the broad area of the sociology of place, considerations of suburbia have tended to be crowded out by the attention commanded by the city and work centring on the urban 'problem'. Yet the suburbs were conceived of as solutions to city ills where urban overcrowding and squalor were substituted with aspirational space. In considering popular culture the book raises key questions around both the public visibility of the suburbs which are paradoxically associated with the private realm and the agendas of those doing the portraying. Methodologically a textual approach is employed with analysis of novels, television programmes, films and popular music. These different mediums are each approached by separate chapters in order to examine to what extent suburban portrayals follow or subvert conventions of genre and how far they further our understandings of suburban life. Narrative structure and content will be twin considerations, after all popular culture can legitimate social practices and help us make sense of understandings of phenomena in selecting and presenting material to us with its often subtle unstated theoretical/ political/ideological frameworks. Suburban-set cultural products and figures will be discussed including hopefully some lesser-known candidates alongside the emblematic. Some of the examples discussed pride themselves in 'social realism' – perhaps the ultimate being the reality television show, while in others suburban characters and situations appear as comic foils or light relief. The book aims to be comprehensive in coverage but makes no pretentions to be exhaustive. Suburbia is often portrayed as backdrop rather than subject of these cultural products (e.g. the films *Donnie Darko* or *Hope and Glory*).

Culture and representation

'Culture' too is not easily defined but since the 1869 version quoted at the top of this chapter the social sciences have undergone what has been described as a 'cultural turn' which one suspects Mathew Arnold would have approved of. Many have proffered differing explanations including Scott and Marshall (2005:132–3) who in their *Oxford Dictionary of Sociology* define culture as 'all that in human society which is socially rather than biologically transmitted . . . a general term for the symbolic and learned aspects of human society'. They elaborate that popular culture is 'more widespread and accessible to everyone' (ibid. 2005:504). At the same time it seems that both popular culture and suburbia have constantly needed justification in academic circles as subjects worthy of being taken seriously. Stuart Hall (1981) has powerfully argued that popular culture matters and called it a 'battleground', a potential counter-hegemonic site of resistance against a culture of the powerful. The devaluing of the study of popular culture can be seen in debates on 'dumbing down' that have been propagated both in the United Kingdom and United States in the past couple of decades (e.g. Medved 1992; Washburn and Thornton 1996; Scruton 1998). The accusation largely made here is that the pre-twentieth century ideals of the cultural experience as enriching and civilizing as described by Matthew Arnold above or Raymond Williams (1976:77) has been crushed under the weight of sensationalism, titillation and quite simply junk. The pros and cons of the subject as an area of academic scrutiny polarized between defenders and those claiming falling standards seem to have been a perennial topic for example in the trade journal of the UK academic the *Times Higher Education Supplement* (*THES*). Colin McCabe has argued that there is no agreed precise definition of popular culture telling the *THES* that 'Contemporary culture is effectively impossible to analyse, not least because it cuts across the humanities and social sciences in ways that make it a very resistant object to disciplines that were constituted at the end of the 19th century' (Davies 1995). Indeed what we could group under its umbrella has grown exponentially. Popular culture as a subject of study is nonetheless popular with students; Davies (1995) lists among its remit 'not only popular entertainment such as *EastEnders*, Hollywood movies and rock music, but also shopping, cooking or the clothes people choose to wear'. The products and processes of popular culture continually change over time; once we might have put the pre-mass produced folk song or musical hall performance into this category; now such phenomena are at best consigned to the history books. Even at the start of this century the web had not reached the all-pervasive influence that it now has in our lives and daily interactions. Cheque books for example have been rendered obsolete by electronic banking and payment by plastic. The old word 'debt' has been replaced by 'credit' which fuels so much of our access to culture as we fill our homes with the spoils of capitalism with consumer durables and lifestyle aids made in China.

What though of representation? Gramsci's concept of hegemony is key to the role of popular culture in constructing versions of suburbia embodying national values as this process is one where no one is forced into anything but consensus instead prevails in the preservation of the status quo. A further staple of many introductory media and communications textbooks is the 'hypodermic syringe' view of the media's function, as propagated by the Frankfurt School of cultural theorists and social scientists in interwar Germany who were greatly influenced by the rise of Hitler and his mastery of the art of propaganda. This broad position saw the mass media literally injecting beliefs, ideas and values into a passive public of cultural dupes. This theory of popular culture as narcotic/anasthesia has been much criticized since its appearance which for its underestimation of the public. Far from being inert, empty vessels with no choice but to be influenced by the messages of popular culture, today's media literate consumers are instead active audiences who are capable of interpreting popular cultural meanings for themselves whether they realize it or not, even if the act of consumption of, for example the act of watching television may be relatively passive in itself, for example having the television on as 'background' to other activities which might including surfing the web.

David Morley has claimed (1998:491) 'In societies such as ours, where increasing numbers of people are quite alienated from the processes of formal politics on which "serious television" focuses, it would be politically suicidal to fail to take seriously the field of popular culture in which people do find their attachments.' The ubiquity of popular cultural forms means that unthinkingly we are almost all constantly processing and interacting with multiple forms of media and popular cultural products which are embedded into our everyday social practices and increasingly complex lives. Counter-hegemonic processes can include using new and social media to answer back. Representations on their own are never complete; they are part of a dialogue with their audience – particularly with internet forums, blogging and tweeting. They reflect ongoing social changes and can in turn inform suburban social perceptions and practices as well as holding a mirror up to them. Images of suburbia in popular culture will be subjectively interpreted differently by different audiences in various ways. Stereotyping is another trait that the observer of popular culture must be aware of (Perkins 1979). This practice often has much in common with 'othering' and in the portrayal of ethnic minorities can render populations as subordinate with simplification and cultural shorthand implying the superiority of 'us' (the majority or mainstream) against 'them' (the other). In communicating social stereotypes popular culture can reinforce dominant discourses but popular culture also has the power to upset received wisdom and alter perceptions as new stereotypes replace the old.

Media manipulation was a notable line taken by the Frankfurt School. Other factors that underpin our current understandings of how both popular culture operates and suburbia has developed were unforeseen by them. Globalization – the process whereby individuals, groups and nations become increasingly interdependent – is now taken as a given. Advocates point out how it diffuses cultural products allowing its consumers to act at a distance in enabling access to them but the resultant heterogeneity of culture could be criticized following Frankfurt logic as illusory: the so-called choice it could be argued is a sham with only different offerings available from within homogeneous mass culture. A pessimistic reading of globalization sees it as eroding the authenticity of 'local' cultures and instead substituting an Americanized 'global' mush which is unreflexive and not related to any real individualization. A sceptical view might see local identities and regionalization as being under threat of being steamrollered by globalization. Converse views are spelt out by David Held et al. (1999) who identify 'hyperglobalizers' as keenest on the phenomenon as opposed to 'sceptics', with 'transformationalists' occupying a third space. He argues that the power of national governments is diminishing as they are unable to control the effects of market processes or environmental threats from outside their borders leading to a loss of faith in national governments among individuals. The consequence is that both nation-states and relations between them are transforming as a result of improved communications, reflexivity and multiculturalism to name but three. These same observations could apply to suburbia at large which has outgrown stereotypical ideas of its remit as unchanging and steeped in tradition.

The suburban context

The rejoinder to the question 'why study culture?' given the intersection of topics under consideration in this book must be 'why study suburbia?' The latter has not historically been an abiding preoccupation of the social sciences. Compared to the copious body of work that constitutes 'urban sociology' looking at disorder and divisions, the suburbs are relatively under-researched for the reason that they are considered to be devoid of problems and instead fairly peaceable and self-sufficient. The intersection of 'suburbia' and 'popular culture' is ever-more pertinent given that the implication one takes away from many forays into suburban territory from the commentariat is that suburbia is something of a cultural void or desert. There is a case to be made for the very fact that suburbs are seen as unremarkable and conformist allowing artistic endeavour to flourish there (MacDonald 2010). The London listings guide *Time Out* magazine in a 2006 feature mused 'Soulless patches of urban ennui or hotbeds of creativity?' neatly summarizing the two sides of this argument.[1] In the same article the poet Tobias Hill declared 'On the whole the suburban dream is unfulfilled. The dystopian emptiness of suburban streets, young people hanging out at bus stops and in train stations, desperate just for a glimpse of strangers, just to collide with anything or anyone.' Yet nonetheless there are multiple suburbias which in the post-war era between them have proved to be fertile ground for fictitious portrayals and more recently reality television. Suburbia then despite being something that is often associated with defensible space and the realm of the private becomes conversely the stuff of spectacle in its onscreen representations, consumed in multiple ways: digitally as downloads or accessed on mobile phones or other handheld devices as well as more established modes such as in book-form in novels or seeping out of speakers and headphones in its sonic and aural representations. There is, as will be seen in the chapters of this book, a powerful suburban iconography served up through popular culture: picket fences, picture windows, sunshine gates, semi-detached dwellings topped off by green lawns and well-kempt hedges. These symbolic landscapes say much about idealized, dominant values fed to us of suburban cultures.

Suburbia is something that we have an intrinsic feel for yet exactly what passes for it seems to have varied from place to place and time to time: specific locales that are considered as suburbs have changed over time with suburban expansion. Dines (2009:31) remarks 'It is unsurprising that people so often deny they live in a suburb even when the area in which they reside confirm to every planner's definition of one.' The word 'suburban' seems to be a pejorative one. It is in some ways suburbia is metaphorical rather than a literal or geographic term, a mindset as opposed to a term of strict definition. One of the narrow features of suburbia that typically urbanites have fled from is whiteness/cultural backwardness. Defining what constitutes a suburb is almost made easier by reversing the question and looking at what it is not. The suburbs have a number of features that sharply contrast with those of the inner city. Suburbia has always evoked the idea of safety and security whereas the inner city has been equated with risk and danger. Suburbs are predominantly residential districts associated with population sprawl to accommodate the burgeoning workforce of the city. The expression 'bright lights, big city' conjures up a pulsating, throbbing buzzy space, ideally suited to the young, free and single whereas suburbia is associated with quiet sleepiness and middle aged familial suffocation. Inner cities are old and sometimes crumbling while suburbia is comparatively new having experienced its most rapid growth occurring in the interwar years in the United Kingdom, or post-war years in the United States. In short the suburb is of the city but positioned at its periphery rather than at its core.

Classic suburbia, as understood in this book, is curiously almost an exclusively Anglo-Saxon phenomenon, the basic tenets of its prescription also apply to Canada, New Zealand and Australia as well as the United Kingdom and United States. MacDonald (2010:30–1) explains, 'The idea of moving up the social hierarchy and out if the city was a distinct process in the English speaking world, making those suburbs a privileged socio-economic belt.' Urban socio-spatial relations are often the reverse of this situation in continental Europe: in France

Table 1.1 Some key events in suburban development

	United Kingdom	**United States**
Victorian advent of modern suburb	Carriage class suburbia built for well to do, alongside railway cottages, for example the three termini of London Underground's District Line: Wimbledon, Richmond and Ealing.	Notion of suburbia embodying the American dream takes root. 1853: Llewellyn Park prototypical gated residential community founded in New Jersey.
1900s–1920s	Popularization of mortgages; Stanley Baldwin (Conservative Prime Minister three times between 1923 and 1937) promoted suburban pastoral values tapping into this vital votebank.	Shift in suburban developments as the car-owning lifestyle becomes central to them and their character is less planned around public transport.
1930s	J. B. Priestly on three phases of England (1934); 4 million houses built in interwar years.	Great Depression 1934: Federal Housing Administration established.

(Continued)

Table 1.1 Continued

	United Kingdom	**United States**
1940s–landscape in transition	War-time bombing damages some of urban landscape, for example Coventry Cathedral. Anderson shelters installed in a nation's suburban back-gardens.	1944: GI Bill (Serviceman's Readjustment Act) aimed at increasing supply of Federal Housing Authority guaranteed property. 1947: First Levittown opens at Long Island, New York.
1950s–post-war optimism	Austerity gives way to boom years as fruits of consumer capitalism popularized. Britain's aristocrat Prime Minister Harold Macmillan declares during 1959 election campaign 'you've never had it so good'.	Critiques of suburbia in influential sociological studies including Riesman's (1950) *The Lonely Crowd*, Whyte's (1956) *The Organization Man* and Mumford (1961) decry suburban conformity/ homogeneity.
1960s	Swinging London. Hippie and counterculture movement, student sit-ins on higher education campuses and in suburban art-schools.	Home ownership rocketed from 40% of the population at the start of the Second World War to 60% by 1960. From 1945 to 1960 gross national product grew by 250%, particularly under President Eisenhower. Betty Friedan's second-wave feminism.
1970s	World economic crisis. Right to Buy policy introduced by Margaret Thatcher's governments (1979–90) triggering the sale into private hands of former suburban council houses.	1973 oil crisis, Watergate and aftermath of failed Vietnam war often seen as contributing to weakening in authority of American way of life.
1980s	Barrat homes, private new build estates as council house building slows. Retro developments such as Prince Charles' Poundbury village.	Reagan-omics, neo-conservative ideology promoting individual values triumphs.
1990s and on	Exurbia and rise of retail parks and out-of-town shopping. Archetypally suburban Prime Minister John Major followed by Middle England-loving Tony Blair Collapse of retail chain-stores in shift to online transactions and out of town shopping changing landscape of suburban high street..	Strip mall suburbia as less well-defined city centres, United States as world power in decline both in terms of political influence and as tiger economies of China begin to challenge it in manufacturing output.

peripheral districts at the edge of cities are more frequently associated with crime, unemployment and immigration than British or American suburban tranquillity to the point that many English language chroniclers of the country leave the word 'banlieue' (literally 'suburb') untranslated as seen in the gritty film *La Haine* (1995). Here attititudinal factors make it at odds with the dullsville/pleasantville British or American suburb. Across the Anglo American divide there are distinct shared recognizably suburban traits however there are importantly differences of scale and history. Table 1.1 attempts to capture these. While the words of Jackson (1985:188) writing in US context that 'No other invention has altered the urban form more than the internal combustion engine' applies on both sides of the Atlantic, it remains the case that car culture is more pronounced in North American and Australasian cases. UK cities and their corresponding suburbs were often planned around public transport and their infrastructure survives and is constantly being updated. Canadian band Arcade Fire's celebrated 2010 album *The Suburbs* reminisces on the title track about a key rite of passage associated with a suburban upbringing:

> In the suburbs/ I, I learned to drive/
> And you told me/ I'd never survive
> Grab your mother's keys, we're leaving.

For a teenager growing up in London with its comprehensive transport network a driving licence would not necessarily be a requirement of suburban adolescence.

To some extent suburbia captures stereotypical features of what we take as characteristically national traits in the United Kingdom and United States. For Dines (2009:13), 'houses speculatively built after the Second World War, unfenced and reminiscent in their styling of early ranch homesteads, evoke the wilderness of the American frontier . . . the desire for freedom and opportunity that residents share with the early pioneers of the west'. Complicating any satisfactory definitive comprehensive list of overarching British features is the fact that the United Kingdom includes Scotland, Wales and Northern Ireland as well as the more obvious component of England. Most attempts at conceptions of 'British' values have almost always meant white 'English' ones. Parekh (2000:16) elaborates: 'these range from the humble cuppa to the grandeur of monarchy and parliament'. Prime Minister John Major in a paraphrase of George Orwell referred to 'invincible green suburbs' in his characteristics. Parekh (2000) reminds us that a distinct attempt was made to fuse this ill-defined notion of Britishness revolving around nostalgia and commemoration with elements of multiculturalism and modernity in the 'cool Britannnia' project of early Blairism.

British suburban house design has espoused the twin traits of (i) derivative (traditional brick-built construction and touches such as, neo-baronial turrets, stained glass details in windows and the whole style of Mock Tudor) and (ii) futurism (art deco modernist semis). Suburban houses have had to move with the times. Combined retrospection with cutting edge design meant that by the 1930s houses were being built to house labour saving devices of consumer capitalism and with garages to accommodate car-owning families. For Gardner (2003) their magnetic pull to the Americans is understandable:

> Lower crime rates, cleaner air, homogeneous settings, home ownership, and good schools have drawn millions of Americans to this middle landscape. In the arts, however, cities continue dominate their suburban neighbors. The arts were never a part of the lure of suburbia, so, as C.G. Vasiliadis points out, 'the relative absence of culture in suburbia is one of the major reasons for its stereotyped image of blandness'.

Although the suburb was conceived of as a refuge away from the negative aspects of the city, later cultural depictions of suburbia often portray it as a place to escape *from*. Ernest Hemingway is said to have commented that Oak Park, the middle-class Protestant Chicago suburb he was raised in, consisted of 'wide lawns and narrow minds' (Lynn 1995). Continually in the memoir suburbia is seen as a site that authors left behind. The now discontinued British ITV 'quality' arts documentary series the *South Bank Show* for example in its programmes on subjects as wide-ranging as film director David Lean, author Hanif Kureishi and the band Blur took their subjects (in the third case singer Damon Albarn) back to their suburban childhoods, literally in the latter two cases of Bromley and Colchester, Essex and in interview with Lean who grew up in Croydon. The implication was that these now-cultural-sophisticates could not wait to escape, this is heard in the narration of Melvyn Bragg with Lean and pictured with Kureishi and Albarn whose journeys back to their childhoods by train have a 'Return of the Native' quality about them. Channel 4 in 2010 screened a series *The House that Made Me* in which over four programmes celebrities were confronted with recreated interiors of their childhood homes in the exact locations: one per week. The Channel 4 website explains 'Famous figures take an emotional trip back to meticulous recreations of the homes they were brought up in, exploring how their past shaped who they are today.'[2] In the show physical recreations of interior contexts of the respective celebrity's childhood homes made it the highly graphic televisual equivalent of the documentary series *The House I Grew Up In* from Radio 4 (2007–11). In the case of comedian Michael Barrymore and the singer Jamelia this meant a narrative of how they had 'made good' after growing up on council estates in the 1960s and 1990s respectively. With comedy actor Sanjeev Bhaskar and singer Boy George the programme in each case focused on how they had escaped the suffocating clutches of their suburban origins (Heston in the west London Borough of Hounslow and Eltham in South East London respectively). Both expressed surprise at social change in their hometowns since the 1970s the period in which the reconstruction was set – although as Peter Hall (2007) has pointed out the murder of Stephen Lawrence in 1994 long after George O'Dowd left means that Eltham is now in the minds of the general public forever associated with this event. The inclusion of Kureishi (born of an Indian father and English mother) and Bhaskar (a second-generation Hindu Indian) as archetypes of suburbia are testimony to its social transformation, although in the interviews during these programmes when they were taken back to these roots, both pointed out how when they were growing up Bromley and Heston were predominantly white.

This disavowal of suburbia tendency is continued in the printed page as suburb has often framed autobiography. Dartford for example is ever present in the early chapters of Rolling Stones guitarist Keith Richards's (2010) book *Life* as are Ealing and Richmond where the band played early gigs. The film director John Boorman (2003) named his effort *Adventures of a Suburban Boy* which begins with his experiences as a schoolboy in Sutton, South London, before the outbreak of the Second World War formed the basis of his film *Hope and Glory* (1987). Its parochial child-eyed innocence at unfolding events from an unthreatening semi is a stark contrast from some of his other directorial examples which include the dystopian nightmare of *Exorcist II* (1977) and the Burma-set *Beyond Rangoon* (1995). J. G. Ballard named his autobiography *Miracles of Life: An Autobiography Shanghai to Shepperton*. The writer Tim Lott's book *The Scent of Dried Roses* (1996) in its 2009 reissue as a Penguin classic gained the subtitle 'One family and the end of English Suburbia'. The publisher's website promises an elegy to 'the pebble-dashed home of his childhood and the rapidly changing landscape of post-war suburban England. It is a story of grief, loss and dislocation, yet also of the power of memory and the bonds of family love.'[3] The suburb that he describes is Southall, West London, home of light industry and scene of Lott's youth which experienced waves of migration from the Irish, the Carribeans and best known Sikh Punjabis. For his brother and him 'We bolted . . . Southall was a dump . . . predictable, safe, conservative, limited in scale and possibility' (Lott 1996:29). In later years, Lotts's mother took her own life naming the downhill trajectory of the area in her suicide note. The book has been the subject of academic controversy provoking a response article from Brah (1999) who rejected the book as a coded racism; something Lott has always denied. Indeed Southall is far from predictable. Although Southall railway station's sign helpfully announces the destination in Punjabi as well as English, among the area's newest inhabitants are Somalis who have their own stretch of cafes on South Road and mosque just off it. The retro-styled jacket designs of Griff Rhys Jones *Semi Detached* (2006) and Andrew Collins' *Where Did it All Go Right?* (2004) also suggest youthful surrounds of suburban security although these two examples are more nostalgia-tinged than Lott's invective. In all of these examples there is a sense though that the authors eventually 'outgrew' the spaces inhabited by their childhood selves, as with the *South Bank Show* portrait of the artist shows mentioned above (apart from Boorman and Richards fleeing through). Higher education can be another motor of social change with relocation to study away from suburbia. The effect of the trebling of university fees, a policy due to be introduced by the UK government may cut off this exposure to city living that the tertiary sector used to bring suburban youth.

Suburbia and shifting national norms

The building of improved public transport routes and arterial road networks (ribbon development in the United Kingdom, highways in United States) connecting what was often former farmland to the city made expanding populations in the suburbs feasible. The distinction of suburb versus inner city positing salubriousness and space on one side with urban decay and built-up environment on the other is as I have argued elsewhere (Huq 2007, 2008a,b, 2013) (and as the examples to follow will illustrate) hopelessly outdated. Another way of thinking about the city is of the 'sprawling metropolis' but it is precisely this sprawl which the suburbs are defined by. While the city is a competitive thrusting place where the machismo bravado of the male breadwinner thrives the suburb is more a domain of domesticity where the wife is left behind with their offspring. This dynamic can be seen in numerous portrayals: the classic (and remade) *Stepford Wives*, *Desperate Housewives* through to *Mad Men*. Yet the coming of the dual-earner household and increasingly common same sex coupledom single-parent family or even single-person household have changed these old stereotypes. Gender politics are explored further in Chapter 6 but the issue needs flagging up here at the start as gender is a running theme throughout all of this book's content.

Of course culture has a long history in suburbia but in forms that urban elitists may not approve of: as a physical presence public examples exist in high street department stores, shopping centres, bingo halls and cinemas; even if the fortunes of some of these attractions has waned in recent years to be replaced by the multiplex or retail park positioned more out of town. In the United Kingdom, well-known high street chains like Woolworths have disappeared, olde English pubs have become Polski Sleps (Polish delicatessans) or even Tesco supermarkets. Given that suburbs have been so associated with a consumerism it is entirely fitting that other aspects of suburban popular culture have become more privatized than ever: the home cinema system is an update of the age-old cultural pursuit of the television set. The age-old saying dictates that an Englishman's home is his castle: both the home itself and car-culture, a by-product of being houseproud spawn their own rituals, for example weekend gardening, DIY or washing the car on a Sunday. Yet suburbia has transformed, as has society at large. It could arguably be described in keeping with national culture as being less privatized and more than ever a product of modernity and consumer capitalism. Blake Morrison (2012) has claimed: 'The British invariably perceive the countryside as being under threat, whether from bombs, developers, tourism, climate change or the passage of time. This makes our literature nostalgic – a land of lost content.' In the face of the release of the UK 2011 Census Results detailing how more mixed-race, foreign-born and less god-fearing and married the United Kingdom had become, right-wing commentators alleged that Britishness itself was threatened, yet this has always been an amalgam constantly undergoing transition even if it rests on (declining) tradition.

The suburbs are in many ways ordinary: according to estimates some 80 per cent of Britons live in them (Barker 2009). America meanwhile is often described as 'the world's most suburbanised country' (Jack 2008). It gave us mall culture for example that is still unfolding in UK developments like the chain of Westfield centres. Suburbia importantly embodies aspiration in both the United Kingdom and United States. The suburbs have tended not to be a subject of sociological concern in the same way as the urban question has preoccupied because it has tended to be seen as relatively unproblematic and even self-sufficient. Sociology has frequently tended to engage in a quest for social problems to be approached in problem-solving terms hence the fascination with the urban seen as synonymous with danger and deviance. Indeed the implication has repeatedly been said that the inner city was hollowed out with de-population to the suburbs. An associated term is that of 'white flight' (Frey 1977; Avila 2006) and the associated notion that those who could (usually white) go out in search of a better quality of life away from the squalor of the inner city. The suburbs were invested in with much hope presenting an optimistic vision of lifestyle removed from the frenetic pace of metropolitan existence. The exodus from the city positioned the suburb as refuge as well as imbued with optimism. Raynor (1969:21) talks of 'the great migration . . . towards the suburbs and residential towns by the middle class, who have been searching not only for better physical surroundings but also a more exclusive and superior social environment by which they could distinguish themselves from people in the manual classes'. The suburb then despite being patronizingly sneered at by intelligentsia and treated with condescension is a place of aspiration and having 'made it'. Thompson (1982:16) describes the traditional model 'new suburbanites . . . desert[ing] the old town centres, escaping from increasing dirt, noise, stench, and disease, dissatisfied with the social confusion of mixed residential areas and with the inconvenience of traditional town houses for the style of life they wanted to pursue'. In this sense suburbs were initially a site of choice as opposed to the constraint of the city. Correspondingly depictions of suburbia have captured the hopes and made statements about issues of their times; these can be the times they were written in as well as the era they are set if they are looking back, for example homosexuality was beneath the radar of mainstream popular culture in the 1950s and 1960s but the film *Far from Heaven* (2002) and series *Mad Men* (2007–present) both designed for modern audiences incorporate this into their narrative. *Far from Heaven* (2002) and *Safe* (1995) both directed by Todd Haynes include Julianne Moore as the American suburban housewife as does the multi-temporal *The Hours* (2002). Some variation is in *A Single Man* (2002) where she is plays an English divorcee living in LA and in *The Kids Are Alright* (2010) depicting a lesbian couple (making it unclear exactly who is the 'wife') and their family situated firmly in suburbia where they instil middle-class values into their children including sending thank you notes for presents received. This final example shows the variety of family forms in post-millennial times as the only one of these films set in the present.

In the United Kingdom suburban variants include council house suburbia: Becontree in Dagenham, on the East London Essex border or Burnage in Manchester are examples. Conversely in the United States, a country where state provision is treated with suspicion (witnessed recently in the ferocious opposition mounted against Obama's healthcare plans which by British standards are restrained) the American dream translated easily into suburban self-reliance. US suburban layouts are generally more spacious than their British counterparts of semi-detached and terraced homes systematically laid out on a grid-plan system with enclosed front and back gardens. There are touches of neo-baronial grandeur in the garrison effect of the heavy front door or turreted and stained glass stylings but the average square footage of the suburban semi is comparatively modest, certainly in comparison to the detached affair we see in the film version of Richard Yates' 1961 novel *Revolutionary Road* pointed out by the estate agent, played by Kathy Bates as a 'sweet little house'. The yellow-coloured blue collar cartoon family of the Simpsons of Springfield too inhabit a home on its own plot despite Homer's everyman status. Both of these houses from two very different portrayals of suburbia show square footage that would be considered fairly vast compared to that occupied by the average British suburban home. As an *Economist* (18 December 2010) feature on the joys of baking claimed with commendable succinctness 'Britons yearn for tradition, but these days live busy, rather atomised lives. . . . [in] . . . their tiny, expensive homes'.

The central importance of public transport as key stimulus to the advent of suburbia can be seen in the classic fiction since seen as archetypal suburban novel *Diary of a Nobody*, which began as columns in the satirical magazine *Punch*. Here key character Charles Pooter travels from his home comforts in Holloway to 'the city' home of his workplace by bus and conveys commuter grumblings to the reader. The Cheap Trains Act of 1883 heralded a dramatic rise in the number of affordable suburban rail services linking outlying districts to London's city centre first by rail and then by underground. The same pattern can be seen in the US railroad. In early series of the television drama *Mad Men* for example (2007–present) the central character Don Draper makes the daily journey to Ossining Metro-North (an express station), the last stop on the line on his commute home on the Hudson Line from Madison Avenue in New York. There is a clear demarcation between city/work and home/family. Ossining was also home to John Cheever an extensive early chronicler of suburbia in novels such as his Wapshot series (Bueka 2004) and short stories such as 1964's *the Swimmer* which became a film starring Burt Lancaster. The latter is centred on the suburban pool which is a rarity in British houses but can be seen in various US representations from *The Graduate* to the very first episode of *Desperate Housewives*. Later UK suburbs/new towns and US examples were more reliant on car culture offering utopian possibilities positioned near a convenient junction of the freeway or orbital ring road. This meant for less social mixing in the jostle for rush hour space documented by the fictitious Mr Pooter and more privatized space between inhabitants. Indeed motorized transport is a prerequisite for visiting some of the more recent variants of suburban developments on the physical landscape, for example the state-of-the art air-conditioned multi-screen cinema and leisure complex in place of the old suburban picture palace or the out of town superstore and retail park in place of the hollowed out high street and its sometimes worse-for-wear 'department store'. Some of these nouveau quasi-suburban creations combine elements of all of these, for example Manchester's Trafford Centre with attractions including the high-end department store Selfridges and multiplex located at the intersection of major motorway junctions making it accessible to most of the north of England, the midlands and also Wales. These developments could legitimately be described as 'exurban', that is in areas beyond the original suburbs. They constitute what Garreau (1991) calls 'edge city' as they are always located by arterial fast roads and home to plate glass office space, retail parks and leisure complexes.

Rising living standards are commonly associated with the advent of suburbia. For this reason it has also often seen as a shallow by-product of capitalism as can be seen for example in the scathing early criticisms of commentators such as Whyte or Mumford. Paul Barker (2009) has stressed the importance of easily available mortgages to the rise of UK home ownership. Via the character George Bowling in the novel *Coming Up for Air*, which is discussed in Chapter 2, George Orwell (1939:14) has written 'Nine-tenths of the people in Ellesmere Road are under the impression that they own their houses', a falsehood that they have accepted when they are in reality at the mercy of the money-lenders. In the United States the GI Bill paved the way for an expansion of suburban housing and people who had been raised in rural Hicksville or city tenements to the new suburban frontier. Federal funds helped particularly under President Eisenhower who instituted the network of freeways that linked these suburbs to cities. Quoting figures from the US Federal Reserve which show a rise of car registrations by 67 per cent from the period 1948 to 1959 and increase from 20 million suburban residents to 55 million in the 20 years from 1940 to 1960, Winters (2008) remarks: 'The postwar suburban household was home to Formica counters, Tupperware containers, and plastic Hula-Hoops. Once-exotic materials moved from the laboratory to the store shelves with amazing speed. Indeed, the 1950s saw an explosion of all manner of former luxuries that became mass consumer items.' Further figures he quotes from the Federal Reserve capture the wider industrial effect of this burgeoning market in showing US industrial production of consumer goods increasing steeply by 67 per cent from 1948 to 1959. Certainly consumerism was another culture that shaped the creation of suburbia, particularly in its post-war expansion era. The US writer Scott Donaldson (1969:73) wrote: 'Steadily the suburbanite fills every inch of available space with the "latest" in furnishings and equipment, and the overall impression is one of cramped clutter.' Indeed this pressure to constantly 'keep up with the Jones" is continually seen in films picturing suburbia, sometimes with humour, poking fun at this most suburban of traits. In the time-travel film *Peggy Sue Got Married* (1986) when the main eponymous character rewinds back to 1960, her father buys an Edsel, the car that famously flopped on the American motor market and the rest of the family cannot work out why Peggy Sue falls about laughing remarking that her father 'was always doing crazy stuff'.

In latter decades inner-city gentrification has been a notable socio-economic and cultural fact that has doubtless led to shifting perceptions of what the form and function of the suburb is and contributed to a mismatch between what suburbia was meant to be and what it has become. This has been witnessed at its most intense in London in, for example Islington and Clapham but also in other cities such as Manchester's northern quarter with its warehouse conversions making real estate in the spaces of industrial decline. Once those who had the means to 'get out' of the inner city did, but post-gentrification the inner city has become both desirable and financially unobtainable to many of those who now live in the suburbs resigned to the fact that where they are is 'the next best thing'. The popularity of the gentrifying movement back towards the city from the 1980s onwards represents something of a suburban backlash often practiced by those who had grown up in suburbia and come to value the advantages of the inner city in the interwar and post-war years as a reaction to what they saw as bland placidity. The two processes are inter-linked. Popular wisdom dictates that suburbanization occurred as the city expanded outwards to satiate the demand of speculative builders, homeowners, local authorities (and indeed social housing tenants) seeking a better way of life in the interwar and post-war years. Gentrification happened when the potential of housing that had been left behind (which had often fallen into disrepair) was realized by a city-working population who valued the mixed environment of the inner ring of residential districts offering a shorter commute to city central work and leisure facilities. Under Thatcherism such people were termed yuppies (variously taken to connote 'young upwardly mobile professionals' and 'young urban professionals'). Gentrification is in some ways the flip-side of suburbanization with its racially coded undertones. In suburbanization city populations abandoned the inner city to undesirables (i.e. immigrants) instead seeking contained territories of respectability/safety: in sum bequeathing a state of affairs that Avila (2006) after George Clinton calls 'chocolate cities and vanilla suburbs'. Gentrification placed their descendants back among an environment of at-worst post-industrial danger or at best unpredictability. Many of those now inhabiting the suburbs have no historic roots in inner cities that the stereotyped suburbanite had fled from for reasons of squalor. Some would dearly love to be in districts closer to the city's core but cannot due to being priced out. There is always a ripple effect around what is desirable; thus, Acton for some becomes an affordable alternative to Shepherds Bush in West London or Northenden the next best thing to Didsbury in South Manchester as property prices rise.

By the twentieth century suburbia was a part of the problem 'state of the nation' debates. In *The City in History*, Lewis Mumford (1961/91) described lifeless suburbs as shrines to uniformity, inflexibility and mass production. William F. Whyte (1956/2002) in *The Organization Man* fused elements of business studies and sociology in dissecting cultures of employment and middle management. People's solidarity with each other, it was claimed, had been crushed by their loyalty to corporations – in their adherence to corporations at work and consumerism at home, which was the efficient dormitory suburb. These allegations of suburbia as breeding conformity along David Riesman's (1950/2001) book *The Lonely Crowd* followed up by an essay entitled 'The Suburban Sadness' (1958) are now American classics still frequently cited today but this tendency has UK equivalents. In *English Journey*, an account of travels along the length and breadth of the country predating Orwell's (1937) better known and more political *Road to Wigan Pier*, J. B. Priestly (1934) concluded by drawing a distinction between (i) old England of minsters and manor houses where everyone knew their place, (ii) nineteenth-century industrial England and the most repellent of all and (iii) 'the third England', which is essentially the suburban. This is described as 'the new post-war England, belonging far more to the age itself than to this particular island. America . . . was its real birthplace. This is the England of arterial and by-pass roads, of filling stations and factories that look like exhibition buildings, of giant cinemas and dance-halls and cafes, bungalows with tiny garages, cocktail bars, Woolworths, motor-coaches, wireless, hiking, factory girls looking like actresses, greyhound racing and dirt tracks, swimming pools, and everything given away for cigarette coupons' (Priestly 1934:401). Difference is a marker of contemporary suburbs. In an age where wireless broadband is a must in any suburban home, lottery scratchcards are more common in suburban detritus than cigarette cards and Woolworths has long disappeared from the suburban high street due to recession; the description sounds quaint but it says much about the whole 'condition of England' debate, suburban culture and Americanization which today must be broadened out to address globalization in a wider sense.

Structure and omissions: Popular culture missing in action

Suburbia can be conceptualized in a number of different ways but this book has chosen popular culture centring in on cinema, television, pop music and the novel as its focus. It is not intended to be a political critique in the same way as early writers such as Whyte (1956/2002) or Mumford (1961/91) – although I have attempted that elsewhere (Huq 2013). By choosing this cultural framing approach inevitably other considerations and methods are neglected. The chapters that follow do not systematically examine stage-plays, poetry or memoir/autobiography which all have their own sub-genres of sometimes overlapping suburban-themed examples. Over the years for example we have also gained an understanding of the potential pitfalls and advantages of suburban living from advertising – slots between the television programmes or radio programmes or films at the cinema we watch or the print ads that break up press articles. Particularly memorable running British suburban sagas have been the 30-second-long mini-dramas of the Oxo family advertising stock cubes or British Telecom's Beattie (BT), a Jewish grandmother who prided herself on being 'suburban' with an outer-London phone code unlike her 'inner city' friend as shown in when two dialling prefixes were introduced for the capital in 1990 to replace the old 01 code. Space and time limitations do not allow a systematic examination in any great detail in this book however.[4] Sport is similarly neglected although following, or playing for, clubs and teams are part of the cultures of suburbia.

The suburban interior has been reproduced in numerous theatrical productions from classical drama to contemporary dramatic works. Henrik Ibsen's 1879 play of middle-class mores *A Doll's House*, originally set in small town Norway, is in present day stagings often situated in suburban context in, for example in recent years in Connecticut and suburban Scandinava as in a US and UK 2010 and 2012 production respectively.[5] At the time of writing a film version was in production in suburban Cincinnati. The play with its theme of a wife and her unhappiness despite outwardly having a prefect life was cited by Betty Friedan in her best-selling treatise *The Feminine Mystique*, a work of second-wave feminism (i.e. from the second half of the twentieth century) returned to in Chapter 6. Friedan's book was released in 1963, the year of Kennedy's assassination, arguably a key event in the US psyche that began to puncture the mythology of the American dream. Dashed suburban hopes have been a running theme that persist. When Lisa D'Amour's *Detroit* was first staged at Chicago's Steppenwolf Theatre one review remarked of its setting that it 'wouldn't have to be Detroit, it could be outside almost any urban city in the U.S . . . older, with smaller houses built about 40 or 50 years ago during a time of American Optimism . . . By 2010, when the play takes place, the original houses are starting to fall apart along with the lives and dreams of its mostly middle-class residents' (Brewer 2010). During its National Theatre run in London the play about two sets of married couples was accompanied by publicity claiming: 'The dial is set to suburban dysfunction and spiritual blight in this wry, raucous, searching comedy.' *The Daily Telegraph* (Spencer 2012) review referenced UK suburban playwrights in commenting: 'The play often seems like an American take on Mike Leigh's *Abigail's Party* and the darker comedies of Alan Ayckbourn in its comic depiction of fraught lives spinning out of control.' The play, a dark comedy, showed the suburbs in recessionary America with anxiety behind the superficial pleasantries of inviting the neighbours to a barbecue. In the Chicago-set Clybourne Park by Bruce Norris (also 2010) a black family moves to a white suburb in 1959 which becomes multi-ethnic then gentrified by whites by 2009.

Alan Acykbourn himself has repeatedly revisited social mores in the English suburbs in stage offerings such as *Absurd Person Singular* (1972), *How the Other Half Loves* (1969) and *The Norman Conquests* (1973). A review of the festive play *Season's Greetings* (Letts 2009) comments that Alan Ayckbourn 'has an ear for failure, for suburbia's silent grieving . . . This show will give you many Christmas laughs but will also make you look afresh at the outer suburbs and ponder the darkness amid the twinkling lights'. Ayckbourn himself has said of suburbia 'It's not what it seems, on the surface one thing but beneath the surface another thing. In the suburbs there is a very strict code, rules . . . eventually they drive you completely barmy.'[6] A BBC press release on the radio broadcast of his *Norman Conquesst* trilogy has called Ayckbourn 'Chekhov of the Suburbs' (BBC 2009a), although this epithet has also been applied to novelist John Cheever (Collins 1982). Mike Leigh's work is discussed in Chapter 4 in his incarnation as a film director but he began as a dramatist. Perhaps the best-known example of British suburban drama through its one-off BBC television play is his *Abigail's Party* which originally began life as a stage production. This suburban satire has become so iconic that BBC4 has staged an *Abigail's Party* theme night of nostalgia inflected programmes in October 2007 on its thirtieth anniversary revolving around the play as centrepiece and newly made 'making-of' documentary *All about Abigail's Party*. The storyline is about a doomed suburban soiree with a fatal finish. Again discomfort and repression ooze through the script with the furnishings and costumes making this very much a period piece (Raphael 2007).

Betjeman's poetry and in particular his references to Metroland and the Berkshire town of Slough which he only saw as fit for human habitation if it were bombed are also well known. As a popular cultural figure his 1970s

BBC television series helped bring him to prominence as a household name. He will not receive sustained analysis in this volume but it is worth drawing attention to him at this point. Stevie Smith quoted at the top of this chapter was another portrayer of suburban satire in novels and drawings but her best-known work was poetry. Both academic and non-academic commentary on her life and work always remarks on how after being born in Hull she lived in the North London suburb Palmers Green (Bluemel 2003; Light 2004) until her death as a spinster, having been a one-time secretary at the BBC *en route*. These experiences shaped her lifeworld: the poem quoted at the start of this chapter satirizes the long-running anti-suburban prejudice among British intellectuals practiced among others by poets W. H. Auden, E. M. Waugh and novelist Graham Greene (Carey 1992; Gardiner 2010). In 2005 the Poet Laureate, Andrew Motion, unveiled an English Heritage blue plaque to Smith at 1 Avondale Road London N13, an unremarkable redbrick slice of Edwardian terrace by any other indicator but made remarkable by officialdom fêting its most famous occupant. Others who have documented the suburban grind when they could have shown us the joys of suburbia include cartoonists. Noteworthy historical examples include Osbert Lancaster (1908–86) and Sydney Strube (1892–1956) who chronicled the tastelessness of 'stockbrokers' Tudor' and the commuter hell of the 'Little man' respectively. Nonetheless only the latter gets a brief mention in passing in Chapter 2 of this book. My logic of inclusion is in part dictates by the limitations of space. It has also in great degree shaped by my own access to culture; which television series I have seen or have been exported to the United Kingdom where my own suburban reality is.

The penultimate two chapters of this book depart from the cataloguing of suburban popular culture medium-by-medium and instead take a cross-cutting approach in looking first at women in suburban portrayals and then at ethnic minority representation and more specifically 'Asian London' across all of the art forms discussed. Other salient candidates could have included social class, however this has not been dealt with in its own chapter as (i) to some extent US popular culture has been less muted on this (with white collar-blue collar being the key binary) reflecting the lessened significance of the concept in American society generally and for the reason that (ii) it is hoped that class is present throughout the whole book. Given that we are dealing with a subject of socio-spatial significance Bourdieu's concept of habitus which fuses cultural capital with locational factors is particularly relevant here. Another area that could have been candidate for its own chapter where examples can be seen in different spheres of popular culture is consumerism. 'Mall culture' seems to be an identifiable feature of the contemporary suburb, having inspired the last novel of the prolific suburban-based British storyteller J. G. Ballard and visibly present in a slew of suburban-centred US teen movies. Long before this suburbs were marketed by advertisers with consumerist advertising techniques, for example in London's environs in tandem with the extension of the London Underground network. The desirability of a (mortgaged) suburban home in which one could store consumer comforts can be seen in the enduring existence of the annual Ideal Home Exhibition at London's Earls Court exhibition centre sponsored by the most suburban of daily newspapers the *Daily Mail* and documented academically by Sugg-Ryan (1997, 2000). Developments in the architecture of the suburban home reflect changing consumer-led vicissitudes that capture changing class relations: once the smarter homes in Victorian districts designed for the 'carriage classes', would include servants sculleries but by the advance of the twentieth century labour saving devices were being promoted as the service classes declined and instead garages and car-ports became a new norm of suburban dwellings.

By looking at a number of cultural forms over a wide sweep of time (the sample material) this approach has attempted to take an overview of the suburban popular cultural landscape in much the same way as many pictorial images of suburbia take an aerial view – shots of an earth spinning on its axis before we close in on the suburbs can be seen in the film *The Burbs* and the opening titles of the tv show *Weeds*, for example. As a UK-based writer it is unsurprising that the United Kingdom's capital London features so heavily in art forms and this megacity of super-diversity is the subject of Chapter 7. New York and its suburbs are omnipresent in US examples across different popular culture forms. Long Island features in F. Scott Fitzgerald's *The Great Gatsby*, children's adventure story series *The Hardy Boys*, *Jaws* and the 1997 film *Love and Death on Long Island* to name just a very few. Connecticut also was setting of *Far from Heaven* (2002), the film and book versions of *Revolutionary Road*, the *Ice Storm* and the fictional town of Stepford of the Ira Levin novel and two films.

I have not practiced a strict content analysis by quantifying instances of different phenomena but wanted to undertake an analysis of message and meaning to detect patterns. As someone who has taught research methods for well over a decade I am all too aware that methodologically subjective readings of cultural texts can as an approach be easily open to criticism for privileging a single cultural interpretation at the expense of wider audiences or a holistic intertextual view and potentially false-freezing in time what it is looking at. Some cultural works have a shorter shelf life than others with their 'critical reception' often helping to seal their permanence or otherwise. Categorizing representations however does have strengths as a method of data analysis. In its defence an attempt will be made where possible to contextualize what follows in respective historical moment and popular and critical reception. Theoretically the concept of structures of feelings 'concerned with meanings and values as they are actively lived and felt' as propounded by Raymond Williams (1977:132) is a useful one in considering media reception. The case material selected between them provide cultural snapshots of suburbia past and present. Between them scenes unfold depicting the evolving nature of the suburbia and wider society in the United States and United Kingdom. It has been an intention to not necessarily concentrate on the obvious, for example John Cheever, Updike's 'Rabbit' novels or the *Sopranos* which have been much celebrated but go for newer examples, for example Gautam Malkani (2006) the author of *Londonstani* (not to be confused with Melanie Philips' 2006 diatribe against multiculturalism *Londonistan*). Works which will no doubt go on to be considered classic dealt with include Franzen's *Freedom* (2010) and Arcade Fire's album *The Suburbs*. It is impossible with a subject as vast as this to ever achieve completely comprehensive coverage. In 2011, in the United States ABC launched the comedy *Suburgatory* about a single father who moves with his wisecracking teenage daughter away from the temptations of the city to the boring 'burbs. The *New York Post* applauded the show: 'At long last, a TV sitcom that doesn't idealize suburban family life to the detriment of the tried-and-true TV notion that cities are horrible, scary, no-place-to-raise-kids hell holes' (Stasi 2011) as did *Time* (Poniewozik 2011). Yet the show had many echoes of earlier representations of suburbia as repressive and inauthentic as seen in the daughter intoning 'A box of rubbers landed me in a town full of plastic' after her father discovers condoms in her bedroom prompting the move. Indeed whole notion of 'suburban dysfunction' has now become a cinematic genre in its own right – it exists as a category in Amazon as well as Netflix – two recent ways of accessing media that illustrate how far we have come from film being about 'a night at the pictures' see Table 4.1 on p. 106. One could argue this strain of suburban condescension is becoming somewhat tired.

The voices of the represented have not been a part of the methodological approach. The film *Rita, Sue and Bob Too* (1986) which started life as a play was set on Bradford's peripheral Buttershaw estate where its writer Andrea Dunbar grew up drew local criticism. As the *Bradford Telegraph and Argus* put it: 'a tatty sink estate where old mattresses and armchairs festered in overgrown gardens, family slanging matches spilled out onto the streets and teenage girls pushed prams around like trophies . . . many Buttershaw residents were offended at the portrayal of their community and resented the fact that nothing positive had been highlighted' (Clayton 2008). When Sarah Ferguson fronted *The Duchess On The Estate,* in which the former royal was dispatched the Northern Moor estate of South Manchester's large council development Wythenshawe, before the show was even aired a resident was quoted as stating 'The preview is portraying Northern Moor as the worst area in Britain to live. We haven't got gangs of gun-wielding, knife-wielding yobs. It's a very, very, very safe and lovely area for families with children' (BBC 2009b). It is not just suburban council housing estates that have been accused of being subject of misrepresentation. When the 1997 film the *Ice Storm* was released the *New York Times* (Nieves 1997) quoted Janet Lindstrom, the president of the New Canaan Historical Society similarly remarked: 'People always seem to be involved in schools and family, the kinds of things that have made New Canaan such a wonderful place to live. It's not to say that what was described in "The Ice Storm" didn't happen here. Maybe it did. I just know a very different New Canaan.' The film was set in 1973 and recalls the unhappy adolescence of its writer Rick Moody there showing debased morals in well-to-do Connecticut suburbia including wife-swopping 'key parties' which the Historical Society President had never heard of. Although with reality programmes that the defence of dramatic or poetic licence might not seemingly apply, programmes like *Made in Chelsea* and *Made in Essex* depart from the ostensible 'camera never lies' original reality formula and instead offer the oxymoronic-sounding 'scripted reality'.

Conclusion: New popular cultural paradigms

It might seem a little odd to be seeking popular culture in a milieu that many have decried as a cultural void. Malik (2007:89) for example talks of '"uncool suburbia" as compared to the "cool, urban, hip" status of LA'. However suburbia is a space where modernity has been on display since its foundation symbolizing progress in conceptualization and everyday lived social practice. As the following chapters will detail, the suburbs have been a rich source of popular cultural material: be that as the butt of jokes in television sitcom or as a security blanket to rail against by exponents of punk rock. Several common themes can be discerned from the phenomena under discussion. In the 1960 film *Please Don't Eat the Daisies* discussed in Chapter 4 a family relocate from their crowded Manhattan apartment out to the wilds of Connecticut. The characters in the film describe this as 'the country' but the home they buy on the Hudson railroad would now be considered as prime suburban real estate. *Diary of a Nobody* is often taken to be the prototypical suburban novel, still described as a 'superb satire on the snobberies of middle-class suburbia'[7] yet it was set in Holloway, now an inner London location. Indeed much of what we since consider to be suburbia (e.g. the entire Metroland development eulogized later by Betjeman) was at the time of its writing, open fields waiting for the bulldozers of the twentieth century to move in and redevelop aided and abetted with expanded road networks and improved public transport. The precise locations that we now classify as suburbs may have shifted and technology may have altered the scope of popular culture but the question of the representation of the suburbs is still a pertinent and under-researched one. Popular culture now has a history. From the standpoint of the early twenty-first century, representations of suburbia now have a legacy behind them. The cumulative social effects of these have helped to define suburbia in the popular imagination. In an era where consumers of popular culture are more media literate and knowing than ever and in which popular cultural practices are continually shifting, questions may need refining as both popular culture and suburbia undergo a process of redefining. Popular culture has made suburbia which was founded on the principle of privacy and defensible space visible and available in the public sphere.

Importantly there are many suburbias. The leafy stereotype of 1930s semi-detached houses which often springs to mind in the United Kingdom only refers to one. Ditto the white picket fence bounded detached home of American drama. The principle of 'homes fit for heroes' referred to the boom in UK housebuilding following the 1914–18 war which took place both by speculative builders on private estates and in proto-municipal and council developments providing social housing in suburbs for those who had been raised in slums. Not all of these estates have aged well. The Channel 4 comedy series *Shameless* (2004–present) offers a British version of the working class suburban experience. The series has since been remade in the United States. Its setting of the fictional post-war Chatsworth Estate is located somewhere unspecified in suburban Manchester and has been filmed variously at West Gorton to the city's east and Wythenshawe at its southern border. At times we see lifestyle-crackdowns enforced as the Manchester city council officials flood the estate looking for benefit cheats. Creator Paul Abbott has cemented his suburban credentials by writing the foreword of the second edition of singer-songwriter Paul Weller's lyric collection *Suburban 100*, a book that would not have been possible had Weller not grown up in the London commuter-town of Working. Popular culture then serves as a means to connect the reader/listener/viewer to suburbia whether they live there or not, making it part of their lived experience. Its forms multiply all the time: in the early 2000s *The Sims*, a computer game set in a simulated suburban environment near SimCity where players with avatars build communities became a runaway hit. A decade later the agrarian-themed *Farmville* played via Facebook reportedly numbered 300 million users demonstrating how far technology had come since long-running Radio 4 series *The Archers*. Some analyses attributed its popularity due to the fact that self-reliance was popular in a recession (Penny 2010); boredom at suburban life could easily be a related reason. In suburban novels or music and screen representations, everyday situations are elevated to become exceptional and social/moral issues are highlighted.

Bourdieu was well known for his theorization of distinction (1984) cultural capital and the 'taste cultures' that this spawns, an argument closely linked to questions of social class. However arguably as a by-product of mass-produced popular culture we are seeing more convergence of cultural practices and tastes despite the increased volume and type of source material available. In 1941 George Orwell (1968:77) wrote: 'In tastes, habits, manners and outlook the working class and the middle class are drawing together.' Indeed this has been a longstanding process facilitated by mass communication. Yet despite Frankfurt school fears about massified models there is also increasing divergence of the availability in what we can consume culturally and the ways that we consume it: the listening/viewing/reading public are more and more disparate and discerning than ever before. Again technology has dictated this cultural shift. Long gone is the era in which whole families would view prime time tv offerings collectively in rapt attention. Longer away still in the mists of time are instances such as the handed-down tales of entire streets crowding into the one household in relative proximity to them with a television in order to view for example the current Queen's coronation in 1953. Even further back in the depths of time are the family sing-songs round the piano. We are no longer in a mass broadcast era. Television catch-up services mean that the programme does not have to be watched at its intended scheduled slot (with meticulously pre-selected adverts). Twenty-four-hour news channels provide current affairs 'at the click of a mouse' making current news consumers the most informed and in turn changing the news cycle away from previous times when announcements were planned for big bulletin impact. In the journalist Hugo Young's posthumously published papers the late Labour minister Robin Cook was reported in 1996 remarking 'Politics has got far more difficult . . . because of the media. When I started, there were three terrestrial channels. Now there are four nationals, many locals, and several satellites. This requires many responses, often very fast. One aspect of all this is that one has to learn to say less and less' (Young 2008). The situation is dramatically different today as camera crews are sometimes stationed outside the houses of those deemed newsworthy broadcasting the front door as a reaction to the breaking news of the moment is awaited. One recalls Mrs Duffy's pebbledashed council-built semi taking centre-stage during the 2010 British general election campaign with the world's 24 hour news media waiting for the twitch of a net curtain following 'bigot-gate' in which Prime Minister Gordon Brown was caught off-gaurd on radio mic. Official media (national broadcasting) and newspapers used as mouthpieces for their proprietors no longer have between them a monopoly on communicating news and shaping opinion. Even before the Leveson enquiry into press ethics brought former news giant Rupert Murdoch down to size by forcing his appearance, the blogosphere had rebalanced relations by opening up new channels. Twitter and YouTube viral videos also have the potential to disrupt established news cycles. Technology means that the e-book and kindle offer alternatives to the hardback and paperback. The chapters that follow will look at suburbia in many forms and its cultural framing in television, film, novels and pop with a detailed focus on the treatment of women. Inevitably these images are interlocking and overlapping and the results will appear dated almost as instantly as they are committed to the page but it is hoped that the snapshots from suburbia offered are of use to those negotiating this complex terrain.

Notes

1 'Suburban Special: What Is a Suburb?' *Time Out*, 1 December 2006, at: www.timeout.com/london/big-smoke/features/2331/Suburban_special-what_is_a_suburb.html.

2 www.channel4.com/programmes/the-house-that-made-me/episode-guide.

3 www.penguinclassics.co.uk/nf/Book/BookDisplay/0,,9780141191485,00.html.

4 Although it is noticeable that in more recent campaigns for BT the post-traditional family has been reflected in depicting a single mother setting up home with a younger man with various offspring in tow. McDonalds' UK television advert of 2013 also showed a boy bonding with the new boyfriend of his mother following a reluctant start after he gets taken out for a burger. Between these two examples we can see a collapse of the ideal of the nuclear family.

5 See www.ctpost.com/entertainment/article/Long-Wharf-sets-Doll-s-House-in-suburbs-465133.php for 2010 article 'Long Wharf sets "Doll's House" in suburbs' and www.telegraph.co.uk/culture/theatre/theatre-reviews/9390146/A-Dolls-House-Young-Vic-review.html for review of 2012 play at Young Vic, London.

6 Quoted in Ann Leslie/BBC (1991) documentary *Think of England: Dunroamin*, screened in BBC2 on 5 November 1991.

7 www.penguinclassics.co.uk/nf/Book/BookDisplay/0,,9780140437324,00.html#.

2

Writing Suburbia: The Periphery in Novels

I came to live in Shepperton in 1960. I thought: the future isn't in the metropolitan areas of London. I want to go out to the new suburbs, near the film studios. This was the England I wanted to write about, because this was the new world that was emerging. No one in a novel by Virginia Woolf ever filled up the petrol tank of their car.

(J. G. Ballard in an interview with Campbell, 2008)

Perhaps somewhat befitting their positioning vis-a-vis the city, the suburbs still manage to be comparatively marginalized in overview considerations of fiction. There is a *Penguin Book of the City*; an anthology of fictional writing capturing stories spun in the metropolis. Presumably due to its perceived naffness, there is no equivalent volume dealing with the suburb. Yet the examples of such work are voluminous and vary vastly. At one extreme the futuristic *Neuromancer* by William Gibson (1984) which contains the first ever mention of the word 'cyberspace' describes a postsuburban 'edge city' (cf. Garreau) environment where business and technology are emeshed with multinational corporations in a sprawl called BAMA, the Boston–Atlanta Metropolitan Axis in which the entire American East Coast from Boston to Atlanta, have merged into a single urban mass. At the other extreme of suburban fiction can be found the historical sweep of events and moralistic undertone of the Delderfield 'Avenue' books set from 1919 to 1940. Just as any writer of non-fiction feels the need to justify their subject of enquiry as urgently needing elucidation the first volume of these *The Dreaming Suburb* maintains 'The story of the country-dwellers, and the city sophisticates, has been told often enough; it is time somebody spoke of the suburbs, for therein, I have sometimes felt, lies the history of our race' (Delderfield 1958:xi). This reference to 'our race' implying a monocultural entity feels distinctly an anachronistic read now at a time when multi-ethnicity is now widely taken as a given, not just by sociologists as seen in recent furores over, for example UK television's *Midsomer Murders* and Aidan Burley MP's remarks that the 2012 Olympic opening ceremony was 'leftie multicultural crap'. The idea of purity in a suburban race in London, the suburbs of which the books were set in, is even more odd given how very few residents are indigenous Londoners or even born in the city let alone able to trace back multiple generations. Since Delderfield wrote these words multiple changes have occurred in suburban society on both sides of the Atlantic involving ethnicity, gender, technology, class and sexuality which have all been reflected in suburban novels directly and indirectly.

The US suburban novel enjoyed a boom period in the 1950s with works such as that of John Cheever and Sloan Wilson's *The Man in the Gray Flannel Suit* (1955) (later a film with Gregory Peck), an expression still synonymous with suburban way of life for a generation who had known war. This chapter however begins with the United Kingdom. A range of examples dealing with 'Asian London' are dealt with in Chapter 7 but in the beginning there is the social satire of Mr Pooter, a character dating from Victorian times.

The twenty-first-century suburban novel is inevitably shaped by earlier antecedents. Just as when a brand name becomes part of the English language we know that it has entered immortality, for example 'the Hoover' for the vacuum cleaner, or 'the walkman' for personal stereo, or 'kindle' for e-reader, the impact of a novel can be seen to have been profound when its characters become words in the English vernacular. Charles Pooter, the central character of *Diary of a Nobody* serves as an example of how a fictional creation has given rise to the adjective 'Pooterish' to connote an ingrained suburban mentality since the book's appearance in 1892. Roy Porter (1998:382) has refereed to how 'Pooterish sorts – decent fellows living in the inner, and later the outer, suburbs.' In 2007 *The Guardian* remarked of 'suburban everyman . . . Pooter, as recognisable now as he was in 1888' and a theatre review from 2011 noted of the book's chronicling of everyday woes: 'in the age of the blogger, we are all potential Mr Pooters.'[1] Pooter's joyless commute to the city by bus or sharing with readers how he was at his happiest banging in nails in an age before the B and Q DIY superstore set the template for much of what we expect as suburbanite preoccupations. Numerous writers who have talked of the 'Pooterish' suburb connoting residential districts dating from the late nineteenth century include: Kidd and Nicholls (1999), Royle (1982), Tinniswood (1999) and Weightman and Humphries (1983). Pooter's corner of North London was Holloway, now considered part of the inner city but was a suburban location in the Victorian era before much of what would now be thought of as suburbia was yet to underwent major development in the interwar years, for example Betjeman's metroland locations were at the time mostly open fields. Anne Perkins' use of the term 'Pooterish suburb' similarly refers to Brixton (2007:128). One of the most important conclusions we can draw from this prototypical suburban novel is not in anything that author and illustrator Grossmith and Grossmith actually intended us to take away from its content. The fact that support from housebuilders and railway expansion have helped these Pooterish suburbs transform into inner city locations over the past century demonstrates how the city has edged ever-outwards and the way that yesterday's suburbia can become the inner city of the future.

Pre-war antecedents: The narrative of English decline in *Coming Up for Air*

George Orwell's 1939 novel *Coming Up for Air* documents the uncontrollability of suburban sprawl, a phenomenon much revisited, for example in Franzen's (2010) US 'state of the nation' novel *Freedom* (Colebrook 2012) explored further below. The anti-hero travelling salesman George Bowling decides to secretly escape his predictable suburban lot with loveless marriage and joyless kids to the Oxfordshire countryside of his childhood with some illicit gambling winnings for a short sojourn. His road is

> A line of semi-detached torture-chambers where the little five-to-ten-pound-a-weekers quake and shiver, every one of them with the boss twisting his tail and the wife riding him like the nightmare and the kids sucking his blood like leeches.

He steals away by car under the cover of a business trip to Birmingham, before his story unravels. This desire to preserve a bygone pre-immigration England is an enduring trope that Prince Charles' speeches and John Betjeman's *Metroland* musings lamenting the countryside's destruction continued in later years. At the time of Orwell's writing too critiques of suburbia among the intelligentsia were numerous. Chapter 1 has referred to Priestley's (1934:401) notion of an Americanized 'third England' which is fundamentally suburban in character. In 1928 Williams-Ellis likened the spread of suburbia to the grabbing tentacles of an 'octopus' (Hunt 2004) in his book kick-starting the rise of the Campaign for the Preservation of Rural England pressure group. Meanwhile in the book Bowling replays incidents from his life including the trenches in the First World War while yearning for the simple pleasures in life such as fishing, only to find on arrival that the Edwardian genteel countryside of his boyhood too has become another suburban settlement with his vividly remembered rural paradise now site of mass-produced houses aimed at the £1,000 pounds a year income bracket. He visits the graves of his parents and the church he attended as a boy but he goes unrecognized by both the vicar who has remained the same and an old flame he spots who in his eyes has deteriorated in looks to the point that he can't understand what he ever saw in her.

Alluding to Orwell's prolific parallel career as an essayist and factual writer Raymond Williams (1971:52) argued 'Instead of dividing [his works] into "fiction" and "documentaries" we should see them as sketches towards the creation of his most successful character, "Orwell". *Coming Up for Air* is written in the first person and one can only assume Bowling in some respects was a mouthpiece to ventriloquize the author's own predilections even if Orwell was the son of a civil servant educated at Wellington and Eton who fought in the Spanish civil war and the narrator the son of a simple country seed merchant who was in combat in the First World War. Bowling remarks of his humdrum existence (p. 74): 'I'm fat and forty-five and got two kids and a house in the suburbs.' Orwell was dead by the age of 47 in 1950. In many ways his works of fiction were like his well-known essays. In his 1946 essay 'Why I Write' Orwell reportedly replied that his motivation was fourfold: 'sheer egoism, aesthetic enthusiasm, historical impulse [and] political purpose' (Williams 1971:32). The same realization follows for George Bowling in *Coming Up for Air* who wants to revert to the simple pleasures of fishing and spending time by himself rather than continue taking the bait of the suburban situation he has bought into. The character literally comes up for air as the Second World War is about to hit.

Orwell's distaste for all things suburban, if we do take his writing to narrate his own opinions, can be seen as repeatedly voiced throughout his novels. In the early example *A Clergyman's Daughter* (1935/69:175) there is a description of:

Southbridge . . . a repellent suburb ten or a dozen miles from London . . . labyrinths of meanly decent streets, all so indistinguishably alike with their ranks of semi-detached houses, their privet and laurel hedges of ailing shrubs at the cross-raods, that you could lose yourself as easily in as a Brazilian forest.

The suburban jungle idea continues in *Keep the Aspidistra Flying* where the hateful houseplant of the title becomes the symbol for stultifying suburban mores. Gordon Comstack who begins the story working in a bookshop but ends up in advertising expresses disdain for a life as a suburban wage-slave at the book's start:

> The types he saw all around him made him squirm. That was what it meant to worship the money-god. To settle down, to Make Good, to sell your soul for a villa and an aspistradra! To turn into a typical bowler-hatted sneak – Strube's 'little man' – the little docile cit who slips away in the six-fifteen [a suburban train service] to a supper of cottage pie and stewed tin pears, half an hour's listening in to the BBC Symphony Concert, and then perhaps a spot of licit sexual intercourse if his wife feels 'in the mood' What a fate! No it isn't like this one was meant to live. (Orwell 1936/2000:51)

The reference to 'Little Man' was the popular interwar creation of cartoonist Sydney Strube an umbrella-ed, bow-tied and bowler hatted gent who appeared in the *Daily Express* from 1912–48 as a national symbol of the long-suffering man-in-the-street, 'with his everyday grumbles and problems, trying to keep his ear to the ground, his nose to the grindstone, his eye to the future and his chin up – all at the same time'.[2] Indeed in a phrase that seems to echo hangings, Comstack's other put-down for the commuting classes is as 'strap hangers' referring to the overhead ceiling mounted device for passengers to hold onto in overcrowded tube carriages. Criticism of commuters here seems to construct them as lifeless, dull and unafraid of risk-taking although Comstack ends up submitting to the suburban cycle by the end.

Coming Up for Air also satirizes after-effects of the speculative suburban house-building boom of interwar years which saw the United Kingdom become a nation of home-owners due to relaxations in lending policies. By 1930 it became as cheap to buy property as to rent it (Rogers and Power 2001:71). Mortgaged property became the most popular mode of housing tenure. Orwell through Bowling is unsparing in his venom for the building societies responsible for the dramatic rise of owner occupation in Britain which he sees as 'a racket'. Read through the prism of the US subprime mortgage crisis which sparked the economic recession which began in 2008, this characterization seems strangely prophetic as does the observation from the 1940 essay *The Lion and the Unicorn* that 'All criticism broke itself against the rat-trap faces of bankers and the brassy laughter of stockbrokers.' There is almost a parallel with Marx' notion of false consciousness with Bowling's remark 'Nine-tenths of the people in Ellesmere

Road are under the impression that they own their houses' (Orwell 1939/75:14). Some passages relating to the role of the building societies are mocking rather than in sympathy with the lower middle classes, for example

> We're all respectable householders – that's to say Tories, yes-men, and bumsuckers . . . And the fact that actually we aren't householders, that we are in the middle of paying for our houses and eaten up by the ghastly fear that something might happen to us before we've made the last payment, merely increases the effect . . . Every one of those poor downtrodden bastards, sweating his guts out to pay twice proper price for a brick doll's house that's called Belle Vue because there's no view and the bell doesn't ring – every one of those poor suckers would die on the field of battle to save his country from Bolshevism. (Orwell 1939/75:16)

In this way the view that the ruling classes need a consenting population to govern with their consent rather than outright coercion is reinforced, an idea that that has been rehearsed many times in sociology in varying degrees from Marx' notion of false consciousness to Gramsci's concept of hegemony and beyond. These individuals are ultimately selfish and as economic actors must keep up a process of constantly consuming on order to service the market and its demands for whom commodities must be churned out including mortgages that give the illusion of ownership. Marxist arguments see the industrial revolution as having resulted in an unequal classist society where freedom for the wealthy and powerful depended in the coercion of the working class and their continual exploitation. Bauman (2004:23) has written 'the chance to enjoy freedom without paying the harsh and forbidding price of insecurity (or at least with creditors demanding payment on the spot) was the privilege of the few; but these few set the tone of the emancipation idea for centuries to come.' In the early twenty-first century the availability of mortgages increased with lenders further relaxing criteria allowing borrowing on higher salary multiples and offering interest-only mortgages which make Orwell's 2:1 ratio for repayment look almost generous.

On his return Bowling has trouble recognizing his beloved Lower Binfield: 'All I could see was an enormous river of brand-new houses . . . several acres of bright red roofs all exactly alike. A big Council estate by the look of it' (177). There are distinct similarities with the sentiments Bowling voices here and as will be seen in the next chapter the songwriting of Paul Weller in the Jam's track *Tales from the Riverbank*, a composition which also borrows much from Kenneth Grahame's *The Wind in the Willows*. Indeed Grahame in an 1892 essay *Orion* quoted by Hunt (2010:xi) declared as a statement of fact 'the desolate suburbs creep ever further into the retreating fields'. The since much-copied pastoral whimsy of Grahame can be seen in *Wind in the Willows* chapters 'The Riverbank, Piper at the Gates of Dawn' (inspiring a Jam track and the title of Pink Floyd's first wistful, pre-prog rock album) and the murky presence of the 'wild wood' which became the title of Paul Weller's second solo album. The book has been seen to capture the rise of the clerkish suburban nobody preoccupied by home improvements as well as wealth and display. Hunt writes (2010:xi): 'The mole has about him the air of a respectable suburban clerk, a Mr Pooter figure straight from the pages of George and Weedon Grossmith's *The Diary of a Nobody*.' Toad of Toad Hall by contrast is loud and ostentatious representing 'new money'. Betjeman too in his television documentaries repeatedly lamented a vanishing England with the countryside rapidly disappearing at the mercy of suburbanization. There is a parallel to the description of Bromstead in H. G. Wells' political novel *The New Machiavelli* (1911:38–9): 'Roofs of slate and tile appeared amidst and presently prevailed over the original Bromstead thatch . . . Residential villas appeared occupied by [people] who deemed the place healthy.' In sum 'all the delight and beauty of it was destroyed' (Wells 1911:43) including its main river the Ravensbrook which becomes a dumping ground. George Orwell via Bowling as narrator reacts in horror at the change and decay around him: 'There was nothing left of the woods. It was all houses, houses – and what houses! . . . faked up Tudor houses with curly roofs and the buttresses that don't buttress anything, and the rock-gardens with concrete bird-baths and red plaster elves you can buy at the florists' (p. 214). A similar dislike of mock Tudor comes over in the passage in *Keep the Aspidistra Flying* when Gordon and Rosemary take a day trip to Burnham Beeches, Buckinghamshire some 25 miles from London described as 'the country'. The decline which is the backdrop to the book takes place on multiple levels. The empire which Orwell hated so much and which he was a product was coming to an end as well as the decline of the ruling classes now that the fast suburbanizing middle class was undergoing expansion.

Post-war Americana

In settling on what we can deem to be 'the Great American Novel' there are multifarious works of twentieth century vividly fiction chronicling their times from depression era Steinbeck through to the 1960s rebellions of J. D. Salinger and Jack Kerouac and the 1980s yuppie satire of Tom Wolfe. Yet within this broad bracket is the rich vein of suburban novel, a significant subcategory. Among the best known exponents are John Cheever for his Wapshot books set in the New York suburbs. After his death in 1982 his local suburban public library honoured him with a Reading Room named after him, dedicated to 'Ossining's Chekhov of the Suburbs'. Citing one-off suburban novels Kenneth T Jackson (1985:281–2) and Scott Donaldson between them list numerous examples: *Mr Blandings Builds His Dream House*, *Please Don't Eat the Daises*, *The Crack in the Picture Window*, *The Mackeral Plaza*, *Rally Round the Flag, Boys* and Richard Yates' (1961/2001) *Revolutionary Road* which has a back cover describing it about 'a couple bored by the banalities of suburban life'. Perhaps best known however is Sloan Wilson's *The Man in a Gray Flannel Suit* forever cited in descriptions of US suburbanism. In describing the ageing rockstar Richard Katz and his associates in the contemporary *Freedom* it is said of his bassist (Franzen 2010:151) '[his] dishevelment and disorganisation made Richard look like the man in the grey flannel suit in comparison'. Franzen incidentally wrote a forward to the most recent re-issue of the book. In series 2 of *Mad Men* the be-suited central character Don Draper attracts the disparaging epithet from a foe in the hippie commune he starts to frequent of 'hey, it's the Man in the Gray Flannel Suit', suggesting that like the book he too epitomizes the 'straight' suburban mindset unlike the bohemian name-caller. Indeed the book has inspired numerous subsequent academic works spanning articles (Jurca 1999), and analyses which see it as symbolizing the triumph of big corporations (Spector 2008; Panayiotou 2012) including the book *Beyond the Gray Flannel Suit: Books from the 1950s that Made American Culture* (Castronovo 2004).

Dissatisfaction seems to be prevalent in many of these post-war examples. Indeed Donaldson (1969:199) goes as far as to brand this strand of suburban fiction as 'hysterical'. In *Revolutionary Road* (Yates 1961) the estate agent convinces the Wheelers of the merits of the suburban house in the aforementioned road despite their misgivings. 'I don't suppose one picture window is necessarily going to destroy our personalities', ventures Frank as they view the house that eventually April feels trapped by and the suburban sell-out from their bohemian past begins (Yates 1961:29). This new way of living initially offers a solution to their haphazardness. We are told 'The gathering disorder of their lives might be sorted out and made to fit these rooms, among these trees' (Yates 1961:30). Of course it doesn't take long before they are at each others' throats. 'I don't happen to fit the role of dumb, insensitive suburban husband; you've been trying to hang that one on me ever since we moved out here, and I'm damned if I'll wear it', Frank rages in an argument (Yates 1961:25). The book is more harrowing than the brightly shot film it became later starring Kate Winslet and

Leonardo DeCaprio. A later strain of revisionist fiction looked at suburbia past from the vantage point of the 1990s, for example Jeffrey Eugenides' suburban gothic *Virgin Suicides* (1994) and Rick Moody's *Ice Storm* (1994) – both set in affluent 1970s suburbs of New York and both made into films. The same fate befell Updike's earlier *The Witches of Eastwick* (1984) with critics predictably panning the film for not living up to the book. Cunningham's (1998) ambitious *The Hours*, set in three time periods and locations focusing on three women in respectively (i) present-day Manhattan, (ii) late 1940s US suburbia and (iii) the suburb Richmond in Greater London also was subject of a film. In the story the overlaps between parallel plotlines only become clear at the book's close. For Nash (1963) the advantage of the suburban novelist over the sociologist as their vantage point allows them to make powerful statements '[u]nburdened by even vague claims to statistical representativeness'.

In his essay on celebrated US novelist John Updike, Tanner (1987:39) states that suburbia is a 'compromised environment' where nonetheless most Americans live with 'all their joys and fears within its ailing routines and numbing geometrics'. Such declining if not quite discarded traditions documented by Updike include marital fidelity and the Christian church. The social realism is underlined by brand names and description of the mundane details of the everyday. Middle-class suburban mores were examined in his best-known work, the 'Rabbit' books, four titles chronicling the life of basketball star turned used car salesman Harry 'Rabbit' Angstrom, a suburban Pennsylvanian, through the lifecycle from high school graduate to old age mirroring the vicissitudes of American life across the decades from the 1960s to the 1990s from *Rabbit, Run* (1960) to *Rabbit at Rest* (1990) where generation gap and marriage under pressure surface. Suburban routine is further unsettled in the *The Witches of Eastwick* (1984) which is complimented by his final work *The Widows of Eastwick* published in the year of his death 2009. For Tanner (1987:55) Updike professes 'qualified, or intermittent, support for the suburban environment which has sometimes provoked the criticism of writers and critics who feel that the writer's repudiation of American society should be more total.' Newman (1988) sees continuities between the classic study into American suburban society *The Organization Man* by Whyte (1956) and the society described by Updike (1968) in his novel *Couples*. She describes the local town hall busybody committee structure (also the premise of *Rally Round the Flag Boys*, Shulman 1958) with its 'suburban ethos of acquiescent participation' that swallows people up (Newman 1988:28). Here 'no real issues are debated [only] schools, highways, sewer bonds and zoning by-laws'. It sounds like a petty and parochial bureaucratic nightmare rather than the stuff of radical politics with the potential to achieve social change. One taboo that Updike was not averse to dealing with was suburban sex liberated from its pro-creational function by the contraceptive pill.

Sex and the suburbs

Predating the hugely successful 1990s series and film spin-offs *Sex and the City* were representations of sex and the suburbs, for example in Yates (1961). Updike often took upper- to middle-class suburban life and failing marriage with partners playing away as his focus. The shock value of his 1968 novel *Couples*, a work combining social commentary on the US suburbia of JFK, cocktail parties, Town Hall and PTA meetings with some graphic sex scenes was reinforced when he appeared on the cover of *Time* magazine the same year with the caption 'The Adulterous Society'. The feature inside asserted 'The fact is that beneath this suburban idyll, Updike's couples are caught up in a black mass of community sex.' In his obituary the *Wall Street Journal* declared 'Mr. Updike spoke as the high priest of the sexual revolution, with all its concomitant adulteries and divorces'. His *USA Today* obituary included the observation: 'The idea that people think *Desperate Housewives* is new and edgy – it was all there' (Minzesheimer 2009). As Paul Barker (2009:63) reminds us 'It's undeniable that the quiet privacy of suburbia has always led to the assumption of mysterious temptations.' The recurring idea that what goes on behind closed doors is never all that it seems pervades throughout depictions of suburban sex in both the United Kingdom and United States.

Leslie Thomas's wifeswopping tale *Tropic of Ruislip* (1974) is more of a page-turner or potboiler rather than a work from the canon of great literature that makes English syllabi, but nonetheless the book made an entry into the *Guardian* list of '1000 novels everyone must read: the definitive list' (23 January 2009) under the 'comedy' category.[3] It is set in the inbetween-land imaginary northwest London location Plummers Park, 'thirty miles from Central London, in the latitude of Ruislip, in the country but not of it. The fields seemed touchable and yet remote' (Thomas 1974:11).[4] The book recounts that one can hear the rattle of the Metropolitan underground line, which terminates at Watford, its furthest outreach from central London making John Betjeman's 1973 BBC documentary *Metroland* an obvious reference point. A picture of promiscuity in a society dominated by pettiness and snobbery is painted where unfulfilled local newspaper hack Andrew Maiby supplements his frustration and onset of middle age with an extramarital fling with a girl from the wrong side of the tracks: the council estate from down the hill. The two public/private housing developments are juxtaposed from the start. Plummers Park is a picture of respectability shielding sexual tension and frustration. Its monotonous inertia of car-polishing, G-plan furniture and golf clubs is broken up by the bit of rough in the nearby social housing with addresses reflecting municipal socialism such as 22 Morrison Way, Atlee Park. There is a clear division between these two discrete bounded territories despite their physical proximity to one another:

> Beneath the station burrowed a pedestrian tunnel nervously joining Plummers Park to the council estate. To venture through it was to leave one country for another: on one side fuchsias, and on the other sheets of newspaper drifting in the street winds . . . Trouble was rare between the tenants on the one side of the railway and the residents of the other . . . people were not well enough acquainted to fight. They were merely strangers. (Thomas 1974:13)

There also seems to be ethnic as well as class segregation. At a house-party the arrival of a group of West Indians is initially greeted with hostilities, with guests remarking 'Invasion! Plummers Park is invaded! There's a whole lot of blackies coming up the road!' (Thomas 1974:107). The revellers gain entry and the party becomes 'two distinct ethnic groups at each end of the room . . . it was an uneasy armistice' (Thomas 1974:109). The book's political incorrectness is seen not only in its treatment of women returned to in Chapter 6 but in ethnic references such as the description of the Jewish pensioner Herbie Futter who collapses as a 'prostrate old Jew'. In a pub exchange the following depiction of the suburb as uncorrupted by foreign or noxious influences occurs (Thomas 1974:54):

> 'Plummers Park is very, very nice.'
>
> 'Very, very, nice,' nodded Andrew with exaggeration. 'Very, very nice. Heaven in Hertfordshire.' He recited
>
> Bring your kids, bring your dogs,
>
> We've fresh nice air, and we've got no wogs.

If the same geographical area were to be written of today it is likely that a good number of 'the monster council-housing development built to rehouse families from slum London' (Thomas 1974:12) would have been sold under the Thatcher governments right to buy legislation and inevitably a proportion of those would have turned into buy-to-let or sub-let properties. Remaining houses with social landlords might have gone into tenancies under the control of housing trusts or other arms-length management organizations. In the 1970s *Plummers Park Men* the expectation was that men would play around in a 'boys will be boys' way. The character Geoffrey describes the reason why he left his wife as his realization of his impending sense of mortality (Thomas 1974:101):

> [E]xcruciating boredom. Every day I used to get on the train to London and I'd be sitting there wondering what the hell I'd do to escape, and every day on the dot, that bloody great overcrowded cemetery at Kensal Green used to straggle past the window. I tried not to look at it but I still used to. Miles of it. Sometimes I could hear the sods laughing at me. So one day I met Cynthia and I ran off with her.

His adultery is explained by a desire to break free of the suburban rat race, although he settles in Plummers Park with Cynthia who becomes his second wife, replicating the suburban routine he wanted to unshackle himself from with a newer model. He later has an entanglement with the already-married Ena who becomes pregnant and proposes that they move to New Zealand. This bawdy romp has much in common with other cultural depictions of suburbia of the time including the series of films begun by *Confessions of a Window Cleaner* (1974) in which a peeping Tom character was more likely to end up in attractive female clients' beds than on the exterior side of their windows with bucket and mop.

The newness of the estate is apparent from the descriptions of its flat rooves and iconoclastic 'Flat-Roof Man'. It is also evidenced in the touting for congregation by the vicar Reverend Boon who is told by the nonchalant resident Polly Blossom-Smith that 'I don't know. They go back to the places they came from originally for such things as Christenings and weddings. I suppose they think things are more *established* there.' Thomas (1974:133). The words 'established' with original emphasis is a play on words of the church as remarked on by the vicar but this has gone un-noticed by Polly. It appears that these are a godless people who have not put down roots in their new community. When Herbie Futter, an elderly character is taken ill and medical aid is slow at coming forward, Gerry remarks in anger 'We're like a flaming outpost of Empire here' (Thomas 1974:214). Futter dies on the spot. It seems that the public services cannot cope as the old (monogamy, a job for life, community bonds) is giving way to the new (mobility, promiscuity, impatience) and Futter represents something of an anachronism in this. Upward mobility and suburban dynamism is discernable at the close of the book. We learn that an empty property has been bought by a young couple from the council house on the 'other side' of whom the character Audrey remarks 'It shows that as soon as they can afford it they hop across the railway line as quick as they can. As long as they don't have washing hung everywhere it will be alright, I suppose' (Thomas 1974:256). At the close of the book it occurs in conversation that 'half the neighbourhood are moving south of the river [Thames]'. The advantage of chosen destinations Wimbledon and its environs are described as an antidote: 'It must be the attractions of Victoriana after Plummers Park.' Here the classic idea of urban leapfrog is invoked. Traditionally this moving up and moving out phenomenon refers to city-to-suburb population displacement but we see an example of suburb-to-suburb in this instance. The revival of period property is anticipated here, realized in the gentrification of Victorian-built areas like Islington.

Tim Lott (undated) has often cited Updike as a key influence to the point that he has claimed that his novel *Rumours of a Hurricane* was fashioned an attempt to create an English Rabbit. In *The Love Secrets of Don Juan* the onset of middle age frames the suburban experience as anti-hero/chief protagonist advertising copywriter Danny 'Spike' Savage finds himself through divorce condemned to live further and further away from central London. Things begin in a bedsit in Acton and conclude with him settling a few streets away from his original family home in Hanwell although his parents by then have moved to Watford, like himself they are suburbanizing further and further out as the story progresses. Spike muses 'Here on the westernmost drift of central London, the dull double-glazed terraces face out towards the lusher suburbia of Chiswick and Ealing. I used to live in Hammersmith, and before that Shepherd's Bush, so I'm gradually being edged outwards, by some impersonal historical source' (Lott 2004:3). As he traces the anatomy of his marriage collapse through past failed relations he describes how with his first live-in girlfriend in his twenties 'Helen and I were in that suburb of hell that is a failing dependent relationship' (ibid. 2003:170). Suburban realities for Spike include parenthood. His desire to be a lothario is curbed by the reality of a 6-year-old daughter who spends alternate weekends with him, usually having to be prised away from her mother to do so. There are some deftly aimed sidewipes at the perceived tacky tastelessness of suburbanites. A nightmarish incident is described on a rainy day at noisy fit-to-bursting a suburban softplay centre he takes her to, a 'Heath Robinson in Hell array of contraptions' (p. 149). Seated at the side of the play apparatus, he has to endure an ill-tempered couple trading insults and effing and blinding at each other before foraging for reading material which he has neglected to bring (p. 149): 'There are a few abandoned newspapers and magazines in the rubbish bin. It seems that the *Economist* and *New Yorker* are not much in demand, but the *Sunday Sport*, most of the red top tabloids and variations on *Hello!*, *Ok!* And *Chat* enjoy an enthusiastic following.' Then Poppy, his daughter. becomes trapped. It is only when Spike begins bellowing and cursing at the top of his voice in this huge, crowded space with no staff to assist that he seems to make any impression and attendants appear: 'This seems to penetrate the indeterminate padding that passes for brains in this postcode' (153). The afternoon ends with a visit to his parents further up the A40 Western Avenue in Yiewsley when he realizes he has left his filofax (nowadays this would be a smart phone) in the mêlée and thus has no wallet to treat Poppy to McDonalds. The visit home sees him becoming infantilized with his father shouting to him to go to his room.

From Orwell (1936/2000:51) in world weary prose describing how the put-upon suburban husband needs to make do with a 'spot of licit sexual intercourse if his wife feels "in the mood"', descriptions of sex seem to have got ever more graphic in recent suburban novels. In the thoroughly twenty-first-century tale *Freedom* by Jonathan Franzen events including the migration of the early 1990s Berglund family from Sweden and the rape of Patty as a teenager are flashed back into the unfolding of the marriage between Patty and Walter Berglund. Various infidelities and sexual encounters are described, including lengthy accounts of masturbation in the middle section dealing with son Joey's college years. Franzen sealed his status as a chronicler of American suburban life when he penned the introduction to the 2008 reissue of *The Man in the Gray Flannel Suit* and made the cover of *Time* magazine in a rarity being the first novelist for ten years and one of only a handful at all including Updike in 1968 and 1982 and Orwell long after his death in 1983. The caption claimed that this was a great American novelist writing about the way we live today. Not shying away from sex scenes is another parallel that can be drawn between Franzen and Updike. In a review of the 1970s-set *The Witches of Eastwick* Baym (1984:165) complains that this tale of suburban occultism and sorcery is 'deadened by Updike's joyless pornography'. Indeed there are references to sexual organs almost from the book's start as seen in the description of choosing tomatoes in a kitchen suburban setting for the evening's dinner: 'Picking up the watery orange-red orbs, Alexandra felt that she was cupping a giant lover's testicles in her hand' (Updike 1984:6). When a mysterious dark newcomer appears on the block extra excitement is injected into the three witches lives and the shared experience of 'the sorority of pain that went with being the dark man's lover' (Updike 1984:208–9). Illustrating the crossover between the different cultural products that inform this book, the novel was later by common consensus turned into a near-sacreligious film starring Jack Nicolson in 1987, then a Broadway musical.

By the time of its follow up *The Widows of Eastwick* set in post-9/11 times old-aged sexlessness is a running theme of it as the all newly widowed trio of central characters who had 30 years earlier 'practiced a half-baked suburban variety of witchcraft' (p. 16) are aged around the 70 mark. Alexandra (Updike 2009:46) remarks when the three are reunited 'Just thinking about those days – aren't you glad all that's behind us? Sex, and all that lost sleep, all that hard hearted scheming that went with it.' At a later point she observes watching teenagers outside a chain Ben and Jerry's ice-cream parlour that had been a parade of independent traders (ibid. 2009:235): 'Eastwick's children, flaunting their growing power, ignoring the old woman sitting in a parked car, vying for attention with their peers, with female shrieks and boyish jokes, testing freedom's limits . . . *Little do they know*, Alexandra thought, *what lies ahead for them*: Sex, entrapment, weariness, death.' Other descriptions are offered of the ladies' calluses, arthritic conditions and other physical tics, for example Alexandra looking at her hands which 'resembled two fat lizards' (p. 265). Even Sukie wearily states of the daily suburban assault course that amounts to life (p. 232): '[T]hese milestones. Weddings and funerals. Graduations and divorces. Endings. Ceremonies get us through. They're like blindfolds for people being shot by a firing squad.' The three's children are also in middle age: on second marriages, balding, etc. They return to literally rehaunt their old haunt Eastwick and like George Bowling are shocked to see how it has become taken over by commercialization/corporate chains, for example a sports bar replacing their old watering hole the Bronze Barrel. The diner they used to hang out in too is in the process of a takeover. Sukie adds writes to Alexandra with no apparent irony that there is some mitigation 'Dunkin Donuts has promised to preserve some of its historical features in their renovation.' Their old powers are failing them just as the landmarks they once knew and objects of their earlier extramarital affairs have been wiped out or are rendered unrecognizable in a changing world. A one-time young virile beau of Sukie has had an arm mutilated in an industrial accident, has become shrivelled and is dependent on his wife. The Italian plumber who would come round at the drop of a hat to unblock a drain or perform other services has died, compelling anyone wanting to get their drains unblocked to ring an impersonal national call-centre. The local amateur orchestra-conductor has also met his maker, recounted with a dash of casual anti-suburban snobbery: 'Poor Ray, trying to bring culture to this backwater where all people cared about was games and the tax rates and the cod catch' (p. 147). A suburban séance goes fatally amiss. Sex is largely talked of in the past tense. Alexandra comments how she does not miss it, much in the same way as her admission 'I think my magic's about used up. Just the thought of casting a spell nauseates me.' The same applies to many aspects of Eastwick. It is a realization that the wild abandon of the seventies of both Eastwick and Plummers Park had to give way in the end, buckling under the weight of AIDS and more importantly old age. We only get a sex scene towards the end where in a twist Sukie takes up with the bi-sexual Christopher who was a boy when they left and now is an actor leading him to make the remark that most sex was acting anyway (Updike 2009:296).

Macabre suburbia

Despite its supposed ordinariness suburbia has often been constructed as the sort of place where out-of-the-ordinary events occur in novels. The immediately post-war American suburb was even seen as a safe haven to escape to in the event of a nuclear attack, which against the backdrop of the cold war was painted by politicians as potentially imminent literally engendering a 'bunker' mentality – seen literally in the 2009 film of Christopher Isherwood's 1964 set *A Single Man* where the man character George's neighbours are building bomb shelters. Alienation and mental illness were themes of Jeffrey Eugenides' suburban gothic *Virgin Suicides* (1994) and numerous works by J. G. Ballard who once wrote 'The suburbanization of the soul has overrun our planet like the plague' quoted by Humes (2003). Crime in suburbia was seen in Nigel Williams UK novel *The Wimbledon Poisoner* in which the idea of the suburban busybody resurfaced a century after Pooter in the neighbour-characters of Maple Drive SW19 including Mr and Mrs Is-the-Mitsubishi-Scratched-Yet, the Nazi Who Escaped Justice at Nuremberg at number 42 and 'Dave Sprott, the northern dentist at 102, whose carefully preserved northern accent had always seemed . . . a way of criticizing the London suburb in which he found himself' (1990:108–9). In Ballard's *Running Wild* (1998:83) the children of the newbuild idyllic mock tudor modern suburban Pangbourne Village are the culprits of their parents' murders. The suffocation of their environment is given as the reason for being 'trapped within an endless round of praiseworthy activities . . . far from hating their parents when they killed them, the Pangbourne children probably saw them as nothing more than the last bars before they could reach out to the light' (Ballard 1998:83). The unhappiness of the Lisbon sisters is the cause of the string of five deaths in *The Virgin Suicides* in Grosse Pointe, an upscale suburb of Detroit. The story is seen through the eyes of the local boys who are in awe of the girls. There are clues to the environment 'They drove past the Little club, the Yacht Club, the Hunt Club' (Eugenides 1994:139).

Like the coverage of the Pangbourne murders on *Newsnight* the Lisbon murders become national news, worrying the authorities with its adverse publicity and other bodies, for example 'While the suicides lasted, and for sometime after, the Chamber of Commerce worried less about the influx of black shoppers and more about the outflux of whites' (Eugenides 1994:99). Gershuny (2005) has argued that busyness is a badge of honour in modern life and the impression from these titles seems that suburbia is a pressured environment in many ways. Even for Poppy the 6-year-old daughter of soon-to-be-divorced Danny Savage in *The Love Secrets of Don Juan* (Lott 2004:148) of whom we are told 'She's bored by books. She's bored by the theatre. She's bored by vegetables. She's bored by violin lessons. She's bored by the whole white middle-class fantasy. She likes to watch tv and eat crap.' The children of suburbia seem to rebel against the cloying safe confines of their suburban upbringings which may also explain the process of inner-city gentrification.

The late science fiction author J. G. Ballard's literary mark is evidenced by the inclusion since 2005 of 'Ballardian' in *The Collins English Dictionary* (Baxter 2008) refering to 'dystopian modernity, bleak man-made landscapes and the psychological effects of technological, social or environmental developments'. Suburbia was present both in Ballard's lived reality but was also a theme across his books, for example *The Unlimited Dream Company* (1979), which begins with a stolen aircraft crashing in Shepperton (where the author lived) and features a narrator who can cannot ever leave the suburbs, or *Running Wild* set in upscale gated community suburbia and Ballard's final novel, *Kingdom Come* (2006) about mega-shopping mall the Brooklands centre, 'a self-contained universe of treasure and promise' (2006:218). Early on in the book the chilling barren territory is described (p. 6): 'Warning displays alerted each other, and the entire landscape was coded for danger. CCTV cameras crouched over warehouse gates, and filter-left signs pulsed tirelessly, pointing to the sanctuaries of science parks.' The futuristic exurban suburbia as described also feels like a hollow, burnt-out carcass of its former self. Ballard (1997) has called his longtime base of Shepperton, Middlesex off the M4 motorway as 'a suburb not of London but of London Airport. The catchment area of Heathrow extends for at least 10 miles to its south and west, a zone of motorway intersections, dual carriageways, science parks, marinas and industrial estates, watched by police CCTV speed-check cameras, a landscape which most people affect to loathe but which I regard as the most advanced and admirable in the British Isles, and paradigm of the best that the future offers us'. This sounds a lot like Brooklands described thus by the character Maxted[5] (p. 101): 'This isn't a suburb of London, it's a suburb of Heathrow and the M25. People in Hampstead and Holland Park look down from the motorway as they speed home from their west-country cottages. They see faceless inter-urban sprawl, a nightmare terrain of police cameras and security dogs, an uncentred realm devoid of civic tradition and human values.' Fascism, violence and consumerism all concepts coalesce with each other in a populist amalgam of demagogery. Shopping is described as a religion: the Brooklands centre's media relations manager quips (p. 60): 'It' like going to church. And here you can go every day and you get something to take home.' This sounds extreme but then the suburbs as described in the book are not merely sleepy and unremarkable but hold pent-up frustration and violence.

The science fiction of the 1950s onwards has many common features with this prescription but many of the extra-terrestrial landscapes woven in stereotypical examples are unrecognizable to the average reader. By contrast Ballard takes the quotidian shopping mall exaggerating its negative features making mundane, unremarkable surroundings threatening. Instead of aliens alienation is the key theme. The nightmarish scenario includes violence perpetrated by men dressed in St George's cross clothing despite the ever-present uninformed security staff and CCTV. The brass band in the shopping centre sinisterly plays 'All Hail to the Chief'. Casual racism flares up towards 'Asians, Kosovans, Bosnians' (p. 58) among others. At one point the first person narrator Richard Pearson distinguishes between different racisms, for example '[N]ot in the bully-boy way of the street thugs who had driven the imam from the suburban mosque, but in the more cerebral style of the lawyers, doctors and architects who had enlisted in Hitler's elite corps' (p. 56). The Brooklands centre even has its own cable television channel which commands greater ratings than BBC2 with a messiah-like host who Pearson remarks is 'The Oswald Mosley of the suburbs' (p. 100). Again he has in his own words argued that the capital city has become antiquated by comparison with the modernity of suburbia: 'By comparison with London Airport, London itself seems hopelessly antiquated. Its hundreds of miles of gentrified stucco are an aching hangover from the nineteenth century that should have been bulldozed decades ago.' Such words are almost heretical in an age where period property is revered by people who celebrate past architecture but perforce inhabit modernity: two processes brought together in gentrification. Although H. G. Wells' later works of science fiction are more often about time travel and alien beings in his early novel *The New Machiavelli* (1911:45) he describes the advance of suburbia in Bromstead as 'a new order . . . a multitude of incoordinated fresh starts, each more sweeping and destructive than the last, and none of them ever really worked out to a satisfactory completion . . . It was a sort of progress that had bolted; it was change out of hand, and going at an unprecedented pace nowhere in particular.' This foreshadows the fictitious Brooklands: is a world of modernism, technology and progress tempered with anxiety, doubts and fear.

Suburbia literally served as a backdrop to Ballard's own creative processes. Ballard insisted that interviewers come to his eccentric suburban lair. Billen (1994), for example noted 'Perhaps the best thing about visiting J. G. Ballard is getting a chance to marvel at his house, a peeling semi-detached in Shepperton [which] . . . makes no concessions to celebrity, fashion, cleanliness, the money he made . . . or, indeed, anything else.' Noting a clear mismatch between theory and practice, Campbell (2008) commented that the experience was tantamount to 'stepping through the looking glass . . . Ballard's electrical fixtures would interest the curator of the Design Museum. On a cold day, the rooms are warmed by small heaters positioned in the middle of the floor. The sleek stylist of western consumerism never got round to installing central heating.' Ballard has claimed in an interview that he always equated suburbia with new designs for life and the future, which is striking given the recurrent analyses of surburbia as anti-modernist. Indeed much popular cultural imagery at the time that Ballard began his career was often steeped in the past, for example bodice and top hat/bow tie cinema and the literary form of the novel which was frequently historical and/or nostalgic. In the interview he has explicitly repudiated the play *Look Back in Anger*: 'With all due respect to Kingsley Amis and others, I didn't feel that the angry young men were responding to what was really important about society. The same goes for John Osborne's plays. The laying down of the M1 was much more important than anything Jimmy Porter's in father-in-law thought about this or that . . . I thought: here is a fiction for the present day. I wasn't interested in the far future, spaceships and all that. Forget it. I was interested in the evolving world, the world of hidden persuaders, of the communications landscape developing, of mass tourism, of the vast conformist suburbs dominated by television – that was a form of science fiction, and it was already here' (Campbell 2008). This continues the futuristic impulses attributed to suburbia by H. G. Wells, at the turn of the twentieth century, another visionary who had suburban origins. In *Running Wild* (1988), a high-end housing estate built as a neo-suburban gated community 30 miles from London with ever-present CCTV witnesses a series of murders conducted simultaneously in macabre circumstances: one resident is crushed by the wheels of her own car and another at her exercise cycle for example. Among initial police theories are that the perpetrators were people from northern England exacting revenge at southern Thatcherite prosperity – a reminder of the 'North–South divide' much talked of at the time. This is ruled out when a more sinister explanation unfolds.

Detractors of suburbia have been in existence since the concept came into being. In opposition to these familiar criticisms of the urban intelligensia there is almost a superiority inherent in the suburban-inflected Ballardian worldview towards the metropolis with the dwindling significance of the city that unfolded over a series of short stories and novels, for example *The Concentration City* (1957), *Chronopolis* (1960), *Million Sands* (1973) and *Crash* (1973).[6] The position is stated clearly in *Kingdom Come* (Ballard 2006:101): 'People in London can't grasp that this is the real England. Parliament, the West End, Bloomsbury, Notting Hill, Hampstead – they're heritage London, held together by a dinner party culture. Here, around the M25 is where it's really happening.' In the book the community described rather than being organic is peopled with actors within wider schemes and systems. The landscape of Brooklands, a public–private space, is not a green and pleasant land but beneath an eerily efficient superficial surface lies a dysfunctional suburban wasteland. Belief in god, family and morality appear to have been suspended with every man (most characters are masculine) for himself. The only loyalty people seem to have is to the cult of the centre: when it is under siege towards the end of the book there is still 'a hard core of supporters who had forsaken everything, their homes and families, their jobs and cars and loft extensions to defend the Metro-centre' (p. 232). The centre has become a substitute for community. David Cruise, the public face of the complex echoes Mrs Thatcher when telling a group of housewives in a televised gathering '"community" . . . That's a word I hate. It's the kind of word used by snobby-upper-class folk who want to put ordinary people in their place. Community means living in a little box, driving a little car, going on little holidays, obeying what "they" tell you to obey . . . For me, the only real community is the one we've built here at the Metro-centre. That's what I believe in' (p. 176). This seems to echo early detractors of suburbia such as Whyte whose arguments were outlined in the previous chapter. There are also echoes of Thatcher's famous utterance 'there is no such thing as society'. It seems to be no accident that the building is topped with a dome, sealing its neo-religious significance. In *Milleneum People* (Ballard 2004) it is middle-class revolt at service charges and parking restrictions that lead to rebellion and terrorist incidents. At one point a video rental store in suburban Twickenham is blown up and at another it is the National Theatre.

Not all suburban fiction is held in high regard by the literary world. The self-described 'far fetched fiction' of Robert Rankin fits between fantasy and sci-fi for its absurdist plots that are low on realism. The suburban landsape of the Brentford trilogy encompasses the Flying Swan public house, golfing, the allotment and 'the council' in titles including *East of Ealing* (1984), *The Sprouts of Wrath* (1988) after Steinbeck, *The Witches of Chiswick* after Updike (1984) and *The Brentford Chainstore Massacre* (1997) alluding to the *Texas Chainsaw Massacre* film directed by Kaufman (1974) about Millennium celebrations. Literary allusion via punning titles continue in Rankin's other titles outside the trilogy – a series with far in excess of three titles, spanning to nine at last count up to *Retromancer* (2009) after William Gibson's *Neuromancer* set in Brentford circa 1967 and during the Blitz. *The Witches of Chiswick* (2003) is clearly derivative of Updike. Again like Leslie Thomas or R. F. Delderfield or the suburban strain of chick-lit that has included *The Rise and Fall of the Queen of Suburbia* by Sarah May or the *The School Run* by Sophie King, Rankin is unlikely to be considered literature yet his loyal fanbase extends to the Order of the Golden Sprout Fan Club who have a website and regular gatherings. The books are cultish in their dogged following but mainstream as they command consistent sales figures. They do not fulfil the 'critical acclaim' marker as they are the type of books that literary critics would not trouble themselves with yet they represent an important current of suburban writing. *The Sprouts of Wrath* (Rankin 1988) for its plot based around seeking a Brentford Olympiad complete with futuristic stadium can be seen as prescient and not so far fetched in 2012 as it may have seemed in 1988. The editor of the *Brentford Mercury* (Rankin 1988:48) thanks god for getting a break from the usual predictable suburban news-cycle of mundanity and greets the news with the sentiment 'Twenty years in this game. Twenty long years of flower shows and boy scout jamborees and now. . . .' He has finally hit on the big one in terms of career-scoops whereas by the time of the *Widows of Eastwick* (Updike 2009) the local paper Sukie used to write on has gone out of print, crushed by the weight of blogs – familiar fate of the local press in the United Kingdom today, matched by falling circulations of national newspapers.

Conclusion: Suburbia in the post-millennial age and continuities with the past

The chronicling of suburbia in fiction continues in post-millennial and post-9/11 novel which also includes Richard Ford's Bascombe books (Knapp 2011). Examples used in this chapter such as Updike (2009) and Franzen (2010) commonly contain wry barbs about the direction of modern US suburbia into exoburb territory and references to contemporaneous popular culture. The three widows who become two are all acutely aware of their own mortality. After her insistence at being an old lady Alexandra's 8-year-old grandson tells her matter-of-factly (p. 271) 'Life sucks, and then you die. Kurt Cobain wasn't afraid to die. He wanted to do it. It's no big deal, the way they do it now. These bombers in Iraq, they commit suicide all the time.' Others who make appearances in conversation are Bush and Mubarak. It appears that the trio are somewhat baffled by modern mores and innovation such as the word 'partner' and the trackball mouse function of the contemporary laptop. On attempting to reach the Godess and cast a spell Jane jests 'Doesn't she have a cell-phone yet?' (p. 200).

Franzen describes suburbia's reverse process of gentrification at the start of the book with the young pioneering Berglund couple buying and renovating an inexpensive yet spacious, ramshackle Victorian in a rundown part of Minnesota with Patty rejecting her own bourgeois upbringing in the upscale New York suburban hinterlands. Multiple moral dilemmas present themselves including trust/betrayal throughout. In the early part of the book we are presented with the need of the teenage Patty's parents to placate eminent local Democrat party dignitaries after her rape by their son. When Patty complains to husband Walter how she hates her family he cheerfuly rejoinders (Franzen 2010:124): 'We'll make our own family!' Needless to say this is not all straightforward. The marriage experiences many pressures: their rebellious son Joey leaves home to move in with the white trash girlfriend next door while still at school before becoming a Republican think-tank apparatchik in contravention of his parent's liberal upbringing and Democrat heritage. The temptation of Walter's best friend from college who was also Patty's college crush resurfaces. Latterly there is the environmental activism versus corporate interests conundrum that the bicycling Walter must wrestle with and depression too features heavily. Such issues intersect: the personal is political to quote the old phrase. All three components of the post-war popular-youth cultural trilogy of sex, drugs and rock and roll emerge as the characters age over several decades before after several *rebondissements* the central couple come full circle again as moving back to New York city after selling their land to make an exclusive suburban housing development, the resassuringly derivatively named Canterbridge Estates for which virgin land has been bulldozed.

Inter-textual references are common in suburban novel: sometimes recurring as motifs such as *Madame Bovary* (returned to in Chapter 6) or *the Hours* constructed around the novel *Mrs Dalloway* in which writing, reading and literary promotion are all central. General pop culture also abounds. In

Little Children house-husband Todd plays his 3 years old nursery rhyme CDs but we are reminded that once he was an avid grunge-fan. Tim Lott's (2004) creation of the soon-to-be divorced dad Danny tries to get his 6 years old to sing the Sex Pistols but 'Anarchy in the United Kingdom' sounds all wrong delivered in his daughter's angelic, mellifluous tones. In some ways in these post-millennial sagas some of these details already feel dated demonstrating how fast technology moves. The advent of cellphones and email is present in Tom Perrota's *Little Children* (2004) but the adulterous Todd and his wife share one between them making the conduct of extramarital affairs troublesome – something fairly unimaginable now. In Updike's (2009) *Widows of Eastwick* again cell phones have been normalized but the smartphone has not arrived. In the latter sections of *Freedom* (Franzen 2010) blackberrys are with us but perhaps now it should be the tablet, android or iphone. At one point the contrast is made between Walter's concern for the preservation of bird species and the modern nature of communications technology which operates at a largely surface level. 'There was plenty of tweeting on twitter, but the chirping and fluttering world of nature . . . was one anxiety too many' we are told (Franzen 2010:546) although Facebook appears not to be as embedded into the characters' lives as it is now becoming. In the story part of the rift between Patty and Joey who once enjoyed a close mother–son relationship is her disapproval for his liking of the suburban sitcom *Married . . . with Children* and edgy rap star Tupac Shakur, hence cultural references are deployed to signify generation gap.

This chapter has been about changing contours of suburban representation in popular literature. Many features unite the titles discussed. Both the two Avenue novels of Delderfield and *Freedom* offer the reader epic multigenerational family drama but while the former is somewhat puritanical in some respects the latter was unbridled in description of sex enough to be recipient of a nomination for the 2010 Bad Sex in Literature Award for his, alongside such distinguished company Tony Blair for a passage in his memoirs (Freeman 2010). Even those written subsequently but set in the past where hindsight has coloured our understanding of the era which they describe can be seen as a way of understanding their respective historical period and appreciating commonalities. One can see distinct similarities between the pen portraits of J. G. Ballard (2006:165):

> Dual carriage-ways and used car-lots. Nothing to look forward to except new patio doors and a trip to Homebase. All the promise of life delivered to door in a flat pack.

Or the observation of Orwell's (1939/75:214) George Bowling of Lower Binfield: 'It had merely been swallowed. . . .' The same sentiment can be discerned in H. G. Wells' (1911:46) description of Bromstead as

> a dull useless boiling up of human activities, an immense clustering of futilities. . . [where] prentenious villas jostle slums, and public-house and tin tabernacle glower at one another across the cat-haunted lot that intervenes.

Or even the lament of the witch Jane (Updike 2009:139)

> I remember Eastwick as a fun hick place. . . but it's gotten homogenized – the curbs downtown all fancy granite, and the Old Stone Bank twice the size it was, like some big bland cancer gobbling up everything.

Certain themes of the great suburban novel or simply suburban reading matter are enduring including descriptions of sex which have become ever more daring. In 2012 when the runaway hit novel *Fifty Shades of Grey* overtook Harry Potter to be the fastest selling paperback of all time, a filmed CBS newsreport announced 'It's sweeping through suburban bedrooms like wildfire' and labelled it as a 'marriage-saver' for its detailing of submissive sado-masochist sexual acts in its story of seduction and lost innocence.[7] This sits alongside many other factors such as the descriptions of suburban interiors. In the 1970s Britain this meant polishing G-plan furniture from Leslie Thomas (1974) or Kureishi (1990:51) via Karim describing 'The things people in Chiselhurst would exchange their legs for: velvet curtains, stereos, Martinis, electric lawnmowers, double-glazing.' We often feel that we have inhabited these spaces before, be it in a real or imagined sense. In the contemporary US suburb Eastwick at Macy's place the exterior resembles 'a stranded-looking leftover from the Levittown era' (Updike 2009:156) while inside '[t]he living room bespoke a gauche prosperity' (p. 157) in which oversized leather armchairs and an unfeasibly large flatscreen television dominate. When Joey in *Freedom* visits the upscale home of his college room-mate in Virgina we are told (Franzen 2010:261): 'Despite having grown up in a home he'd considered book-filled and tasteful, Joey was staggered by the quantity of hardcover books and the obviously top quality of the multicultural swag that Jonathan's father had collected during distinguished foreign residencies.' He is described as floating through the beautiful rooms as if on helium. Artefacts and furniture gathered from overseas heritage rather than simply work attachments/holiday trips around the world or religious significance, for example Islamic wall hangings of the *kaaba* at Mecca or Jewish *menorah* candleholders might just as easily be found in the suburban homes of today. It is narrow-minded and blinkered to reduce the diversity of the contemporary suburb to a space populated by one-dimensional characters who are backward in cultural taste. Nash (1963:35) writes that the characters of Max Shulman 'are not so fixed as casual reading of much popular sociology of suburbia would suggest' citing their ability to experience love as evidence that makes them more than mere automatons or victims of their envoronment.

The main examples discussed in this chapter are all of fairly classic status: Weedon and Grossmith began the trend towards the suburban novel with the daily life chronicles of Pooter first in *Punch* columns but then collected in book-form. The form has sustained through Orwell's critical reflections, Delderfield's historical sweep of documentary through to post-apocalyptic science fiction have sustained the suburban tendency in fiction. However new examples add themselves continually to the list of fictitious works representing the lived realities of suburbia. If we are looking for suburban happy endings they are not always present but often things seem to come to full circle. Bowling in *Coming Up for Air* ends up crushed. Following his return from the trip down memory lane signifying 'loss, disillusionment, disenchantment' (Williams 1971:49) he has no will or energy to explain to his livid wife Hilda that he hasn't been with another woman in his lost week away because the truth is even less credible to her. *Keep the Aspidistra Flying* ends with one-time penniless rebel Gordon Comstock having taken a regular job and about to marry his on–off girlfriend with the couple now expecting a baby. As responsibility beckons he undergoes a realization that suburban mores have much to recommend them and the aspidistra plant that has been a constant of all his suburban-rented lodgings is not such a symbol of all that is bad with the world after all. Williams (1971:39) remarks 'most of Orwell's important writing is about someone who tries to get away and fails. That failure, that reabsorption happens, in the end . . . though of course the experience of awareness, rejection, and flight made its important mark.' It is again a submission to conformity but the self-loathing anti-hero of both of these novels anticipates the angry young men novels of the 1960s that followed them, predating and yet prefiguring the kitchen sink drama that Orwell never lived to see but would probably have approved of. In *Freedom* (Franzen 2010) the Berglunds begin by gentrifying their first area of residence and effectively suburbanizing it. Their marriage emerges renewed at the end despite the tribulations it undergoes. Our faith in the American suburban way of life is intact indicating essential conservatism.

This chapter has looked at books about the suburbs and set in them rather than enjoyed by readers there. The latter could have included Dan Brown's historical fiction, the Harry Potter novels, the Mills and Boon franchise of romantic fiction that has been long been popular among a suburban readership and more recently the escapism of the bondage book *Fifty Shades of Grey*. The suburban novel uses a range of devices and flourishes, for example the letter in *Widows* (Updike 2009), or multiple voices and perspectives in a non-linear narrative where all stories join up at the end (Cunningham 1998; Franzen 2010) or even a story partially told in a journal completed at the insistence of a character's therapist which itself changes events (Franzen 2010). Suburban motifs are long-running in fiction, for example, 'the sinister suburb' is a trope running through the work of Victorian novelist Wilkie Collins dating from his novel *Basil* (1852) onwards. The number of books named in this chapter that have been converted into film or television adaptation is testimony to their potency ranging from the screwball suburban comedy of *Rally Round the Flag, Boys* to the melancholia of suburban alienation in say *Revolutionary Road*, *Little Children* and *Virgin Suicides*. Also powerful is the sense of suburbia's detachedness from the thrusting city but umbilical connection to it. Leslie Thomas' in between status of Plummers Park is also echoed in a letter Sukie writes to Alexandra in which she confesses 'The thing about all these suburbs is that having such a big city, *The big city* as far as the US is concerned [New York]", keeps us on our toes and at the same time is rather demoralizing because we don't *quite* live there, we just live in its aura, so to speak' (Updike 2009:73). We do need more nuanced readings of suburbia than some of these well-known examples have offered. As Delderfield attempted to show by celebrating it some decades ago, suburbia is not simply a trap for its inhabitants as has often been suggested. Despite abundant hype about new forms of popular culture suburban fiction is an old form which has long expressed cultures of suburbia spanning hopes, dreams and anxieties which looks set to continue. The formats may change with the e-book and kindle complimenting hardbacks and paperbacks and purchasing options shifting from bookstore to websites capable of recommending what others with your profile purchased but as this chapter has many of the same debates around class, culture and context remain the same while suburbia is subject to continual renewal.

Notes

1   See J. Wilde (2007), *The Guardian,* arts blog 23 April, 'I hope Diary Of A Nobody is in safe hands', at: www.guardian.co.uk/culture/tvandradioblog/2007/apr/23/ihop

ediaryofanobodyisin?INTCMP=SRCH and L. Gardner (2011) 'Diary of a Nobody: Review', *The Guardian*, 15 March, at: www.guardian.co.uk/stage/2011/mar/15/diary-of-a-nobody-review?INTCMP=SRCH.

2   www.cartoons.ac.uk/artists/sidney-conradstrube/biography.

3   www.guardian.co.uk/books/2009/jan/23/bestbooks-fiction.

4   Plummers Park is believed to be based on Carpenders Park, Watford, Hertfordshire. This remains an open secret to the point that estate agents for the area acknowledge this notoriety in present-day advertising for houses, for example: a December 2010 advert for a £330,000 bungalow includes the words 'the area gained some notoriety as Plummers Park, the setting for Leslie Thomas' *Tropic of Ruislip*' www.fairfieldestates.co.uk/Property-For-Sale-St-Georges-Driv e-Carpenders-Park-Watford-PI-755.htm.

5   Maxted is also a character in the best-selling part-fictionalized autobiography Empire of the Sun (1984) about his formative years in Shangai.

6   For full details, see 'J. G. Ballard – Summary Bibliography', at: www.isfdb.org/cgi-bin/ ea.cgi?259.

7   http://newyork.cbslocal.com/video/6792758-fifty-shades-of-grey/.

3

The Sound of the Suburbs:
Noise from Out of Nowhere?

Although the song became famous in its own right, for me – as for any Scousers – it was simply an ordinary suburban junction where I went to the barber's shop. (It also led loads of people to nick the road signs . . .) I think we sometimes get seduced into believing that extraordinary people and places are, somehow, extraordinary by nature – but they are often simply cases of the ordinary being given some extra significance. At the end of the day, Penny Lane is still just a road – and extraordinary people bleed and laugh and weep like the rest of us. As an ordinary Christian I think this is really encouraging.

(Nick Baines, the Bishop of Croydon, BBC Radio 2)[1]

All right Morrissey you thunderously appalling great ponce, tell me if you would, how much f***ing time did you spend in Dagenham researching this one? Spend time in the pub with the panel beaters, wideboys and assorted f***ing hoolies, get drunk with them, get in a few f***ing fights, really found out what makes them tick? Did you f***. You just warbled the first bollocks that came into your f***ing head, didn't you?

(Mr Agreeable on Dagenham Dave)

From hip hop's urban violence and anti-police messages to earlier examples, for example the Jam's 'In the City' there has been an abiding pop fascination with urban imagery in pop and denigration of the suburb, as seen on the Sex Pistols' track 'Satellite' in which Rotten snarls 'I don't like where you come from/It's just a satellite of London.' Nonetheless there is a rich vein of pop documenting post-war suburbia on both sides of the Atlantic dating from 1960s beat combos, through 1970s punk via *The Pet Shop Boys* in the 1980s with their single 'Suburbia' and 1990s grunge up to the award-winning 2010 album by Canadian indie outfit Arcade Fire *The Suburbs*. In tone these have oscillated between a commiseration of suburban drudgery and a celebration of the periphery and its possibilities. Pop has long had a centrality in post-war youth culture offering escape routes to its practitioners and to its listeners, alternatives to their routine surroundings in the form of emotional escapism. The suburbs have not only been spaces where pop music is listened, to or consumed but it has also been the inspiration and locale in which much pop was created or produced. Pop's practitioners frequently have been drawn from suburban locations which have provided much impetus to pop's messages and meanings. It has both reflected the suburban surroundings of its creators and provided a soundtrack for its suburban listeners whose lives were played out in box bedrooms at the edges of cities. The significance of place and its relationship to popular music at large is a growing area of academic enquiry. Socio-spatial interest in pop soundtracks appears to have intensified in an era of increased globalization within the music industry: perhaps because of the inescapable pull of such tendencies. Studies concentrating on the significance of the 'local' usually in music-making have included those of Bennett (2000), Finnegan (1989) and Fornäs and Lindberg (1995) but each concentrated on their own locales rather looking at the broader category of suburbia. This chapter attempts to address this imbalance by looking at the field of suburban pop and how music has reflected multiple suburbias and how in tone it has shifted from optimism to *ennui*.

Suburban sensibilities in early popular music

On the blues song 'I'm Gonna Move to the Outskirts of Town' sung by Ray Charles the desire for the quiet life and privacy in suburbia is expressed as solution to the hustle and bustle of the city 'cos I don't nobody always hanging around'. The narrator nonetheless says that eventually they will have children there although woe betide her wife if she is in any way unfaithful – 'they all better look like me'. Luxury consumer comforts, the very trappings of the suburban life, are mentioned by brand-name.

> Let me tell you, honey/We gonna move away from here
>
> I don't need no iceman/I'm gonna get you a Fridgidaire.

The song was not a huge hit on its release but was later covered by Jackie Wilson, B. B. King and Rod Stewart and featured on the *Sopranos* (episode 73 of season 6). The suburbs flourished under President Eisenhower in the United States with his emblematic GI loans offering mortgages for returning servicemen. Suburbanization away from cramped living conditions was meant to be an optimistic movement as the song implies however negativity towards the supposedly bourgeois suburban ideal was also expressed in the song as postwar youth culture took root becoming a full-fledged consumer-led market in both the United Kingdom and United States.

Young people no longer faced the shackles of the immediate post-wartime austerity and rationing was ended in Britain. As well as lessening material restraints, structural conditions improved: UK compulsory national service was dispensed with, full employment and lack of family obligation allowed the young disposable income. The ridiculing of suburban domesticity is also evident on the 1963 Pete Seeger hit 'Little Boxes' (written by Malvina Reynolds) which is scathing about speculatively built hastily constructed 'ticky tacky' dwellings 'all the same'. The song, used as theme tune to suburban comedy *Weeds* in several different versions including world music and hip hop variants playing in a show which ran on US television four decades after its appearance, predicts that the cycle will repeat endlessly:

> And they all play on the golf course and drink their martini dry
> And they all have pretty children and the children go to school
> And the children go to summer camp
> And then to the university
> And they all get put in boxes, and they all come out the same
> And the boys go into business and marry and raise a family
> And they all get put in boxes, little boxes all the same.

The song sounds like these inhabitants are being condemned to coffins – it is almost a checklist of American suburban clichés, which in the United Kingdom would have to be matched by references to net curtains and privet hedges. In attitudinal as well as spatial terms 'suburbia' nurtured youth culture's accelerated growth as the restlessness at the sterility of their surroundings was a key factor in the pop expressing suburban ennui, stimulated by the UK art school in particular. Of the pioneering performers of homegrown youth culture in Britain, the magnetic pull of the United States can be seen in a fascination with all things American. The still musically active Cliff Richard was the United Kingdom's answer to Elvis who was born in India under colonial rule but grew up in Cheshunt, Hertfordshire to the north of London. Diana Dors who was originally from Swindon, Wiltshire, was fashioned as the UK equivalent of Marilyn Monroe. It was not until those other enduring favourites, the Beatles from suburban Merseyside and forever synonymous with Liverpool that British pop found its own voice in suburban English accents. By 1967 Beatles copyists the Monkees (based in the United States) on 'Pleasant Valley Sunday' penned by Goffin and King poured scorn on suburban aspiration when they sang: 'Another pleasant valley Sunday/Here in Status Symbol Land.' There is even a satirization of the suburban ritual of outdoor barbecue party: 'Charcoal burnin' everywhere/ Rows of houses that are all the same/And no one seems to care.' The Beatles later rivals the Rolling Stones hailed from Dartford in Kent. The increased affluence was a seedbed for the fertile growth for post-war pop. Participation in post-war pop could be buying into the youth cultural dream by starting a band oneself (an example of the activities listed in 'Pleasant Valley Sunday') or at the level of purchasing the end-product records substantiating the claim of Prime Minister Harold Macmillan in a 1957 speech that 'most of our people have never had it so good' referring, to improved living conditions.

While the Beatles were influenced by US musical trends (in their Hamburg incarnation their set almost entirely consisted of rock'n'roll standards) the band's recorded output was noteworthy for its Englishness. The influence of Albion was underscored by their singing in English accents and subject matter sometimes dealing with mundane almost kitchen sink subjects or venturing into melodramatic territory, for example on the songs *Eleanor Rigby* (1966) and *She's Leaving Home* (1966). These twin tendencies were accentuated further throughout the band's career as they grew in confidence musically to the point that the McCartney contribution 'Penny Lane' immortalized the line 'here beneath the blue suburban skies' sung in an approving manner on a song with a generally upbeat, optimistic register. Daniels (2006) has devoted an entire article to this single and its double A side the more surreal 'Strawberry Fields' as symbolizing a genre he calls 'suburban pastoral', a variant on the quintessentially English 'rural idyll'. Unlike the imaginary 'Blackberry Way' (the Move) or 'Itchycoo Park' (the Faces) or 'Detroit City' sung about the same year by Welshman Tom Jones in an American country drawl, both 'Penny Lane' and 'Strawberry Fields' were actual names of real places from Lennon and McCartney's childhoods. By the time the double A side was issued the band had dropped their now considered clean-cut although at the time shockingly long haired be-suited earlier image for even longer hair, moustaches and beards and hippie inspired clothing. Nick Green (2005:261–2) claims Strawberry Fields was revolutionary for its psychedelic noodlings however 'it is McCartney's Penny Lane that gets to the heart of the idealised English suburban way of life, safe from the dangers of the city itself, peopled by unthreatening characters who lend a feeling of steady continuity

[and] . . . capture everyday suburban life'. The banker, fireman and barber of the song are analogous to the fictitious butcher, baker and candlestick-maker of any English suburban high street before the onset of chainstores and out-of-town shopping began their decline, later sealed with the rise of online transactions. As the Beatles became a purely studio band, the two chief songwriters reverted back to their suburban origins for inspiration. The band had earlier been faces among the throng of 'Swinging London', celebrated for example on French *chansonnier* Serge Gainsbourg's satirical 'Qui est "in", Qui est "out"'. Here they were taking a more introspective, whimsical and personal view of Englishness.

From the exterior Mendips, the home of John Lennon's Aunt Mimi who he grew up with looks like an indentikit 1930s semi as found in suburbs all over the country: Edgbaston bordering Birmingham, Withington in Manchester or countless examples in Leeds, Coventry or London. Norman (2004:6) describes it as 'a semi-detached villa designed for the aspirational lower middle class, with mock Tudor half-timbering'. He calls Woolton where it was situated 'a respectable, desirable and featureless suburb'. Of the other half of the song-writing partnership we are told how in 1955 the 13-year-old Paul escaped to suburbia: 'the McCartneys left Speke and its pallid factory smog . . . [for] a council house in Allerton, one of Liverpool's nearer and better suburbs. It was a definite step-up for the family to move to 20 Forthlin Road, a double row of semi-detached houses small and neat enough to pass for privately-owned villas' (Norman 2004:16). At the time that the pair lived at these addresses: two different types of suburbia that show the contrast between private and social housing, it could not have been envisaged that both would become quasi-stately homes to be taken over by the National Trust and run in the same way as say Osborne House, Queen Victoria's Isle of Wight retreat and numerous other 'national treasures'. The Bee Gees grew up in Manchester. Band-member Barry Gibb re-bought the house that had been the family home in Keppel Road, Chorlton, when it came up for sale in 2002 and he and the late Robin were conferred with honorary degrees from Vice Chancellor Anna Ford and a posthumous award for Maurice, at Manchester University two years later. The house is now rented out but in 2008 featured in a BBC1 *One Show* item when Robin, who died in 2012 of cancer, revisited the property.[2]

As they grew in confidence both the Beatles and their arch-rivals the Rolling Stones dropped the r'n'b standards that they initially played covers of and began to document the everyday in their own original composition. Old suburban haunts are revisited and daily routines chronicled in English accents on various Beatles tracks, for example 'Good Morning Good Morning' with its observation 'nothing has changed, it's still the same' and on 'Day in the Life' where the surrealness of Lennon's section (4,000 holes in Blackburn, Lancashire) is counterbalanced by McCartney describing the commute to work and the reverie of escapism of smoking on the bus – an act no longer permitted. The band employed English musical tradition in their character sketches. However the Beatles' commentary of suburbia reached its apogee in 'Penny Lane'. The Stones attempted social commentary on 'Yesterday's Papers' and probed the disturbing side of the suburban dream on 'Mother's Little Helper' about the plight of the housewife addicted to prescription drugs to get through the day.

Daniels (2006) notes that the rivalries between Lennon and McCartney continue in death as both have had their childhood homes become potentially competing visitor attractions under the umbrella of the National Trust (two words Lennon sang sarcastically about on the White Album's 'Happiness Is a Warm Gun').[3] Presumably both properties are visited by near-equal number of people as part of the pop-tourism industry that has grown up around the band and their city of birth: if outsiders are making the trip to Liverpool it surely makes sense to visit both. Guided tours can be conducted of both and there are accompanying brochures for the two rather modest houses.[4] After the McCartney's council home 20 Forthlin Road was bought, restored and opened to the public in 1999, Lennon's widow Yoko Ono bought the house of John's Aunt Mimi for £150,000 to donate to the National Trust, stumping up £75,000 restoration costs herself. Philip Norman's (2004) rewrite of his Beatles biography *Shout* includes in its photographic plates Yoko pictured outside Mendips in 2002, the year of its opening ceremony. Norman (2004:431–2) remarked: 'One can now therefore belatedly examine every detail of the genteel home which that self-professed "working class hero" never completely got out of his system . . . the "morning room" with its defunct servants' bells . . . the glass front porch to which Mimi banished him for so many hours of solitary guitar practice. Here is the sub-baronial staircase to the seven-by-ten front room [recreated], with its red-quilted bed and pin-ups of Elvis and Bridgette Bardot, where he . . . drafted the first eccentrically spelt versions of songs that would one day captivate the world.' The house had been in private ownership until 2002 so replica fixture and fittings needed to be sourced in several areas, for example the front room art deco armchairs and even the front door with its stain glassed windows had to be replaced as the original had been bought by a Japanese fan some years earlier. The example shows how the mundane almost becomes sacred. The houses in landscapes of ordinariness become extraordinary.

The press at the time painted rivalries between the Beatles and Stones centring on their North versus South and working- versus middle-class backgrounds whereas they also had much in common including their suburban roots. The same dichotomy was to be drawn later in Britpop between Oasis and Blur. The description of the Rolling Stones's home county of Kent is described in terms stereotypically applied to suburbia by Norman (2002:25) as 'ranks of suburbs barely distinguishable from one another, crossed by railway bridges, whose names are synonyms for dullness and decorum – Bexley, Bromley, Beckenham, Dartford, Sidcup, Sevenoaks and the rest'. Meanwhile Keith Richards also was from Dartford but from the social housing end of the town and Templars Hill an 'estate [that] was brand new, dumped down on raw new tarmac roads without amusements or amenities' (Norman 2002:39). Various suburban compass points featured in the band's early history including Sidcup Art College where Richards studied and the Ealing Blues club where the band first played (selected as a location when its founder Alexis Korner could not find a central London venue prepared to host it and finally having a plaque unveiled at its former location in 2012 in a ceremony attended by Charlie Watts among others). Band members have long since moved away from their suburban origins but the Stones connection to their hometown is more of a living one than restoring their childhood houses as heritage projects: in 2000 the town's Mick Jagger Arts Centre was opened by the now Sir Mick who came back to unveil an extension in 2010 and pay a visit to Dartford Grammar School. In an audiofile of the event he describes the town as 'an odd place, really urban and suburban, from the playing fields you can see the M25, but then there's also countryside beyond that'.[5] Jagger is also patron-funder of the Red Rooster project in which Dartford primary school children can take up playing musical instruments.

Suburbia connotes territory in a constant state of flux. The suburb does not stand still and there is no singular experience of suburbia. Gentrification can be seen as the polar opposite of suburbanization but suburbia too is reinvented and gentrified with successive generations. The commentary of Swedish writer Lars Madelid (2007:50) who traces rock routes in his guide-book demonstrates an outsider's perception of neighbourhood and locale as seen in his comment: 'I choose to go . . . towards central Muswell Hill. This is where The Kinks have their roots and I am slightly surprised that the district gives such a cosy and inviting impression. I knew that . . . the brothers Davies grew up in an old working class suburb, and I had imagined a considerably more shabby area.' On hits like 'Autumn Almanac', 'Waterloo Sunset' and 'Well Respected Man', 'Plastic Man' and the concept album *Village Green Preservation Society* the Kinks were also erudite chroniclers of London and its suburbs. 'End of the Season' from 1967 begins with birdsong and sounds world-weary and bored of the city explaining 'I get no kicks walking down Saville Row. . . .' George Melly (1970:136) observed 'Despite his carefully grubby and poverty-stricken appearance, and painfully restricted vocabulary, the average young pop fan today is drawn in the main from a middle-class or suburban background and is educationally in one of the higher streams.' The UK art school – dubbed 'state-subsidized bohemia where working-class youth too unruly for a life of labour mingle with slumming middle-class youth too unruly for a life in middle management' (Reynolds 2005:xviii) – often acted as crucible of pop as seen from the backgrounds of Lennon, McCartney, Keith Richard, Pete Townsend of the Who, Queen, Malcolm McLaren and the Kinks. Madelid (2007) voices disappointment that the Kinks' neighbourhood is not as down-at-heel as expected. The reason is the gentrification that has taken place to make the London N10 area a highly desirable one. Horne and Frith helpfully include a table of where these colleges, which were frequently in suburban locations: for example, Hornsey College (attended by Adam Ant), Ealing College (Freddie Mercury, Pete Townsend) and Croydon (Jamie Reid, Malcolm McLaren). The Kinks and Syd Barrett were also 1960s art school alumnae.

Suburban punk and post-punk

Like many musical styles punk has contested roots: the British trace its lineage to the Sex Pistols and the Kings Road, London, however US analyses see it as emerging from the hip New York arty garage rock scene and the CBGBs club. Both versions prioritized musical amateurism and a do-it-yourself ethos. Redhead (1990:87) has remarked: 'Punk is the best example . . . [of] . . . subculture, style and sound shrink wrapped for the pop culture archive. It represents not the end of the pop/rock/youth culture nexus but its most perfect product.' Sonically its boiled down three-chord thrash made it an ideal vehicle for the articulation of anger. Part of the punk mythology is of urban paranoia. Even if punk at first sight was 'white', artists like John Lydon had immigrant backgrounds with their experiences refracted through the faultlines of Irish Origins. Recalling Paul Gilroy's influential theory of the Black Atlantic and circulating migratory and cultural routes, Campbell (1999:158) has written of 'displacement, discrimination and diasporic cultural practices, and the enduring impact that these circumstances have had on second-generation identity', in relation to those of Irish heritage. The now US-based Sex Pistols singer John Lydon who identified himself as 'from Finsbury Park', inner North London on his appearance on the BBC's prestigious *Question Time* political debate show (5/7/12) entitled his autobiography *No Dogs, No Blacks, No Irish* in a reference to now outlawed racially discriminatory wording of lodging advertisements seen up until the 1960s in the United Kingdom. However this immigrant experience has been frequently filtered through suburbia. Jon Savage (1991:72) names the suburban council houses of the Wormholt estate on the Shepherds Bush/East Acton border, modelled on the garden suburb principle: 'Although it was only a mile away from Hammersmith, Wormholt, just over the road from White City was quite different. It was a sprawling council estate that, despite the benefits of thirties town planning, was as much of a rabbit warren as the slums of Dicken's London had been a century before.' Croydon Art School was pivotal in the development of Pistols manager Malcolm McLaren who has been quoted as saying (Your Local Guardian series 2010) 'Croydon will always be remembered as a rite of passage of my life – one night layovers, in the arms of someone, the constant roaming at night through its market streets and thereafter navigating those deep leafy suburbs into the countryside beyond, spending hours looking out of Croydon's art school windows, observing and then struggling to come to terms with these giant triffids of buildings that rise up and spread themselves all along East Croydon's path, using charcoal pencil and anything close to hand. I drew and drew and drew.' Croydon in some ways has characteristics of exurbia as extensive development took place in the 1960s onto its original suburban footprint. It contains gleaming office blocks including the futuristic sounding Lunar House, UK Home Office passport office as well as suburban homes. It has bid several times for city status seeing itself as a conurbation in its own right although it has been constantly knocked back.

The idea of punk emerging from the urban paranoia of towerblock-induced high rise hell perpetrated by its practitioners has tended to obscure its status as outlet for the frustrations of suburban youth articulated in punk soundtracks, particularly in its later guise of new wave. For all its urban posturing, punk was then an intrinsically suburban phenomenon in the 1970s, emerging from a period of crisis in governmental circles reflected in its short sharp shock sound. In the 1970s Bromley-set *Bhudda of Suburbia* central character Karim disapprovingly remarks (Kureishi 1990:130) 'Not a squeeze of anything "progressive" or "experimental" came from those pallid, vicious council-estate kids with hedgehog hair, howling about anarchy and hatred.' Yet the suburb of Bromley on the South London/Kent border has been named by Frith (1997:271) as 'the most significant suburb in British pop history'. Not only did it spawn David Bowie but in the punk era it was the base of the 'Bromley contingent' numbering Billy Idol and Siouxsie Sioux among members that fuelled the early roster of punk personnel. The Banshees' debut single Hong Kong Garden (1978) with its insistent nagging riff at first sounds like it is describing a perfect oriental scene but it was actually about a fight in a Chinese restaurant in deepest suburban Chiselhurst as closer inspection of the lyrics, for example 'Would you like number 23?' referring to a menu item shows:

> Chicken Chow Mein and Chop Suey
> Hong Kong Garden takeaway.

The song actually details suburban violence perpetrated by local racists against the eatery's proprietors. Siouxsie has described the song as her revenge: 'I used to go along with my friend and just be really upset by the local skinheads that hung out there' (Webb 2009). The song's jagged, punchy structure fittingly ends with an apocalyptic single cymbal crash. This taut staccato sound continued on the track 'Suburban Relapse' from the album *The Scream* returned to in Chapter 6.

Many other songs of the era pilloried dull suburban lives. The Jam emerged from the Surrey commuter town Woking on Polydor during the phase of major label punk signings termed 'new wave'. Principal songwriter Paul Weller later had a volume of collected lyrics published under the title *Suburban 100*. Suburban stereotypes are evoked in their pen portrait of pin-striped commuting character Smithers Jones; a regular on the 8 a.m. train to Waterloo:

> Sitting on the train, you're nearly there/You're part of the production line
> You're the same as him, you're like tinned-sardines
> Get out of the pack, before they peel you back.

'Sound of the Suburbs' by the Members from Camberley, Surrey, painted scenes of a suburbia where the car is washed while mum cooks Sunday roast, little Jonny practicing guitar 'annoying the neighbours'. Its title has been more than once unearthed since including by myself (Huq 2007) and as the title of a 1991 Virgin compilation album of 1980s punk and new wave tunes. Their later 1978 single 'Solitary Confinement' delivered a more nuanced look at the suburbs. The opening powerchords usher in the familiar theme of the beginning locating suburbia as somewhere to flee from. Then as the song develops the youth-protagoist who the lyrics are addressed to relocates to 'London' only to find that he has swopped one prison for another: incarcerated in bedsit-land, isolated and trapped once again. The lure of the city 'to live out . . . life in style' did not live up to its promise.

> You are living in the suburbs/And you have problems with your parents
> So you move out to London town/Where you think everything's happening and going down.

The main repeating lyric was 'you're so lonely', echoing the anonymity of the city that is often named as a downside to urban living. The Skids had a track entitled 'Sweet Suburbia'.

US suburban pop sensibilities seem to be less obviously stated in song-titles but more indirectly noticeable in the general impression conveyed and images described. Consumerism seems to be a running motif, for example on 'Rockin' Shopping Center' from the 1977 self-titled LP *Jonathan Richman and the Modern Lovers*. The Sonic Youth track 'The Sprawl' with a title alluding the suburban development has been variously interpreted on web forums as being about prostitution and 'Selling Out'. The lyrics state

> I've gone native/I wanted to know the exact dimension of hell
> Outback was the river/And that big sign down the road
> That's where it all started.

And the chorus:

> Come on down to the store
> You can buy some more, and more, and more, and more.

On the post-punk New York New Wave band Talking Heads' track 'Once in a Lifetime' we are told of suburban routine on a highway which never seems to conclude, chasing the American dream:

> And you may ask yourself /What is that beautiful house?
> And you may ask yourself / Where does that highway go to?
> And you may ask yourself / Am I right? . . . Am I wrong?
> And you may say to yourself yourself/ My God! . . . What have I done?!

Here there is a direct questioning of the hamster-wheel existence of suburban life and realization of the futility of material possessions in the grand scheme of things which cannot compensate for the endless repetition of the cycle of life 'same as it ever was' which can catch up you unawares as it accumulates without your noticing and then gradually ebbs way. In the promotional music video for later 'Road to Nowhere' (another never-ending road that has little of the freedom one might expect of a 'freeway') the succession of expected conventional milestones: growing up education, job, career, marriage, kids are all visualized.

The Alberta-born Canadian songstress Joni Mitchell's album *The Hissing of Summer Lawns* of 1976, for example revisits many of these themes across its ten tracks and is returned to in Chapter 6. Similar suburban dissatisfaction is clear on 'Subdivisions' (1982) by the Canadian rock band Rush with eerie synth backing over a guitar solo of a progressive rock style. In an early biography (Gett 1984) now digitalized[6] the band's Neil Peary is quoted as explaining the song as 'an exploration of the background from which all of us (and probably most of our audience) have sprung'. It is explained how in keeping with other prog rock such as Genesis and Marillion who had sung about mythical landscapes originally, Rush who hailed from the Ontario suburbs had 'a passion for fantasy and science fiction work which provided . . . an element of escapism from the grim reality of everyday life in suburbia'. The song signalled the change from such epic themes to the more everyday with a video filmed in part at a high school in Scarborough, Ontario, featuring evening Toronto newscaster Mark Dailey repeating the word 'Subdivisions' in the chorus. Aerial shots of city sprawl of freeways and flyovers give way to the band performing interspersed with story of a Hank Marvin-like high school nerd who ends up playing arcade games downtown after being ridiculed by cool and trendy classmates. The video also includes shots of a commuter subway station. The verse admonishes:

> Growing up it all seems so one-sided/Opinions all provided
> The future pre-decided/Detached and subdivided
> In the mass production zone.

The chorus references high school halls and shopping malls where one must 'conform or be cast out' concluding

> But the suburbs have no charms to soothe
> The restless dreams of youth.

As punk mutated to post-punk, suburban critique continued. On the Jam's 'Tales from the Riverbank' (1981) which like the Weller solo album 'Wild Wood' appears to have a title derived from the children's Classic novel 'Wind in the Willows' the yearning for an idealized past of open fields 'when we were young' which no longer exist is remembered. The tone is gentle and the tempo slow. The lyric wistfully admits:

> True it's a dream mixed with nostalgia
> But it's a dream that I'll always hang on to/That I'll always run to
> Won't you join me by the riverbank?

The more pugnacious-sounding fast-paced song 'Bricks and Mortar' decries rather than regrets the onset of the bulldozers replacing old, organic communities with gleaming new skyward leaning creations and car-parking in the name of progress:

> Bricks and mortar, reflecting social change,
> Cracks in the pavement, reveal cravings for success
> Why do we try to hide our past/ By pulling down houses to build car parks.

This critique of urban planning sarcastically refers to 'progress' and demands

> Who has the right to make that choice?
> A man whose home has cost forty grand.[7]

The sum of £40,000 sounds laughable when even in the present financial climate a modest house in the south of England might easily cost ten times this amount.

This lamentation of old rural landscape being replaced by suburban symbols can also be seen in the Pretenders' 'My City Was Gone' where a nightmarish situation ensues as Muzak fills the air after the farms of Ohio have been replaced by shopping malls. The sentiments can also be seen in Joni Mitchell's pre-punk 'Big Yellow Taxi' (1970) concerning the suburbanization of California where she relates 'They paved paradise/And put up a parking lot'. The line has much similarity with the Pretenders' verse:

> I went back to Ohio/But my city was gone
> There was no train station/There was no downtown
> South Howard had disappeared/All my favorite places
> My city had been pulled down/Reduced to parking spaces.

Both this and the Jam recall and the Weller interview are reminiscent of the couplet of Betjeman (2009:163): 'The sisters Progress and Destruction dwell/ Where rural Middlesex once cast her spell.' An ironic take on this sentiment is discernable on the latter period Talking Heads 'Nothing but Flowers' which describes a reverse movement of anti-suburban development that takes place as old suburban shibboleths are replaced with a back to nature movement as environmentalism wins out. The narrator sings nostalgically about missing his old suburban way of life with trappings of lawnmower and microwave. The Joni Mitchell line 'Don't it always seem to go/That you don't know what you've got till it's gone' seems appropriate here:

> From the age of the dinosaurs/Cars have run on gasoline
> Where, where have they gone?/Now, it's nothing but flowers.

He feels the new world of open fields disorienting.

> This used to be real estate/Now it's only fields and trees
> Where, where is the town? Now, it's nothing but flowers
> The highways and cars/Were sacrificed for agriculture
> I thought that we'd start over/But I guess I was wrong.

Given the band's previous distaste for the suburban rat-race on song that campaigns around a depleted ozone layer and other ecological issues were prominent in the late 1980s one can only assume that the song is intended with heavy irony. Around the same time the Pixies also sang of a world under threat from toxic waste in 'Monkey Gone to Heaven' and the B52s 1989 album Cosmic Thing (e.g. the track 'Topaz' also highlighted imminent environmental disaster).

In Paul Weller's later work the theme of yearning for the organic communities of old continued; 1985's 'Come to Milton Keynes' with Weller's then band the Style Council was a critique of New Towns to the annoyance of the district council of Milton Keynes. Older and wiser in an interview from 2007 at the age of 49 Weller took his journalist interlocutor back to Woking to promote his book of lyrics. We are told that Weller 'prefers its leafier, sleepier past' (Sandall 2007) to its present. The street that his 1995 solo album was named after Stanley Road is now dominated by offices at one end and a block of flats on the other . He is quoted as commenting 'It's f***in' 'orrible. How can you call this progress?' He recalls playing in the street, now converted to one way traffic, as a child which was possible as car traffic was so rare then. The interview states 'The young Weller's Woking was a place where "affluence and financial struggle were both very apparent, although any problems my family had I never noticed. There was always food on the table. We always had clean clothes". His dad worked in the building trade "on the hod", or on the taxi rank at the station, while his mum was a cleaner at the local 19th-century mosque, one of Britain's first.' Indeed Woking is also the site of a major Muslim burial ground in the United Kingdom (Naylor 2002), where Dodi Al-Fayed's body was flown to after his death at the side of Princess Diana in 1997. During the course of the interview a visit is paid to his parents who still lived at the time in Woking, in an upscale flat (a church conversion) on the edge of town. Of Weller we are told he now lives with his family 'in a house in Maida Vale in west London and, like many suburban boys, Weller is a devoted Londoner'. The narrative of decline is a longstanding one in writing on suburbia: both the character of Bowling in George Orwell's *Coming Up for Air* and the poetry of Betjeman make similar observations about how suburbia destroyed the countryside. In H. G. Wells' *New Machiavelli* too there is a disapproving description of how green fields get carved into parallelograms for suburban housing in Bromstead, painted as anti-progress. Weller seems to be lamenting how the old organic suburbia (he grew up in a two-up two-down terrace) has been destroyed by the new city-suburbia which includes office developments from multinationals such as Norwich Union (since absorbed by Aviva) in the town and blocks of flats.

Other suburbia-related musings present in punk came from a slew of new wave artists, for example the Stranglers who were originally called the Guildford Stranglers as they formed there ('English Towns') and XTC ('Respectable Street' 1981 about nosey neighbours and the jaunty 'Everyday Story Of Smalltown', 1984). The character sketch woven by these artists carry on the tradition of Penny Lane in evoking the 'idealized English suburban way of life, safe from the dangers of the city itself, peopled by unthreatening characters who lend a feeling of steady continuity to a place via a sun-drenched series of vignettes' (Green 2005). In 2010 the lead singer Andy Partridge was interviewed by *The Guardian*'s John Harris for a feature on suburban pop. The band's hometown Swindon had once been a west country railway town but its rapid train connection to London Paddington has almost made it a suburb of the capital and its major twenty-first century employer is Japanese car-manufacturer Honda which temporarily stopped production in 2008 and 2011 due to economic downtown and act of god happenings.[8] To the east of London Essex too has been source of pop inspiration and band personnel. 'Billericay Dickie' is a song by proto-punk Ian Dury on his 1977 album *New Boots and Panties*. His vaudeville theatre style also heard on the Billy Bragg song most associated with Essex is 'A13, Trunk Road to the sea', a reworking of the Rolling Stones' 'Route 66' itemizing places on the major arterial road that link Essex to the East End taking in suburbia en route. Things begin in Wapping taking in Fords, the Dartford Tunnel and the river too, Barking, Dagenham before the further reaches of Thurrock and Basildon before ending up at the seaside paradise of Southend. In his autobiography he has claimed 'I came from the place most kids come from: Nowheresville', (Bragg 2006:16–17). Other Essex post-punk artists included Depeche Mode and the Prodigy whose industrial electro metallic sounds arguably reflected the light industry of the county.

Post-punk's austere indie aesthetic of early recession-hit Thatcherism gave way to more glamorous, colourful 'new pop' as Thatcher moved into her second term. Suburban prime movers included to name but three: (i) the 'pure pop' of ABC fronted by Martin Fry who hailed from Stockport, technically in Cheshire but more accurately a satellite of Manchester; (ii) Wham!, a disco-rap duo from suburban Bushey in Hertfordshire just north of London and (iii) the pop-reggae of Culture Club whose lead protagonist Boy George was from Eltham, South London, an area later to become synonymous with the racist murder of Stephen Lawrence. Around the time of her third victory the maxim 'greed is good' held sway. The television stand-up comedy character Loadsamoney created by comic Harry Enfield attempted to satirize this vulgarity but ended up popularizing the stereotype. The Pet Shop Boys' early hit 'Opportunities' (1986) had a chorus which sarcastically urged 'Let's Make Lots of Money'. Their later track entitled 'Suburbia' was ode to suburban boredom containing the constant refrain: 'I only wanted something else to do but hang around' on the track. The almost spoken word lyrics describe petty rebellion and vandalism:

> Stood by the bus stop with a felt pen
> In this suburban hell
> And in the distance a police car
> To break the suburban spell.

The vision is one of dystopia. The soundtrack reflects this with crashing collision type effects overlaid onto a simple almost nursery-rhyme-like keyboard refrain. As the song progresses this basic melody jostles for attention with panda car sirens and other sounds of urban chaos. In an interview Neil Tennant has stated: 'I thought it was a great idea to write a song about suburbia and how it's really violent and decaying and a mess. It's quite a theme in English art, literature and music, like in Graham Greene or Paul Theroux – that the suburbs are really nasty, that behind lace curtains everyone is an alcoholic or a spanker or a mass murderer. Also, this was the era of the riots in Toxteth and Brixton. I remember some friends of mine having to drive through the riots in Brixton to visit me in Chelsea, and being scared. Brixton was a prosperous Victorian suburb, and eighty years later it had become this decaying inner city.'[9] The quote recognizes that what is and isn't a suburb changes over time. As urban populations sprawl city characteristics inevitably spread to suburbs. The theme here is of faded suburban promise.

Subsequently the 1990s band E17 strongly identified themselves with their outer East London home-district choosing their postcode as name in the same way as NWA had declared earlier that they were *Straight Outta Compton* (1988) on the album credited as beginning the gangster tendency in hip hop with its liberal references to AK47 weapons and an agressively anti-police stance. Their debut album was entitled *Walthamstow,* an area that to date had probably been known to most as the stop at the nothernmost end of the Piccadilly line. *Straight Outta Compton* itself was later parodied in 'Straight Out of Dunwoody' the Suburb Life remix a pop video on the internet that namechecked Birkenstock sandals and explained that the police were called once every two years and littering was frowned upon.[10]

In the quotation opening this chapter from 1995 columnist Mr Agreeable from now defunct weekly music magazine *Melody Maker* criticizes the singer Morrissey for a lack of first-hand research experience in single 'Dagenham

Dave'. From a methodological point of view the quote appears to be a plea for ethnographic responsibility. Yet there is also a parade of stereotypes being displayed about this area of East London overspill that in later years became known for its far-right BNP (British Nationalist Party) vote earning the borough of Barking and Dagenham the epithet the 'the racist capital of the UK'.[11] It is however Manchester that Morrissey and his former band the Smiths are synonymous with. The city featured repeatedly in their work – most famously the picture of Salford lads club pictured on the sleeve of the Smiths album, *The Queen Is Dead*. The Smiths articulation of being crushed by their drab small-town surroundings was a regular a feature of their lyrics. 'William it Was Really Nothing' opens with the observation 'The rain falls hard on a humdrum town/this town has dragged you down'. Similarly 'Frankly Mr Shankly' recalls the plot of Keith Waterhouse's novel *Billy Liar* and a yearning for the narrator to escape the claustrophobia of suburban/small-town origins and answer back to the boss that he despises. 'London' unusually addresses the song's subject rather than being told in the first person. The person it addresses is about to get on the train to Euston and thereby 'escape' his un-named habitus. This scenario again recalls the central plot of the novel and later kitchen sink film *Billy Liar*. On Youtube there has been a music-video of black and white images of the film, a kitchen sink classic, cut to the track which had no original video as it was never originally a single.[12] On the Smiths track 'Paint a Vulgar Picture' the hero seems to enact his solitary revenge from the confines of his box-bedroom lair: 'In my bedroom in those ugly new homes [sic]/I danced my legs down to the knees.' The Smiths' Englishness is all the more paradoxical for their Irish origins, all were sons of Irish immigrants.[13] Morrissey and Marr had both grown up in council house suburbia rather than the privately owned, speculatively built version, although their families had suburbanized out: Morrisey's from Hulme to Stretford and Marr's from Adwick to Wythenshawe. When Johnny Marr was asked 'When was the last time you cried?' in a *Q* magazine interview (February 2003) he answered 'I come from Ardwick, crying was beaten out of me', showing how the inner-city class origins were valorized more than suburban ones.

The 1990s and on: Hip hop, Britpop and beyond

Long before it became the stuff of ring tones and downloads pop music was a tangible product where songs assumed primacy. The 1980s saw the purely aural or sonic dimension of contemporary pop music reception supplemented by the advent of the pop video which was a factor in expanding the popular appeal of hip hop from its urban origins with ghetto associations to suburban bedrooms far and wide – all the more ironic given that MTV at its start only played white artists. Lavish cinematic promo clips were often accused of ostentatiously glamourising 'bling' however a subset of hip hop videos used the suburban idiom often juxtaposing the serenity of suburbia with a subculture that certainly at its outset was originally known for its raw sound tough image. Ice T's 'It was a Good Day' helped satisfy thirst for the 'urban' among young suburban youth with its lyrics that seemed to be resigned to a suburban fate and almost world-weary tone. The video ends with police snipers and gunmen swooping in on him as he walks home through a suburban street. Puff Daddy's memorable 'Bad Boys for Life' music video shows a hip hop crew (including Snoop Doggy Dogg, Ice Cube, xzibit, Shaq) cruising in an open top vehicle into a saccharine peaceful suburb 'Perfectown USA' as a real estate 'SOLD' sign goes up and neighbours' eyebrows are raised. The connotation is of the menacing cultural pollutant hip hop invading the unnaturally sunny picture of suburban tranquillity pictured satirically with humour and bravado. The 'there goers the neighbourhood' theme is evident again in the accompanying clip for 'Dilemma' by Nelly and Kelly Rowlands as a removal truck rolls in to 'Nellyville', which resembles the comfortable, upscale midwestern suburban setting of the US family prime time drama we have seen many times on the big or small screen, for example on *Desperate Housewives* or in the film *The Burbs*. The removal service brings with it the 'Dilemma' of the title as Nelly and new arrival Kelly desire each other although she has a pre-existing boyfriend. Unlike Puff Daddy's Perfectown in which Ben Stiller appears as a neighbour there are no white people in Nellyville and devoid of overt humour or irony, we see Nellyville with the sun shining and also in the rain as the melancholy torture of this love triangle is dramatized. There is no obvious resolution to this dilemma as the song simply fades out. The suburban trope in hip hop videos can also be seen in Trick Daddy's 'I'm a Thug' where our hero goes to 'meet the parents' and a whirlwind of images of high-class hotels, shopping and confusion over gun crime follows. High-end suburbia can also be seen in the video 'Touch'N You' in which Rick Ross can be seen performing in a swimming pool. It seems for these stars their acquired wealth allows them an escape route from humble origins and a passport into classy suburbia much in the same way as the original suburban aspiration dictated. Here the American dream is still present but with flashes of dystopian nightmare as in other genres.

Like punk British Britpop revelled in urban chic while the background of its practitioners revealed suburban roots. Here is a direct parallel with the statement of Gunn and Bell (2003:61) that 'Rejection of a suburban background was de rigeur for artists and writers of the 1950s like John Osborne.' Britpop from the mid-nineties onwards more than most musical scenes identified with the city, in particular London and its fashionable Camden inner-city neighbourhood. The wider Cool Britannia movement was actively championed by the first Blair government, encapsulated in pictures of Noel Gallagher with the PM at a Downing Street drinks reception. Early 1990s group Suede who Bracewell (2002) credits with beginning Britpop injected twisted suburban glamour into their songs in which a fascination for the seedy side of London, reflected and refracted through their origins in Haywards Heath, a prosperous if somewhat faded commuter town in Sussex. Geyrhalter (1996:220) has written on them 'Suede emphasise Englishness as a repressive, potentially perverse attitude towards sexuality. They celebrate London as an inherently sexual experience: "To Brett, London was big, swinging, punky, sexy, dangerous and depraved, the Ultimate metropolis" (*Melody Maker* 2/1/93).' The track 'Asbestos' from the 1999 album *Head Music* talks of 'suburban girls . . . making eyes at suburban boys' and vice versa. Britpop continually demonstrated a fascination with the capital city from those who were more often than not were from outside its boundaries mytholgizing a neo-swinging London also seen in parallel art forms such as the 1997 film *Austin Powers: International Man of Mystery* which also drew inspiration from the same era. In some ways it seemed that the 1990s, with its suburban role models gravitating to caricatured metropolitan culture and a Labour government led by a meritocratic-styled new-broom youthful premier in power, was the 1960s turned upside down.

Blur's second album *Modern Life Is Rubbish* seemed to document the familiar theme of suburban ennui. On the 1995 album *The Great Escape* Blur offers a caricature of 'poor' Ernold Same (possibly a relation of clothes fetishist Arnold Layne in the Pink Floyd song of the same name) that commiserates him for his sad repetitive life of drudgery which carries a life-sentence of commuting to a mindless, meaningless, repetitive, soul-destroying job:

Ernold Same caught the same train
At the same station
Sat in the same seat/With the same nasty stain/
Next to same old what's-his-name/
On his way to the same place/ With the same name/
To do the same thing/ Again and again and again.

The spoken-word rather than sung track is dryly intoned by Ken Livingstone, at the time Labour MP for Brent East and subsequently Mayor of London. There are echoes of the Jam's Smithers Jones. Blur's lyrics have satirized the futile, mundanity of suburban existence. A number of their songs take the form of character sketches centring on the suburban *ennui* theme, for example 'Tracy Jacks' – the civil servant who ran away to the seaside, 'Colin Zeal' – 'looks at his watch, he's on time, once again'. On the aptly named 'Stereotypes' from *The Great Escape* album (1995) opens with a first line that refers to Delderfield before a scene worthy of Leslie Philips unfolds:

> The suburbs they are dreaming
> They're a twinkle in her eye
> She's been feeling frisky since her husband said goodbye
> She wears a low cut T-shirt
> Runs a little B&B
> She's most accommodating when she's in her lingerie
> Wife-swapping is your future
> You know that it would suit ya.

The comedy adulterous behaviour that unfolds suggests another world beneath the surface of the suburbs contradicts the buttoned up 'no sex please we're British' stereotype. It's very title concedes that these type of goings on, seen for example in Cynthia Payne's suburban lair at Streatham where payment was by luncheon voucher was later fictionalized in the 1986 film *Personal Services*, is almost something of a cliché.

Suburbia 'gone bad' surfaced as a theme later on in their career. Far from the cheery pen-portraits and powerchords of earlier outings, the discordant sounding 'Essex Dogs' with its stop–start slow rhythm and reverb drenched bus-saw guitar from 1997's self-titled album tells of a dysfunctional landscape of 'tiny lawns' and what would now be ASBO land (referring to the punitive New Labour youth justice policy of the Anti-Social Behaviour Order) although the term had yet to be coined then. It is largely instrumental but among the spoken lyrics are:

> In this town, cellular phones are hot with teens
> In this town, we all go to terminal pubs
> It helps us sweat out those angry bits of life
> . . . You know you'll get a kicking tonight
> The smell of puke and piss.

This dysfunctional picture of suburbia gone wrong echoes of the Specials 'Friday Night and Saturday Morning', b-side to the number 1 'Ghost town' in which the narrator/hero snacks on pie and chips while waiting to go home after a night out in the city centre, the detritus all around him to the sound of a fairground organ:

> I'll eat in the taxi queue/Standing in someone else's spew
> Wish I had lipstick on my shirt /Instead of piss stains on my shoes.

However in 'Essex Dogs' there is no stated escape; its outright negative tone signals a shift from Blur's earlier suburban analyses which were more in a vein of gentle mocking fictional characters rather than outright condemnation. Blur hailed from Colchester in Essex. Yet pop fans and performers have hailed from many different types of suburbs: including working-class variants. The Gallagher brothers, lead protagonists of northern arch-rivals Oasis grew up in the suburbs of Manchester spending their formative years in the council cottage estate of Burnage. Jon Savage (1996:393) has described this as 'a step up from inner-city ghettos such as Moss side and Hulme: the 1930s semi-detatched suburbs of Burnage and Stretford, the garden city of Wythenshawe . . . ambiguous zones, far from the city centre; superficially pleasant, yet also prone to inner-city problems: broken homes, poverty, unemployment.' Oasis' lyrics were not always terribly meaningful, frequently following a template of nonsense rhyming however the idea of escape from the chains of suburbia does surface seen at times in Oasis' music. On the song 'Half a World Away' Noel Gallagher sings: 'I would like to leave this city. This old town don't smell too pretty.' Given that this was written before the band had made it and when Gallagher was on the dole this could as much refer to exiting Manchester rather than Burnage *per se*. The Smiths track 'London' also takes the capital as escape route. The subject of the song has parallels with Keith Waterhouse's daydreaming anti-hero Billy Liar. The sleeve of the Oasis single 'Live Forever' depicts 251 Menlove Avenue, the home of John Lennon's aunt Mimi where he spent his childhood, now as described above, a National Trust property.

Britpop was vociferously criticized by Fisher (1995) who drew parallels between its 'whiter than white' style and then Prime Minister John Major who predicted 'Fifty years from now Britain will still be the country of long shadows on county (cricket) grounds, warm beer, invincible green suburbs, dog lovers and pools fillers' and in his reference to old maids cycling to communion in the mist namechecking George Orwell, an old-fashioned socialist who probably would have been horrified to have lent support to a Conservative in this way. Since then were the comments of Aidan Burley MP on Twitter decrying the 2012 Olympic opening ceremony as 'leftie multicultural crap'. Much of the content of Britpop was however not in the form of grand statements but micro detail of suburban foibles, for example Pulp from Sheffield and their tales of suburban peeping toms and outdated décor, for example from 'Disco 2000' a reference to textured wallcoverings that had been popular in the 1970s and 1980s: 'Do you recall? Do you recall? Your house was very small with wood chip on the wall. When I came around to call you didn't notice me at all.' Non-UK and non-Western influences were later experimented with by Britpop personnel. Oasis later went on to tour with Cornershop, the Anglo-Asian Wolverhampton band who scored a number 1 hit single with 'Brimful of Asha' with Noel Gallagher guesting on sitar. Damon of Blur departed from Britpop's orthodox template in collaborating with musicians from Mali.

Britpop began with a stated aim to differentiate itself from the US grunge rock tendency with Damon Albarn being quoted as saying 'If punk was about getting rid of hippies, then I'm getting rid of grunge' in a 1993 *NME* interview with interviewer John Harris widely quoted on the web including several Wikipedia entries. Yet there are many continuities between the two styles which articulate suburban alienation, for example the work of Nirvana which tapped into the 1990s slacker/Generation X debates or more recently in a track such as 'Jesus of Suburbia' by Green Day. Again aesthetic and visuals were part of the message. The video for the Smashing Pumpkins track '1979' for example includes scenes showing a raid on a convenience store, youth driving round in circles and a teenage house party with a band. The images look reminiscent of what we have seen in films like *Donnie Darko* and Linklater's *SubUrbia* among others. The 2001 Ben Folds track 'Rockin' the Suburbs' goes further than simply pillorying the suburban lifestyle as Seeger or The Monkees did by delivering an angsty direct attack on suburban life and privilege. The song which is guitar-led begins with the low-key, almost whined lyrics:

> Let me tell you all what it's like/ Being male, middle-class and white
> It's a bitch, if you don't believe/ Listen up to my new CD.

The song builds up in anger on the part of the narrator who threatens to swear because he is 'so pissed off'. Inevitably though the singer is following a long line in his art 'Just like Michael Jackson/Jon Bon Jovi/Quiet Riot did' the difference as admitted is that they were 'talented'. This satirization of the suburban pop experience became the theme tune to the 2003 Dreamworks animation film *Over the Hedge* in which cute furry animals battle the local pest control called in by narrow-minded suburban neighbours. The song in its voicing of suburban ennui has much in common with Britpop. 'Garage' by Weezer also is a grunge track in which the space suburbia affords the status of being a misfit is celebrated by an introverted suburban kid who practices guitar in the solace of the outbuilding of his parents' suburban home. The US powerpop outfit Sparks whose biggest UK hit 'This Town ain't Big Enough for Both of Us' reached number 2 in 1974 also made a comeback in 2002 with the gently mocking 'Suburban Homeboy' describing a very US middle class existence hinting at the following of hip hop in suburbia:

> I am a suburban homeboy and I say yo dog to my pool cleaning guy
> I hope I'm baggy enough for them/ I play my Shaggy enough for them.

The old model saw flight from the city to the suburbs – Robins (1992:118) found this in his study as applying to musicians: 'Most of the people from this neighbourhood who have become successful through music have moved away. Then, typically, "they don't want to know the ghetto no more".' Earlier generations of pop stars have repudiated their suburban origins by buying large country estates such as John Lennon and George Harrison at their mansions in Surrey and Oxfordshire. Britpop alumni have been more mixed. Blur's bassist Alex James bought a Sussex farm after living in Covent Garden at the height of Britpop. Noel Gallagher also moved to Buckinghamshire outside London after owning a London townhouse Supernova Heights in Hampstead, a North London neighbourhood that has was once a suburb and has always retained an aura of exclusivity despite having been swallowed up by the capital's growth and now lying in an inner-city location. *The Guardian* report when he left in 1999 explained 'Tired of London, and presumably of life, he has left Primrose Hill after he and his followers turned the star's home into a den of rebellious behaviour. . . . The collective sigh of relief at Gallagher's departure was about as deafening as his revelries. "There were noisy parties all night; all kinds of people staggering in and out of the place," says a psychiatrist living near by . . . This is not normally an area normally associated with that kind of behaviour' (Wazir 1999). When the late Amy Winehouse who had grown up in suburban Southgate returned to the United Kingdom after a stint in Jamaica her mother sought out a property in suburban Barnet for her as it was felt she would be safe there than with the temptations of Camden. She did not remain in the new setting and it was in Camden that she eventually met her substance abuse-related death. Blur drummer Dave Rowntree meanwhile retrained as a barrister and stood both as a council and parliamentary candidate for the Labour party in Westminster. Paul McCartney has also been a long-term resident of St John's Wood, a smart inner London neighbourhood.

Common themes and future directions in suburban pop

In addition to its recorded aural form, contemporary pop music reception takes multiple forms such as the pop video and live performance experienced at concerts and festivals. Clapson (2003:167) has decried the denigration of the suburbanite in pop history claiming: 'getting lyrical about the suburban plight is a maudlin indulgence, derived from an incomplete understanding of the everyday life of the English suburbs. For the simple fact remains that the suburbs, in their aggregate variety, have grown historically to constitute a massive and complex cross-section of the English people.' Bearing the UK suburban pop standard for the twenty-first century are Hard-Fi whose CV includes the 2007 single *Suburban Knights*. In spite of the words 'from nowhere' in the feature's tag-line the band's Richard Archer has described their hometown to the west of London's Heathrow airport to the *Independent* (Caesar 2005) as a strength: 'The thing about Staines is it's insular . . . but because it's insular it's helped us out. We were never like, "Oh the *NME* and all our mates in Camden are telling us that we have to make this kind of sound." So we just listened to the music that we loved . . . soul, dub, hip-hop reggae house.' Indeed in addition to the lyrics that have been pored over by theorists of pop often treating songs as a written text, music has provided lifelines and alternatives for the suburban listeners who have comprised the adoring audience who were always more than passive victims of their environs on both sides of the Atlantic and beyond. In the United Kingdom transport and the stress of commuting feature in several pop songs of and about suburbia. In the United States where there is more pronounced car culture there have been more descriptions of motor vehicle transport. Apart from such questions of infrastructure, romantic love, boredom and even the ideal of living in spacious surrounds have also inspired suburban pop. Suburbia however is not just the binary opposite of ghetto, there are links between the two in the twenty-first century; the suburbs are not static and the cultural activity alive in them means that they are far from sleepy commuterland or purely one-dimensional residential enclaves that depend upon the city, the modern suburb is complex and multifaceted. It can be argued then that there is more interesting cultural work than in the supposed central sites taking place in peripheral sites and what might appear at first sight to be non-descript suburbia. The group Orbital for example emerged from a sound system that organized raves around the M25. Songs like 'Streets of Your Town' from Australian band the Go-Betweens also show suburban pop pervades in Anglo-Saxon settings other than the United Kingdom and United States.

The best-known album in the recent past addressing the suburban condition is from Canadian band Arcade Fire simply entitled *The Suburbs*. Even if one review remarked 'listening to the Suburbs is almost as boring as actually living in the suburbs themselves' (Meline 2010) most of the critical reception was almost entirely praiseworthy. It amassed a number of gongs including the 53rd Grammy Album of the Year, the Canadian Juno Album of the Year and International Album at the BRIT Awards in 2011.[14] The album is multi-textured as the two tracks with the same name demonstrate. 'Sprawl I (flatland)' is a plaintive number in a minor key with mournful instrumentation including violins and defeatism in its lyrics:

Took a drive into the sprawl
To find the places we used to play
It was the loneliest day of my life
You're talking at me but I'm still far away
Let's take a drive through the sprawl
Through these towns they built to change
But then you said, the emotions are dead
It's no wonder that you feel so strange.

This contrasts with the urgent pounding electric keyboards, sub-disco rhythms and female vocals of 'Sprawl II (Mountains beyond Mountains)', which rhythmically recalls Blondie's pulsating 'Heart of Glass'. The lyrics detail some of the recognizable features of the ever-expanding exurban landscape:

Sometimes I wonder if the world's so small,
That we can never get away from the sprawl,
Living in the sprawl,
Dead shopping malls, rise like mountains beyond mountains,
And there's no end in sight,
I need the darkness, someone please cut the lights.

The album's title track with its jaunty piano riff and chiming guitars, already referred to in Chapter 1, is a generally upbeat track even if it talks of being 'already bored' and refers to the flimsiness and ultimate lack of sustainability of hastily constructed mass produced 'crackerbox' suburban houses of post-war

America (Donaldson 1969) whose uncertain future had been pondered some years ago by Wood (1958) in the line:

> All of the houses they built in the Seventies finally fall/It meant nothing at all.

The vocalist seems resigned to this: it is a fact of life. The collapse of some of the old structures and certainties in recessionary times when old codes of morality, working practices, leisure and consumption have also weakened their grip over the suburbs of yesteryear.

The band also released the accompanying film *Scenes from the Suburbs* shot in Austin, Texas, and directed by Spike Jonze. This 30-minute feature begins conventionally enough showing suburban youth goofing around, fumbling at first love and taking dead-end jobs before a nightmarish scenario of a suburb with troop manned strict border control and the human cost of suburban regimentation unfolds. A brief appearance from husband and wife singers Win Butler and Regine Chassagne as cops can be seen. This sense of suburban paranoia contrasts with 'Mushaboom' by fellow Canadian singer songwriter Feist (2004) which the lyrics describes an idyllic suburban scene and settling down before the realization

> But in the meantime I've got it hard/ Second floor living without a yard
> It may be years until the day/ My dreams will match up with my pay.

The video appears to show the daydreams of a city dweller who wishes to spread their wings but is constrained by finances. Here the suburban dream as a mode of living to aspire to still persists although is increasingly out of reach to average salaries in current economic circumstances.

The music emerging from contemporary suburbia continues to be moulded by multi-ethnicity and other rapid social change. The pickled-in-aspic version of suburbia sung about in twentieth-century pop has experienced dramatic transformations as the urban landscape now has business parks, retail parks, out-of-town leisure complexes and shopping malls among its features challenging the traditional suburban set up. In 2012 the 'misunderstood' tweet of Aidan Burley MP at the Olympics 'Bring back red arrows [*sic*], Shakespeare and the Stones!' rendered him even more ridiculous as rhythm and blues which in the essence of the Stones is intrinsically multicultural, rooted in black America. As Norman (2002:33) describes music was their escape route from suburbia before they adopted their now familiar stage personas: 'Mike [*sic*] Jagger listened to Muddy Waters, Jimmy Reed, Howlin' Wolf, giants of the urban blues with heart-shivering voices, calling and answering their virtuoso guitars, that could change the view beyond the lace curtains from Kentish suburbia to the dark and windy canyons along Chicago's Lake Shore Drive.' Their musical teeth cut the suburban circuit including the Railway Hotel, Harrow, the Crawdaddy club at the Station Hotel, Richmond and scene of their first ever gig the Ealing Club played in 1962 which guitarist Keith Richards mentions several times in his autobiography *Life* (2010).

Melville (2004) describes the universe of British hip hop outfit 'The Streets' as 'distinctly sub-urban – the land of asbos, twockers and daytime drinkers . . . surroundings [reflected] sonically, through word, accent and music.' Grime and dubstep are two suburban genres that have added themselves to familiar lists that have inspired past textbooks (Shuker 2003; Borthwick and Moy 2004). O'Connell (2006) calls the home of dubstep 'the hotbed of sub-cultural creativity that is Croydon', a suburb to the south of London with ambitions to be a city in its own right. An *Independent* article sounds similarly incredulous with the subheading 'The hottest dance sound around wasn't born in the USA. Chris Mugan tracks the new scene down to its unlikely birthplace' (Mugan 2006). For Melville (2004) 'Mike Skinner is the hip hop balladeer of the suburbs, an anthropological humanist . . . marking the unlikely connection between Norman Wisdom, Suggs, Seinfeld and Del Tha Funkee Homosapien.' A Letter to *Croydon Advertiser* (29 July 2010)[15] stated: 'There is a tendency to look for bricks and mortar examples when conveying what is good about Croydon . . . Our senior councillors are probably not aware of developments in the dance music scene [but] "Dubstep" is a new bass driven genre which has taken the world by storm . . . follow[ing] a rich history of musicians from our borough . . . Identifying dubstep as an example of Croydon culture may not be the conventional way to describe this borough, but that does not mean it should be ignored. The next time Councillor O'Connell is at some international municipal conference or on the radio, could he show he's in tune with what's going on in the whole of Croydon.' Escapism has long been a key function of suburban pop but so has the documentation of the quotidian. There are in modern record shops 'urban' racks of mainly dance music. To make a *suburban* category might necessitate use of a whole store's entire stock. Then again the idea of physical racks for classificatory purposes and 'record' shops seems anarchronitsic as music ceases to be a physical product and download culture and laptop DJs now dominate. Grime and dubstep from Croydon are but two recent styles that capture the textures of the modern suburb serving as a powerful rejoinder to conceptualizations of the suburbs as monocultural. Along with all the styles described above including Canadian indie rock these are proof, if proof were needed, that suburbia has provided a wellspring of creativity in pop soundtracking suburban existence in contemporary times.

Notes

1 Chris Evans Breakfast Show, 23 August 2010 at: www.bbc.co.uk/programmes/b00th93y.

2 'It's good to Bee back says Robin' by Marie Burchill, *Manchester Evening News*, 2 October 2008 at: http://menmedia.co.uk/southmanchesterreporter/news/s/1070247_its_good_to_bee_back_says_robin. When the Manchester Metrolink tram route was extended the advertising posters read 'The smoothest thing to come out of Chorlton since the Bee Gees'.

3 A soap impression of his wife/which he ate and donated to the National Trust, this expression is apparently slang for excreting.

4 www.nationaltrust.org.uk/main/w-vh/w-visits/w-findaplace/w-mendips/; www.nationaltrust.org.uk/main/w-20forthlinroadallerton.

5 www.kentonline.co.uk/kentonline/news/2010/july/15/mick_jagger_visits_dartford.aspx.

6 http://2112.net/powerwindows/transcripts/gettsuccess.htm.

7 On its live performance (following 'In the City') on YouTube filmed at the Electric Circus venue in August 1977 the young Weller introduces it with the words 'This one's for fat councillors', www.youtube.com/watch?v=zKaLHbXjcZs.

8 'Honda Swindon closing for 50 days', BBC, 21 November 2008, at: http://news.bbc.co.uk/1/hi/business/7741269.stm. This first 50-day stoppage was due to reduced orders and then in 2011 a halving of production due to a scarceness of parts from Japan in the wake of the Tsunami and earthquake.

9 Interview at 'Absolutely Pet Shop Boys – Unofficial Site', www.petshopboys.net/html/interviews/pleasse005.shtml. The same interview – curiously given how 'English' the band (and the interpretation of suburbia described) seemingly are – also alleges that the song was inspired by the Penelope Spheeris film of the same name about youths in suburban Los Angeles who channel disenchantment and rebellion into gang-life, www.worldgreen.org/living/eco-products-for-the-home/3261-friday-music-blogging-arcade-fire.html.

10 http://zhiphopcleveland.com/3158092/n-w-a-straight-outta-compton-suburbs-remix-video/.

11 www.obv.org.uk/index.php?option=com_content&task=view&id=344&Itemid=127.

12 www.youtube.com/watch?v=clPhtitSpes.

13 In an acerbic interview with BBC Radio 2 DJ Dermot O'Leary, the DJ's Irish roots seemed to be the only thing instilling a modicum of restraint into Morrissey who expressed clear disdain for *The X Factor*, another show that O'Leary had worked on. See www.morrissey-solo.com/content/133-Morrissey-on-Dermot-O-Leary-Radio-2- (30 April 2011, 3 p.m.).

14 It was also Album of the Year at the Canadian Polaris Awards and placed first in best of the year album lists drawn up by critics of BBC 6 Music, *Clash* Magazine and *Q* Magazine and second placed from Shasha Khan, Croydon Green Party for *NME*, *Billboard* and *Time*.

15 *Letter to the Paper on Dubstep*, 29 July 2010, at: http://croydongreens.blogspot.com/2010/07/letter-to-paper-on-dubstepyes-dubstep.html.

4

Pastoral Paradises and Social Realism: Cinematic Representations of Suburban Complexity

> *I never wanted to get into this rat-race but now that I'm in it I think I'd be a fool not to play it just like everyone else plays it.*
>
> (Gregory Peck as Tom Rath, *The Man in the Gray Flannel Suit*, 1956)

The cinema in its literal sense has been both a landmark of the suburban-built environment and staple source of popular culture in the post-war era: with the Regals, Gaumonts, UCGs and ABCs offering relatively cheap escapism from everyday mundanity and routine. The cinema has served the function of a venue for suburban courtship for couples and entertainment for fully formed family units with the power to move audiences to the edge of their seats in suspense or to tears – be that laughter or of sadness. While the VHS and advent of domestic video recorders was seen to threaten the very existence of the cinema, many suburban areas have seen the old high street picture palaces replaced/displaced/ succeeded by out-of-town complexes where suburbia has sometimes been the subject on the screen as well as the setting of the multiplex they are screened in. In the United States the suburb has variously equated with idyllic family dreamhouse, horror-laden land of dark undercurrent and stomping ground for adolescent angst in films from which changes can be tracked from the innocence of the suburbia of the all-American goodlife in the 1950s to its more recent portrayal as shopping mall-dominated territory from the 1980s onwards overrun by slackers by the 1990s. British cinema has tended to pride itself by being in a more 'slice of life' social realism vein. This chapter turns to the silver screen (or DVD release) to discuss full-length feature films featuring suburbia. The consideration of suburbia onscreen will continue in Chapter 5 addressing televisual (small-screen) representations.

'Suburban film' is not usually a categorization that is common to film studies. In discussing genre in film Monaco, (2000:306) names film noir, gangster movies, horror films, musicals, science fiction and the screwball comedy among others while noting that 'In the seventies, the Western fell into decline as increasingly urbanized America lost its zest for wide-open spaces.' Into the space vacated we can see an increasing number of films taking the suburbs as their source and setting which cut across genres. Indeed the suburban films of recent years have included retreads among their number. In 2004 the 1975 classic the *Stepford Wives* based on the 1972 book of the same name underwent a zeitgeist-chasing remake. *The Simpsons*, discussed in the following chapter and Chapter 6 as a television series, merited their own film in 2005 *The Simpsons Movie*. Ali G from Staines in Berkshire to the west of London the anti-hero of indeterminate ethnicity (the character speaks in Jamaican patois, has an Asian-sounding name, is played by a Jew and comes from an area once seen as fairly ethnically 'white'), who first appeared as a comedy insert of a Channel 4 talkshow graduated to his own series and then cinema-released feature film *Ali G In da House*. The trajectory had been followed earlier for example in the film *Bless this House* (1972), an extended film spin off from the popular television series, starring Sid James and an early outing for Terry (Scott) and June (Whitfield) who later got two subsequent spin off long-running programmes in their own right: *Happy Ever After (1974–79)* and *Terry and June* (1979–86) set in Ealing and Purley respectively. The plot emphasized the principle of defensible space and included the theme of generational difference and the two middle-aged suburban couples the film revolved around traded hostilities over the garden-fence while their respective offspring (both rebellious with hippie tendencies) were romantically involved with one another unbeknown to the parents. Many other suburban films are dramatizations of suburban novels as mentioned in the previous chapter.

SubUrbia and *The Burbs* are two US films which ultimately disappoint in content if one is looking for clues as to suburban lifestyles even if their titles suggest that they will address the subject. *The Burbs* (1989) opens with an aerial shot of the earth turning on its axis before the cameras close in on the neighbourhood in which it occurs. It is a 'there's more to things than meets the eye' tale that unfolds. The film can be classified as a screwball comedy with elements of thriller/suspense. It is largely about the neighbourhood's self-appointed upstanding residents taking their suspicions of the newly moved-in Klopek family to be murderers into their own hands. There is not much on display concerning the suburban lifestyle apart from eccentricity. None of the characters are seen going to work and there are few female characters. The Universal Studios set in which the house exteriors were filmed has been used as the location for *The Munsters* and *Desperate Housewives* among other examples. The film was a commercial flop. In *SubUrbia* (1996) a bunch of dead-end kids hang around a petrol station and eat fast food. One of their former members who 'got out' and became a pop star comes back and violence is perpetrated against the heavily accented Indian owner of the hangout. This film was seen as part of the 'slacker' wave of cinema depicting the despair of a downwardly mobile post-baby boom generation. The setting appears to be the type of suburbia suggested by Donna Gaines (1991) but there are no real trends from which one can draw conclusions about suburban living discerable from the 24-hour timespan of the events. These Generation X protagonists' self-absorption can be explained by how they are too satiated by the trappings of consumer culture to have any major material injustices to rebel against. Yet at the same time they are not satisfied with their lives. Muzzio and Halper (2002:252) observe: 'Their parents suburban dream of comfort and security has left them trapped.' In the current circumstances of economic downturn, youth may do well to emulate their parents' suburban ideals: the stalling of the growth model means that the automatic expectation of having higher standards of living than their parents is in doubt.

History and memory: Depictions of suburbia of and from the 1950s and 1960s

In terms of location it is London that looms largest in UK suburban films. Gardner (2003) meanwhile notes that in American suburban films it is often Connecticut that is the by-word for the all-American suburb for its easy commutability to New York. Onset of family responsibility is often seen as ushering in a move to suburbia. Consequently US suburban-set films have frequently placed a great emphasis on idyllic family life. Dines (2009:9–10) remarks that this post-1945 middle-class suburban family fascination was 'in part a reaction to the sustained hardships experienced by most families throughout the years of the Depression and Second World War, but was also a response to Cold War anxieties about Soviet takeover'. Early antecedents of the suburban film include *It's a Wonderful Life* (1946) more accurately about American small town life than suburbia *per se* but setting a trend in its promotion of wholesome all-American values (Beuka 2004; Halper and Muzzio 2011). Based on the novel by Jean Kerr *Please Don't Eat the Daisies* has a family headed by acerbic film critic David Niven and dutiful wife Doris Day escaping their increasingly cramped apartment in New York city to a rambling house 'on the Hudson' and with it accepting a 'long life of commuting'.

One of their offspring is so unaccustomed to seeing flora he attempts to eat the daises growing in the garden, from which the film gets its title. Niven tells the new local school that he will not volunteer when they ask for him to help out as he considers their request to be 'moral blackmail' whereas his wife happily plunges herself into a pivotal role in the school play in what is on the whole an upbeat, sunny film. It later became the basis of a television show from 1965 to 1967. The post-war suburban mindset with a slightly more dramatic edge is seen in *The Man in the Gray Flannel Suit* (1956) based on the novel by Sloan Wilson starring Gregory Peck as a family man experiencing flashbacks on the daily commute to New York from Westport, Connecticut. His wife seems more driven than him so as a result of her ambitions for a better quality of life Peck's character lands himself in a new pressurized work environment (advertising on Madison Avenue). She chides him for turning into a 'cheap slippery yes-man' while he himself harbours wartime secrets and pent up frustration – most explosive of all to his wife that he fathered an illegitimate child. His resolve to do right contrasts with his workaholic boss who is a stranger to his family, long ago sacrificed for their father's climbing the corporate ladder in a television network. When Peck laments that his children are constantly glued to the television, the boss suggests smashing it in. They seem to watch westerns with shoot-outs heavily featured. 'That's seven dead already' his young daughter exclaims at one stage numbed to the carnage, Peck's character is even more unmoved: he has seen this all close up as he killed 17 people in action. The film is more a picture of suburban masculinity rather than the portrayals of female suburban neuroses that are dealt with in Chapter 6. *The Graduate* (1967) has been described as a suburban film (Beuka 2001, 2004; Gardner 2003) for showing Ben's reaction to the suffocating confines of his parents' suburban parameters. Perhaps we can trace the 'turning' of popular culture away for its initially rosy positive picture of suburbia from this point of roughly in the latter 1960s onwards.

More recent suburban films are often self-referential nostalgically harking back to previous stereotypical images of suburbia from 'the good old days'. Questioning the 1950s versions automatically signalling the way to perfection and the 'good life' are encapsulated in the film *Pleasantville* (1998) which punctures the nostalgia-fuelled myth of the good old days of American suburbia and what 'a kinder gentler nation'. The trailer describes the film's fictional setting as 'a place as far from reality as we can imagine' and plot as 'about the loss of innocence and the power of change' has generated a notable degree of academic interest (Muzzio and Halper 2002; Dickinson 2006). The film takes its name from a 1950s television show in the story, that has at time of its taking place is being re-run on an oldies satellite channel where its wholesome image and catch phrases like 'Hi Honey I'm home' have mesmerized the teenage boy lead character who finds himself trapped in the family television set and transported to *Pleasantville* an eerily black and white (literally monochromatic shots) world of repression. Gradually despite the efforts of the old guard to cling on to how it was, Technicolor engulfs Pleasantville with a positive message advocating rebellion and creative culture in suburbia over routine and belief in the acquisition of consumer durables. At the end of the film a hip hop mural gets painted on a wall in Plesantville leading to a court case in which the Town Hall committee's wish to 'hold on to those values that made this place great' proves untenable. Rock and roll is allowed to stay. As for the future, it seems nobody knows with any certainty what it holds anymore. Time travel was also the theme of teen hit *Back to the Future* (1985) which spawned a number of sequels and the more adult *Peggy Sue Got Married* (1986). In both films the main protagonist is able to change events relating to relationships of their parents and own destinies. In the former a suburban 1980s high school student is transported back to his pre-suburban 1950s existence when the same surroundings were a small town yet to become swallowed up by the nearest city of which it became a suburb. The questioning of old suburban values is raised by Spigel (2001a:408–9) who details the plot of a 1999 made for television Disney film *Smart House* in which 'computer-powered versions of an imaginary 1950s housewife . . . [a] full time mother who lives in a suburban dream house and . . . looks after everybody's needs' gradually develops into a nightmare scenario and 'a zillion evil retro mothers, all bent on keeping the family trapped inside'. The imagined suburban perfection of the 1950s and 1960s displayed is more exaggerated than the versions portrayed in the films from the actual era itself.

The rewriting of history to highlight the faults of suburban repression are dramatized in *Far from Heaven* (2002, Todd Haynes), a film styled as a melodrama which is heavily derivative of director Douglas Sirk who was active in the 1950s when the film was set. Things begin by drawing us into a seemingly textbook case of an idyllic affluent suburban scenario: the devoted mother with a respectable standing in the community is married to a successful executive who upholds the standing of 'the company' and works hard to provide financial security for the family, for example ballet lessons and station wagon vehicle. However this world begins to collapse before our eyes with two main transgressions presenting themselves: the secret homosexuality of the husband (who visits a doctor to see if he can be 'cured') and the twin taboo of the (chaste, non-sexual) friendship developing between the film's housewife and her young black gardener across the racial divide. This 1950s depicted is socially conservative and deeply divided.

People use words like 'charming' as a positive adjective, the children respectfully address their father as 'sir', there is a black housemaid and when the son of the family utters the word 'Jeez' as an exclamation he is reprimanded for blasphemy. At Frank and Cathy's cocktail party civil rights unrest discussed: one guest states that the race riots that occurred in Little Rock could just as easily have occurred 'here in Hartford'. Another rejects the proposition because 'for one thing, there's no Governor Faubus in Connecticut. But the main reason [is] there are no Negroes'. The exchange is all the more shocking as it is uttered as the speaker is served a drink by a black domestic servant. The film ends with a divorce being sought and the gardener, a widowed single father, leaving town with his daughter to escape town gossip and disapproval from both whites and blacks. The temporal moment of the 1950s as a golden age when wholesome nuclear-family oriented suburban life was seen as a norm to aspire to in civilization's best interest is punctured. As with *Pleasantville* and *Mad Men*, it can be stated with certainty that these retro-representations of the 1950s/1960s are quite unlike the actual films from the era which tended to portray suburban perfection.

Social realism: Slice of life depictions of British suburbia

The suburbs were not the dominant setting for films in the costume drama period productions of the early twentieth century that helped seal the popularity of the cinema in the early twentieth century. Big costume dramas were often set in country homes or at smart central London addresses rather than mundane districts on the edges. Again the United Kingdom has spawned a number of stylistic film categories: the comedies of Ealing studios were made in the suburbs and consumed by suburban audiences. Elstree studios in Borehamwood, Pinewood and Shepperton were also significant production sites of British cinema located in the suburbs of north-west London. The 1944 film *This Happy Breed* (directed by David Lean from a play script by Noel Coward) portrays the vicissitudes of a stoic south London family between the wars – although its Clapham setting is not a location now regarded as 'suburbia', occupying a Pooterish distance from central London. A broad sweep of history is encompassed from demobbing after 1919 via the General Strike, appeasement and then to the outbreak again of war in 1939. The character that seems to stand out most with the rest is Queenie who rails against the confines of suburban mediocrity in two memorable soliloquies when she declares that she wants more than living in a house identical to hundreds of others making the same tube journey as everyone else. The film has obvious overlaps with the better-known *Brief Encounter* (1945), a tale of repressed suburban desire, by sharing the same writer-director team and actors Celia Johnson and Stanley Holloway. In *Brief Encounter* Johnson's character despite outward appearances as leading a life of respectable middle-class contentment (wife, mother, comfortable home, etc.) falls for a mysterious married hospital doctor (Trevor Howard) in a station refreshment room that develops into an illicit affair which is cut short when she realizes her 'mistake' and ends up back in the bosom of her suburban family, her husband being completely unsuspecting. Every time the lovers meet there is a running subplot of Holloway and Joyce Carey flirting with one another on the other side of the café providing comic relief around, rather patronizingly, the theme of 'how the working classes conduct themselves' in contrast with the more formal register of the central pair. In the decades that followed the best-known British films dealing with everyday life situations (outside period drama) tended to oscillate between ribald comedy (e.g. the popular *Carry On* series of films or the *Confessions* films) and realist drama.

By the 1950s and 1960s the popular wave of 'angry young man' fiction had translated into film with a number of screen adaptations. Directors such as Tony Richardson, John Scheslinger and Karel Reisz dramatized the work of John Osborne, Alan Sillitoe and others contributing to what amounted to the most sustained engagement between working-class British life and the big screen to date, only at all challenged in the early 1980s with the birth of Channel 4. The sometimes depressing images pictured in these 'kitchen sink' dramas often included back-to-back housing and washing hanging up while children played in the streets before the mass ownership of cars filled up roadsides. The semi-detached swathes of the suburbs fell between two stools in British cinema typology. They were (i) not bodice-ripping yarns or (ii) slums ripe for films incorporating social conscience or social commentary meaning that they largely escaped the gaze of film-makers as their ordinariness offered no escapism or statement to the viewer. Sometimes there are references but often constructed in opposition to the more dangerous inner city. In Ken Loach's *Poor Cow* (1968) based on the best-selling Nell Dunn novel of the same name, the ironically named character 'Joy' is married to a crook who gets sent to prison. She inhabits a succession of seedy flats inside terraced multi-occupancy Victorian houses, getting into which means negotiating treacherous flights of stairs with her toddler son Jonny in tow (one is in Wandsworth and we are told that she herself is from a pre-gentrified Fulham). At the start of the film is a flashback to better times 'When Tom was in the money the world was our oyster and we chose Ruislip'.

Their time there is not dwelt on in any great detail but in snatched conversation on prison visits Tom implores Joy that Jonny and her can 'do better' than lodging at her Aunt's flat in cramped conditions where they are forced to move to after his incarceration when the money runs out. Her joyless existence leads her to take part-time jobs in pubs and modelling, in the course of which she falls in with other bad company. The film concludes with her trapped in the inner city.

In veteran director Mike Leigh's films suburbia does nudge its way into the narrative although most typically as seen through the eyes of inner-city dwellers. In *High Hopes* two joint-rolling lefties Cyril and Shirley who live in a tenement block overlooking Kings Cross station are befuddled at the gentrification that has taken place around his elderly mother's crumbling Victorian terrace (filmed in Bow) when they pay her a visit. Looking at her moneyed next door neighbours' smart window boxes Cyril remarks wistfully 'it was a completely different street when I was a kid'. He observes how the houses' function has changed to an investment not dwelling remarking how people 'buy them for sod all, sell 'em for a fortune . . . it's a capital investment'. Meanwhile his sister Valerie is presented as *nouveau riche* suburbia personified with her affected speech and tastelessly decorated house located deep in what Brunsdon (2003:68) calls 'semi-detached vulgarity'. She gets to see the inside of the yuppies' home when she turns up (deliberately late) to collect her mother who has ended up there after getting herself locked out, exclaiming with obvious condescension 'amazing what you can do with a slum'. Brunsdon (2004:69) asserts 'Valerie and Martin live in the no place which is the suburbs'. The surprise birthday party they throw at their house for the mother goes horribly wrong who cannot wait to leave – we are told it will be a £15–20 cab fare back. These characters are a revisiting of John and Barbara in Leigh's earlier film of unemployment and desperation *Meantime* (1983) who live on a modern estate 'about twelve miles' from the city. Barbara offers her jobless nephew Colin money for painting and decorating at her home there. When she gives him directions to their house from Chigwell tube she asks 'you'll recognise it won't you?' rhetorically for reassurance only for Colin to retort 'yeah it's just the same as all the others'. Uncle John only shows a slight flicker of imagination when he enthuses about getting a picture window fitted for the reason that is 'just one big pane', a reference to the couple's strained marriage and sad suburban existence. In both films the city is painted as authentic while the suburbs are characterized as spaces of dull monotony and deadening pain underscored by the loveless marriages both these suburban couples seem to be in – Martin seeks solace in a mistress and Barbara is driven to drink.

Rather than highlighting class differences *per se* it seems (in a situation that chimes with Bourdieu's theory of distinction) here the divide is between the working class inner city worthies versus the tasteless suburbanite ones. The yuppie couple next door to Cyril and Val's mother in *High Hopes* have lived in inner London out of choice, not constraint, and are also portrayed as shallow and inauthentic – their pretentiousness is derided rather than their geographical loaction. As Shirley comments to Cyril 'what do they wanna live round here for?' Indeed conforming Cyril's theory the materialistic wife Laetitia tells Mrs Bender 'you've been sitting on a gold-mine' not realizing that she is a council tenant. Carney (2000:96) quotes a review of Leigh's earlier much celebrated television drama *Abigail's Party* by Dennis Potter that accuses the director of anti-suburban prejudice. Certainly Leigh films do seem to communicate a sense of 'them' versus 'us' often mocking suburban inhabitants for their depthlessness and narrow-mindedness, for example Valerie for her tastelessness. In the 2010 film *Another Year* we see Mary, an emotionally unstable and needy gibbering woman who we laugh *at* rather than *with*, a family friend of Tom and Gerri the pivotal couple who live in middle-class London suburbia. Another fairly cardboard cut-out-like suburban character of Leigh is Wayne from *High Hopes* who appears at the beginning of the film from Epsom as remarkably un-streetwise. He is described by Brunsdon (2004:67) as 'the ingenue from the countryside' and stumbles into the story when Cyril and Shirley put him up in sympathy. A further example of Leigh taking a condescending view of suburban pretensions can be seen in 2008's *Happy Go Lucky* when central figure the Poppy, who lives in Camden, visits her married sister in the sticks. The house has dated decor, a flat-pack table and a doormat husband. Again the suburbanites are derided for submitting to a conformist routine rather than the carefree spirits of the inner city who visit them.

The social realism tradition in a fusing of fact and fiction occurs *par excellence* in the 1994 film *London* and its follow-up *Robinson in Space*. These films feel documentary like: in them the director Patrick Keiller through the narration in deadpan delivery describes the travails of central character Robinson (who we are told teaches at the University of Barking, itself a suburban outpost of East London)[1] around the metropolis. The first film traces a journey in the footsteps of Daniel Defoe taking in locations from Stoke Newington to Brentford. The tone is almost despairing, evoking a hollowed-out capital city and diverting our attention to fairly neglected unglamourous places and spaces. His project of an anti-road movie continues in *Robinson in Space*, which retraces Defoe's *Tour thro' the Whole Island of Great Britain* from the mid-1700s in which Robinson and friend set out on a further odyssey this time from Reading. Among bus-shelters, DIY superstores and motorway service stations the picture that emerges again is a privatization of space and interestingly general flow of cultural resources from the core of the city to the peripheral zones. The narration dryly intones 'We imagined a scenario in which the centre of the city continued to decline and activities previously thought of as occurring in the centre began to take place in the suburbs.' Anger is expressed but in such an urbane way that its impact is not as cutting as the say in a Sex Pistols song. The first two Robinson films were produced under the dying days of Conservative rule although the second had a post-1997 release, the third was *Robinson in Ruins* (2010). This notion of the city way of life under threat from suburban-fixated government seems to have been more applicable to Tory rule than under New Labour who very much prioritized arts-led city centre regeneration. Terrence Davies' *Of Time and the City*, the director's memoir of Liverpool has some similarities in its invective heard in the narration although the film is largely stitched together nostalgic archive footage of working-class popular culture: football matches, seaside outings to New Brighton, etc. The scenes of back-to-back housing in the Hovis advertisement mould make this film more city-focused than suburban but nonetheless it offers a fascinating historical document of evocation of place.

Minorities and the suburban feelgood film

A different image of women and suburbia emerges from female writer/director Gurinder Chadha's films where received ideas of Asian femininity are too on display returned to in Chapter 7. In earlier eras ethnic characters in films were present only to provide comic relief, one of the most striking examples can be seen in the classic light and fluffy 1961 (city rather than suburban-set) *Breakfast at Tiffany's*. New York looks like a candy-store while a heavily cosmetically yellowed-up Mickey Rooney plays Mr Yunioshi, the upstairs killjoy neighbour of indeterminate oriental origin to lovebirds Audrey Hepburn and George Peppard. The portrayal is astonishingly crude and its portrayal of race is one that is cringeworthy to watch; the character is a small man with slitted eyes who barely speaks English, has stick-out teeth and thick lensed spectacles leading one *Times* commentator to remark 'it makes *The Black and White Minstrel Show* look like a government ethnic minority recruitment campaign' (Sanghera 2009). In *Harold and Kumar* it is second-generation ethnic minorities we witness. The stereotypes have changed (having now mastered English language) although the stereotyping hasn't. The title pair are two stoners on a quasi-road trip through suburban New Jersey as they seek a White Castle burger bar in a post-marijuana binge comedown (the follow up was the wrongful imprisonment tale *Harold and Kumar Escape From Guantanamo Bay*). Kumar is a smart Alec Indian who has strayed from his parents' chosen path of a medical career for him while Harold is his long-suffering 'nice guy' Asian achieving friend of Korean heritage, employed as a stockbroker. In their quest they must outwit suburban police officers, students at Princeton (dividing into sexually willing whites and studious orientals), Kumar's heavily Indian-accented doctor father and older obedient brother (no accent) as well as the 'assholes' a white-trash gang from whom the pair are confronted with various popular cultural and ethnically coded insults – their name unwittingly recalls the ear'oles of Paul Willis (1977). Harold gets called 'Mr Miyagi' after the Japanese martial arts instructor of 1986 teen-film *The Karate Kid* and Kumar is referred to as 'Apu', the name of the of the *Simpsons* grocery-store owner by the bullies. His brother by going into the family trade (medicine) like Puppy's brother in the novel *Tourism* as seen in Chapter 7 represents conformity whereas Kumar/ Puppy have chosen a path of rebellion. In a soliloquy delivered at the hospital after Kumar's disastrous failed medical interview his brother delivers a speech in praise of suburban values: 'What the hell's wrong with you, Kumar? Look at me. I own my own house. I drive a beamer [BMW]. And I get laid whenever I want. You can have all that too, if you'd just get off your ass and go to med school . . . When are you gonna grow up and stop with this post-college rebel bullshit?' Meanwhile towards the end Kumar delivers a sermon equating burgers with all that the United States and its immigrants have held dear. He tells Kumar 'Our parents came to this country, escaping persecution, poverty, and hunger . . . they wanted to live in a land that treated them as equals. A land where their kids could study and get into good colleges. A land filled with hamburger stands. And not just one type of hamburger. Hundreds of types with different sizes, toppings, and condiments. That land was America. You think this is just about the burgers? No. This is about achieving what our parents set out for. This is about the pursuit of happiness. This is about the American dream.' The implication is that this has become hollow: Harold's cell-mate when he is imprisoned is a sage-like black man who turns out to be a professor who is there simply 'for being black'.

While the *Harold and Kumar* films portraying Asians were the work of a Jewish scripting and director combination (screenwriters Jon Hurwitz and Hayden Schlossberg, and directed by Danny Leiner) interviews with Gurinder Chadha often impress upon the reader the fact that the director is a Southall-raised Punjabi conferring them with authenticity. A number of US films appear to have convenience store owner as a new mode of Asian stereotype in suburban film: in addition to Apu and the example in *Harold and Kumar* the films *Falling Down* and *SubUrbia* also all include a put-upon small businessman who is under siege from racist violence. Chadha's film deals more with femininity. Her best known work is *Bend It Like Beckham* (2002) which was taboo-busting for taking a football playing Asian girl as its chief subject. *Bhaji on the Beach* (1993) is a story that looks at the intertwined lives of three different generations of Asian women and the decisions that they face in life including accidental pregnancy. A daytrip to Blackpool is the nucleus of the story. This downmarket kiss-me-quick slapstick seaside location becomes the scene of escapism and even exotic retreat. The scenes where old-fashioned elderly gent Ambrose romances the demure be-saried Asha are particularly memorable for their replaying of familiar Bollywood Indian film aesthetics in a faded English seaside town. In Hanif Kureishi's work, characters often cavort around the metropolis they are attracted to the centre having broken free of the shackles of suburbia; London is their playground. Kureishi's 1991 film was entitled *London Kills Me*, demonstrating an ambivalent love/hate relationship towards the capital.

Trade union organization is not a common theme of feature films as a rule but the 2010 film *Made in Dagenham* was a tale of industrial strife in the east London industrial suburb that for years housed the Fords motor works. British cinematic social realism is combined with comedy in a film based on real life events from 1968 when crippling strike action was taken by women sewing machinists at the Ford plant demanding that they be reinstated onto a pay grade that recognized the skilled nature of their work. Women take centre stage: in all the shots. In reality the action led to the 1970 Equal Pay Act. There is a sense that Swinging London's influence was slowly creeping into the ostensibly encapsulated community of Dagenham – there are references to Biba, Mary Quant, C and A, Babycham and Berni Inns – the latter is the eatery of choice for an expense-fiddling union baron. Despite subject matter of some gravity being its central focus the film is very much a feel-good movie. The women portrayed are heroic in standing up for their rights but we are also shown their softer side. Motherhood is portrayed across the social divide as both the strike leader Rita and wife of the Fords boss find their paths crossing at the school gates of the local grammar school where Rita's son appears to be facing difficulties for being from the estate and not fitting in. The shop steward is a carer for her elderly war-veteran husband. The youngest member of the striking group dreams of being a model only to have her dreams regularly shot down by workers with lines such as 'This ain't Knightsbridge it's Dagenham'. The housing pictured is not the vast acreage of the Becontree estate that Dagenham is often associated with but the early 1960s Mardyke Estate, in the neighbouring borough of Havering which looks futuristic in the film and at the time of its setting would have housed many Ford workers. By 2007 the Mardyke was named by a BBC website as 'Havering's most run-down estate, with a reputation for crime and anti-social behaviour' (Diseko 2007). Its scheduled demolition was held off until filming had taken place. The outside world is represented by the 'brothers' at the TUC (Trade Union Congress) Council in Eastbourne and Whitehall where the machinists visit Employment secretary Barbara Castle. People go 'down the dogs' for kicks. The dramatization of real events has been a running theme in British cinema: the runaway success of 2011 was *The King's Speech*. Further London suburban-themed examples include Twickenham-set *Hope and Glory* (1987) based on film-director John Boorman's childhood memories of the blitz and *Personal Services* (1988) based on the story of Cynthia Payne who ran a brothel for VIPs from suburban Streatham. In some cases real-life examples have been poorly received, for example the film *Buster* (1988) based on the Great Train Robbery of 1963 was criticized by the victims' families for making light of a brutally violent episode and making loveable heroes out of criminals.

Dysfunctioning suburbia and suburban alienation

Suburban films have been numerous; reception by their fans are shaped by their eras. For those who were teenagers in the 1980s, *Heathers* (1989) is an iconic angst-filled suburban high school-set comedy with liberal amounts of irony and cynicism. The opening scenes show a genteel suburban setting as a group of girls play croquet on the lawn in a back-garden of a well-to-do house. The plot unfolds with our introduction to various classroom cliques including the 'geeks', again reminiscent of Willis' 'ear-oles' and the fashionable Heathers including the sceptical Veronica (Winona Ryder). Into this picture enters the mysterious JD (Christian Slater), the dark and brooding new kid in town who has attended 'Seven high schools in seven states and the only thing different was my locker combination', with a father in the construction industry who watches videos of his firm doing demolitions of towerblocks for pleasure. After JD and Veronica become an item he leads them into a systematic murder campaign in which the school's most 'popular' students die one by one with each case staged to look like suicide. Veronica increasingly questions the killings and ensuing climate. After each death, television camera crews roll in to Westerberg High to record vox pops. 'Heather, how many networks did you run to?' Veronica says reproachfully to Heather Duke after Heather Chandler's murder. When Veronica's mother chides her for not getting her face in front of the cameras she exclaims with horror: 'All we want is to be treated like human beings, not like guinea pigs to be experimented on and not like bunny rabbits to be patronized.' Her articulation of suburban angst are mocked by her parents. Her dad retorts: 'I do not patronize bunny rabbits' and her mum mocks her as 'little Miss Voice of a Generation', seemingly more rebel without a clue than *Rebel without a Cause*. The film parodies the fiction of suburban perfection and the media saturated age that it came out of: although noticeably it was before mobile phone use as we know it and the internet. JD celebrates the carnage that he has created: 'Chaos is great. Chaos is what killed the dinosaurs, darling, and it's what's going to make Westerburg a purified place to get an education. Face it, our way is the way. We scare people into not being assholes.' The rejection of the conventional dictates of what one must do to be 'popular' is part of a low-on-realism outright repudiation of suburban values. This follows a 'suburban outsider' tradition running through the *Graduate* and *Ferris Bueller's Day Off* (1986) and later *Donnie Darko* (2002) beginning with *Rebel without a Cause* (1955) whose poster proclaimed that it was about 'the bad boy from a good family'. All are about generational conflict with youth rejecting the suburban idyll at the heart of the American dream that their parents bought into.

The darkly comic films of Todd Solondz and Sam Mendes purport to expose the uncomfortable side of life in the comfortable suburbs and hypocrisy of suburban mores. Paedophilia, real and imagined, is present in both. Solondz' *Happiness* (1999) takes the women in a New Jersey family to contrast their fates; the mother's marriage has failed after her daughters have grown up. One of these is a housewife, another teaches English to foreign students and the third a would-be writer. The more mainstream Mendes' *American Beauty* is a tale of what goes on behind closed doors in a seemingly unthreatening generic suburban street. We hear opening narration from Kevin Spacey's character Lester Burnham, a middle-aged middle-ranking advertising office staffer who lives with his family in a tidy villa which from the outside resembles many others we have seen in suburban films before. The picture perfect scenario of the opening title sequence is shattered as a picture of that hackneyed cliché 'midlife crisis' unfolds; he is revealed to have fatalist tendencies and adolescent sexual fantasies. Themes such as incest makes this un-family viewing despite dreamy visuals. We are told in setting the scene 'Both my wife and daughter think I'm a gigantic loser . . . and they're right. I have lost something. I'm not exactly sure what it is, but I know I didn't always feel this . . . sedated.' The cast also includes a gay couple and the homophobic ex-military man who lives next door with Ricky, his drug dealer son who later becomes Lester's supplier. The film has elements of comedy, tragedy and mystery. The deadpanned voiceover and some sharp-tongued ripostes also weave satire into the dramatic mixture. For example on losing his job the following exchange occurs at the dinner table:

> Caroyln Burnham: . . . but you don't want to be unemployed.
>
> Lester Burnham: Oh well, alright, let's all sell our souls and work for Satan because it's more convenient that way.

In the later film *Crime and Punishment in Suburbia* (2000) the father of the family similarly answers 'Spent my day chained to my desk surrounded by scychophants' when asked over dinner by his wife how work was. *American Beauty* invites us to sympathize with Lester who is pictured as being put-upon and hampered by his overly driven, materialistic wife (the same role was played earlier by Betty Rath in *Man in a Gray Flannel Suit*) who is a cut-throat suburban estate agent who has an affair with a male competitor. Completing this all-American dysfunctional family is Jane his sullen, narcissist teenage daughter who longs for more. Lester has desires awakened in himself directed at her cheerleading classmate Angela, initially seen as a dumb blonde but later revealed as a vulnerable virgin. When the girls are bragging about their sexual exploits, which we later learn are more imagined than real, Angela patronizingly retorts 'That's how things really are. You just don't know 'cause you're this pampered little suburban chick', when of course she also is such a specimen. Visually the film has some memorable moments including a wafting plastic bag gliding around in the wind. Even this is artifice. Ricky shows Jane video footage of it which he declares is 'The most beautiful thing I've ever filmed', with a wistful monologue: 'this bag was just dancing with me. Like a little kid begging me to play with it. For fifteen minutes. That's the day I realized that there was this entire life behind things . . . Sometimes there's so much beauty in the world I feel like I can't take it.' The incident proves to be a bonding experience for the couple. The film is mostly shot in neutral colours but there are injections of bright red as roses, rose petals and blood all appear to break up the almost monochrome monotony, for example when he is pursuing Angela. By the end of his opening prediction, 'This is my life. I'm 42 years old. In less than a year, I'll be dead. Of course, I don't know that yet . . . and in a way, I'm dead already', comes to fruition. The film has been described by Muzzio and Halper (2002:550) as 'a sermon on the evils of upscale suburbia . . . envy, disappointment and emptiness. . . . Suburbia in *American Beauty* represents the highest stage of bourgeois inauthenticity.' It was widely seen as being an attack on the vacuous sterility of the suburbs. Yet while tantalizingly presenting the viewer with the possibility of subverting the supposedly suffocating norms of suburbia the film ends with these same values intact.

British director Sam Mendes reprised his role as chronicler of suburban dysfunctionality in *Revolutionary Road* of 2009, a dramatization of the 1961 Richard Yates novel of the same name. In the 'making of the movie' extra feature from the DVD version Kate Winslett (actress of the lead character April Wheeler) has described the film as a 'suburban battle'. Mendes has remarked 'I grew up in the suburbs so it's familiar territory to me even though it's American suburbs and it's period' although he has insisted that the film is principally about marriage claiming that 'The suburbs and city are a background.' He has claimed that the book is the 'grand daddy' of suburban fiction. The film cannot even claim that it reveals suburban nastiness behind a happy facade: almost from the outset we see the film's central couple at war with one another. At all times however the film is brightly shot with glistening lawns and immaculate white picket fences. It serves as a cautionary tale all about being stifled by suburban conformity: a young couple who briefly resuscitate their earlier newly-wed ambitions of European travel and bohemianism eventually shelve their dreams of escape because another one is on the way. Suburban materialism, social climbing, parenthood, adultery and suicide are all elements of the story. The film's stark ending takes April Wheeler's suburban malheur to its logical conclusion. Indeed the accompanying documentary on the DVD release borrows a phrase from Betty Friedan (returned to in Chapter 6) in its title *Lives of Quiet Desperation*.[2] In sum the film is about the perils of suburban sell-out: in this instance trading youthful dreams of living a bohemian existence in Paris for middle-management mediocrity in the conveyor belt of marriage, kids and being a wage-slave/beholden to a mortgage. As in both versions of *Stepford Wives* and in the film *Revolutionary Road* (both originally novels) it is the wife who expresses misgivings about moving to suburbs which was the husband's idea.

Many of the same acting personnel appear in these portrayals – Julianne Moore has been mentioned in Chapter 1 for example. Kate Winslett played the long-suffering *Mildred Pearce* in the HBO mini-series of the same name and while this was first aired on television it had a sweeping cinematic take on its subject faithfully reproducing the book it was named after and with Todd Haynes directing. The film adaptation of the novel by Tom Perrotta's *Little Children* (directed by Todd Field, 2006) again starred Kate Winslett as a dissatisfied suburban American housewife although set in the present day. We are told at the outset by the eerily voiced narrator (with echoes of the 1999 film *Virgin Suicides* derived from the 1994 novel of Jeffrey Eugenides) that as she sat in the playground area of the local park Sarah imagined herself to be 'a researcher studying the behaviour of typical suburban women, not a typical suburban woman'. We only get flashes of 'the remnants of her former self', that is her existence before suburbia wore her down. The story is a study of adultery to compensate for the promise of suburban utopia unfulfilled by two people trapped in loveless marriages. There is a further backdrop of a local felon being released into the community after a period in prison. This character lives with his elderly mother and in his own words has 'a psycho-sexual disorder'. News of his arrival spreads to engender a lynchmob mentality from the locals who believe he should be castrated. The scenario has flashes of *The Crucible* the 1953 Arthur Miller play which takes the Salem witch trials as its subject. Inter-textual references and reminders of the world outside are rare but present. At a meeting of their local book-club that Sarah has reluctantly been cajoled into attending, Flaubert's *Madame Bovary* is under discussion. Whilst the other the gossipy wives are divided on whether Bovary is a liberated woman discovering her sexuality or a 'slut', Sarah, who we discover studied for a PhD in English literature, has the last word declaring that Bovary is commendable for having escaped from the confines of her strait-jacket of a situation and following her heart which she describes as 'Hunger for an alternative, refusal to accept a life of unhappiness' which of course describes her own situation. The film's spatial positioning in the suburbs can be seen in the way Brad the handsome young stay-at-home dad and student lawyer that Sarah has an affair with gets dropped off at the station from the arms of one woman (wife) to another (lover, as soon as it's safe to do so) when the day of the bar exams he is studying for arrives. The wider world is hinted at in the film where Brad's wife is making on children who have lost fathers in the Iraq war. There is a train line that rattles past the ground where Brad plays baseball. The only black character is a police officer. The book allows more detail into Sarah's lesbian past at college and her husband's indiscretions, explaining that he already had a failed marriage with teenage children but that she married him to escape her job as a Starbucks waitresss.

A further example of a community turning on an individual is seen in *Edward Scissorhands* (1990) a film about a creature created by an inventor literally with scissors for hands. Here the predominant suburban motif is the hedge, a marker of territory and privacy rather in the same way that net curtains demarcate space with the added advantage of allowing you to look out but not letting passers-by look in. The message conveyed is that difference has its limits. At first, as a new arrival in an idyllic pastel painted suburb, Edward is welcomed by the locals and admired for his topiary and hairdressing skills. He even appears on a television talkshow. However when he is taken by Peg, the middle-aged mom who adopts him, to the bank to discuss get a business start-up loan they advise him to get a social security number and driving licence (adding that he could also get an 'invalid permit' and park anywhere – a rare mention of disability in a film) and thus become simply another cog in the machine. Such regularization threatens to destroy his uniqueness; a movement that has already been in train since Edward's arrival, for example Peg dresses him in cottons to fit in with his new peers, disguising the goth aesthetic of his original black leathers. Tasker (2002:74) sees elements of fantasy as a standard tactic of the director Tim Burton, seen clearly in the dream-like shots of the suburban surrounds but events take a turn. Edward's vilification and ostracization by the status-conscious local community starts after he fails to respond to the sexual advances of one of the frustrated wives so as revenge she spreads rumours about him. His downfall is cemented by his deliberate framing in which he is caught breaking and entering a house on the estate. Before long the suburban busybodies are out in force demanding blood, shattering the tranquillity of the film's opening.

Postmodern inter-textuality and dreaminess can be seen in David Lynch's *Blue Velvet* (1986) which seals the deal with a golden oldies style soundtrack including the hypnotic sounds of the title track from crooner Bobby Darin and 'In Dreams' a Roy Orbison song lipsynched from a ghetto blaster cassette. Like the suburbia of *Edward Scissorhands* the images at the film's opening are ostensibly a wholesome, comforting idyllic suburban landscape where red roses sway in the breeze and white picket fences bound the green grass all under a dazzling blue sky yet there is an eeriness to this perfection hinted at by the insects beneath. Human life is seen in cheery waving firemen, a school crossing patrol and a man watering his plants collapsing on the spot. For O'Day (2002:250) the assembly of film visuals and soundtrack is evidence of Lynch's postmodern cynicism in adopting 'a tone at once naively innocent and mockingly self-knowing'. Todd Solondz also documents imperfection beneath the surface of suburban America but in a more realist 'warts 'n' all' way than the surrealism of *Blue Velvet* or *Edward Scissorhands*. He has been hailed as an exponent of '"New Geek Cinema": an emerging body of work that . . . give[s] voice to outsiders and the brutalized' (DeFino 2002:314). *Welcome to the Dollhouse* (1995) uses some element of pastiche in recalling the 1987 Guns and Roses track 'Welcome to the Jungle' translated to the tranquillity of the suburbs and shows the unfolding of events experienced by a non-conformist junior high school girl who is bullied by family and schoolmates. Again the suburban landscape is similar to *Edward Scissorhands*. The suburbia pictured in both cases is one of neat lawns, pastel pinks and sunshine although the themes dealt with are unremittingly dark. Other films' examples of in-text references are more direct, for example *Crime and Punishment in Suburbia* (2000) billed as 'a contemporary fable loosely based on Fyodor Dostoyevsky's *Crime and Punishment*'. Dostoyevsky finds himself the subject of classroom discussion in *The Ice Storm*.

The lynch-mob mentality of vengeance-seeking angry suburban dwellers in *Edward Scissorhands* and *Little Children* is seen across other genres. A suburban backcloth has been almost the default setting of many well-known horror films. The pioneering 1968 zombie film *Night of the Living Dead* was shot in black and white adding to its eeriness zombie and set in a Pittsburgh suburb people before attacks take hold all over the eastern United States. The story sees people under siege from zombies seeking human flesh and in many ways shows how with the hippie movement underway, the American dream coming under attack. The setting was not outer space, there were no aliens or ghouls from eastern Europe but under threat was mainstream suburbia. *Invasion of the Bodysnatchers* made twice (1956, 1978) also shows a small town encircled by alien forces which by the remark was a suburb. As one-by-one once dependable locals fall under their spell only one person is left untouched and on the run, prefiguring the same sense of urgency conveyed in *Stepford Wives* (1975, 2004). *A Nightmare on Elm Street* again evokes the terror felt by a small, close-knit community under siege from a child-killing psychopath's posthumous revenge. *Scream* and its sequels are set in California in a suburban area, the first film of the series in particular demonstrates postmodern traits as the teenagers of the story are initially unimpressed by the murders engulfing the locality as they do not measure up to previous films that they have seen. A suburbanite on the rampage is the simple premise of *Falling Down*. McCarthy (1998:42) sees the film as symbolic of 'a general subordination of the interests and desires of women and a pervasive sense that life in the urban centers is self-made hell'. Pfeil (1995) had also used the film as an example of white masculinity in crisis. The film is 'centered around a protagonist, a kind of proto-normative, anomic individual who [can be described as] "out there"', according to McCarthy (1998:41). The film serves as illustrations of a suburbia which has strayed from the rosy picture once seen of wholesomeness or even muted frustration (*American Beauty*, *Little Children*, etc.) to become intolerant and impatient. It seems that while suburban culture was once celebrated in film it has now become an open goal for potshots. Science fiction takes the horror genre even further and some analyses see the dystopia inherent in it as corresponding with some of the negative features of standardization and suffocation that have been attributed to suburbia. Indeed science fiction novels have included reflections on the suburbs since H. G. Wells' *War of the Worlds*. While space (no pun intended) precludes a close examination of this film type, examples include *Invaders from Mars*, *ET* and *Close Encounters of the Third Kind* as examined by Latham (1995). *The Truman Show* (1998) showed the eeriness of modern suburbia as imprisoning and isolating with CCTV surveillance technology dominating life.

Perhaps the most extreme version illustrating the cautionary tale of submission to the suburban ideal is seen in the horror cum science fiction of the *Stepford Wives* (1975) based on the 1972 novel by Ira Levin, itself reportedly inspired by Betty Freidan. The film follows a young family moving to Conneticut from New York in search of a better life. As Walter the husband reminds his wife aspiring photographer Joanna it will be 'perfect for the kids' itemizing: 'Good schools, low taxes, clean air.' From the beginning however both she (and their daughter, unable to sleep at night) are doubtful of the move but suspicions are confirmed as Joanna notices how all the fellow housewives one-by-one become robotic vacuous, drones: devoid of any soul or personality and instead becoming perfect (i.e. submissive) housewives in what can literally be described as a clone-town. The only thing they can enthuse about are recipes and cleaning . Odd repetitive behaviour ensues when they are in any way physically struck, causing their circuits to short, as seen with one neighbour whose car is bumped while she's reversing out of the supermarket carpark and later her best friend Bobby when Joanna sticks a knife into her on realizing that has also 'turned' to have the suspicion confirmed when she doesn't bleed. Both mechanically begin repeating the same phrase. It gives a new meaning to her psychiatrist's warning that 'a city to suburb move for a woman with interests other than children can seem like a jolt to Siberia'. As the realization dawns on Joanna that the women are being programmed by the husbands and their shady 'mens association' to become androids, after a visit to a psychiatrist insisted on by Walter she becomes next in line. Despite attempting to fight the system it ultimately wins. The film has the hallmarks of science fiction. A Mr Big masterminds the takeover from a central control room at the club. However the shots of Stepford itself show the visual perfection of the idyllic US suburb: white picket fence, picture windows and immaculately manicured lawns. Director Bryan Forbes has described how he wanted to shoot a thriller in sunlight rather than a dark house. The trailer calls it 'a modern day horror film'.[3] This is a depiction of surrealism in the suburbs, a world where the nightmare of women as domesticated dummies is realized to its logical conclusion. The title has perhaps even more than the expression 'gray flannel suit' entered our everyday lexicon. In 1997 on the election of 101 women Labour MPs who swept to power with a New Labour government and provided with pagers to remain 'on message', many commentators negatively remarked them as 'Blair's babes'; these were effectively parliamentary Stepford wives programmed to mindlessly accept leadership instructions.

Conclusion

This chapter has looked into cinematic representations of the suburbs although the cinema as a physical presence as an actual building in the suburb is also worthy of mention in recessionary times where suburban high streets are increasingly hollowed out with the collapse of chainstores and small businesses alike. West London's Southall was once home of four cinemas . By the late 1970s, while cinemas elsewhere had shut down or changed function to become bingo-halls in the post tv age, all were showing Bollywood films to cater for an audience who had migrated from the Punjab region of India with samosas as well as popcorn on sale. The Himalaya lasted longest; styled like a Chinese Palace it variously closed and re-opened its doors before shutting for the last time in 2010. In the 1980s it was video rentals and more recently in its second incarnation (following Arts Council restoration) DVDs and multiplexes that hit this 'decaying beauty' (Gates 2010) hard enough to be no longer viable. Chambers has remarked of art deco styled cinemas across the United Kingdom: 'Such "picture palaces" were themselves like film sets, in dramatic contrast to their location in the working-class and suburban areas of Britain's major cities.' Southall with its sometimes chaotic and always vividly diverting Asian commerce in shopfronts and spilling out in stalls onto the pavements has always been more than just another dreary suburb: its proximity to Heathrow airport explaining why Asians opted for this suburban location as opposed to earlier ethnic settlers around the docks that had been their point of arrival. The same applies to Hounslow as the quote of Malkani in Chapter 2 illustrated. Today futuristic multiplexes have alongside hi-tech retail and business parks have supplanted the role of many suburban cinemas; some were subsequently turned into bingo halls which themselves atrophied before long, for example Kingston's Gala Bingo once a Regal then ABC cinema which shut in 2010. Up the road from Southall three miles along the A4020 Uxbridge Road later, Ealing, home of the world famous studios that spawned 'Ealing comedy' at the time of writing has no cinemas at its centre. Nonetheless the cinema has provided representation of and escapism from suburbia in various ways.

When determining what it is we look for when we identify a 'suburban film' the answer is multiple things. Generation is portrayed in many ways for example. The older generation of suburbanites are figures of fun in numerous youth audience-oriented films although in *Ali G Indahouse*, a suburban youth of indeterminate ethnic origin becomes figure of fun in a film drawing on the resources of black youth culture and aesthetic from hip hop. The implication is that the suffering implied cannot translate to the affluent leafiness of Staines-upon-Thames. The actor is Jewish and slang used is adapted Jamaican Patois. Ali G is a masked player, we do not know who he 'really' is. James Dean and Natalie Wood of *Rebel without a Cause* both died young (Dean particularly so) sealing their longevity as anti-suburban cultural icons whereas Mathew Broderick has aged from playing a freewheeling 1980s suburban kid thumbing his nose at suburban parental values in *Ferris Bueller's Day Off* to a fully paid up subscriber of these and stalwart of the sinister Mens Association for local husbands by 2004's *Stepford Wives* comic remake. The UK sitcom spin-off *Bless this House* is another film where middle-aged suburban domesticity and the pompous snob values of the parents generation are contrasted with the hedonistic liberation of their offspring who represent youth. *Revolutionary Road* seems to be a warning against squandering the inheritance of gilded youth for the suburban treadmill. More recently *Fishtank* (2009, directed by Andrea Arnold) is set both in an inhabited and an abandoned council flat in non-descript blank East London suburbia which feels very cut off from anything in the film, bisected by dual carriageways. The main character Mia diverts herself from everyday existence by truanting from her pupil referral unit to try out dance routines by herself. Her mother's latest on–off lover Conor tells her 'You dance like a black.' She follows him home: a Barrat-type newbuild house near what looks like an industrial landscape bordering wasteland.

Portrayals of suburbs in cinema seem to oscillate between the dichotomous representations of utopian promised land or dystopian hell. De Fino (2002) claims that Solondz was motivated by the saccharine 1980s/1990s popular television series *The Wonder Years* which was an affectionate depiction of growing up in an unnamed non-descript suburb through the eyes of a 12-year-old boy. The two can then sometimes overlap in their practice or form a dialogue. Solondz among other things is a Jewish film-maker. In his film *Welcome to the Dollhouse*, the central Weiner family of suburban New Jersey are Jewish although this is not explicitly stated in the script. Solondz has decried what he calls 'a part of society, that's lapsing from the Jewish faith but also wanting to have the cake and eat it too' (Applebaum 2010). Jewish characters have been a mainstay of his work just as suburbia has been home of Jewish residents in the United Kingdom and United States. Golders Green in North London or Prestwich in the Metropolitan Manchester borough of Bury are both now established 'Jewish' suburbs where residents often made outward journeys, for example from London's East or North Manchester's Cheetham Hill. Solondz' interview with the *Jewish Chronicle* includes the following line with interesting implications for the burden of representation: 'On the one hand, people say, "Yes, I'm Jewish and pro-Israel", and at the same time they're getting the nose job and trying to camouflage any signs of Jewishness as best they can.' The same could apply to Asian-inflected popular cultures. The burden of representation is then another consideration that becomes particularly acute in dealing with minority subjects as film-makers must wrestle with to what extent their portrayals of, for example ethnic groups should convey a sense of realism or just be included for purely entertainment/ aesthetic value.

There is an ever-lengthening list of films that are either set in the suburbs or that take suburbia directly as subject matter. Yet while some examples thrive others are written out from the wider narrative. A distorting effect can occur as some films are stubbornly resistant to receive wider airings. The film *Diary of a Mad Housewife* (1970), which was set on Long Island while the husband worked in Manhattan, has never had a DVD release making rare VHS copies sell on this outmoded format for disproportionally high prices on Ebay. Given the advance of technology and the accelerated culture that follows in its wake perhaps it is only now a matter of time that the content is uploaded onto YouTube democratizing it for all. Unlike the British urban kitchen sink epics *Cathy Come Home* and *Up the Junction* which have prided themselves in close-up gritty topicality and realism, American suburban-set drama often contains elements of surreality and fantasy as well as straightforward sensibilities of a mission to entertain: *Edward Scissorhands* seems to be a prime example in its pastel utopia which provides the setting for what is a late twentieth-century fairytale. *Revolutionary Road* and the *Stepford Wives* (both versions) are very different films which share as features wide angle shots and being brightly lit where everything looks sunny at a surface level lending an almost dreamlike quality to the proceedings. Throughout the decades a number of directors including Mike Leigh and Todd Solondz have engaged in what Loukides and Fuller (1991:181) call 'attacking suburban mediocrity, empty affluence, and the ugliness of the rat race' and instead advocating 'the challenge of an adventurous, and ambiguous, rather than pre-planned future'. YouTube

Table 4.1 Suburban-set feel-bad movies: an alternative slice of American pie?

Title	Theme	Year
American Gun	US love affair with firearms.	2005
The Babysitters	Teenage prostitution passing for babysitting service highlighting middle-aged lust practised by suburban men for high school girls.	2007
Burning Palms	Dark comedy, interlacing four separate stories united only by the fact that they take place in different *suburbs* of Los Angeles.	2010
Crime and Punishment in Suburbia	Teen drama 2000 update of Fyodor Dostoyevsky's *Crime and Punishment* with a murder committed in the plot recalling *The Postman Always Rings Twice* (1946 and 1981).	2000
Den du frygter (Fear Me Not)	Move his family into his wife's childhood home in the suburbs; dark psychological thriller addiction in middle-class Copenhagen.	2008
A Dirty Shame	Suburban sexual fetishism and nymphomania receives a comedy treatment as the underworld of sex addiction in suburban Baltimore is uncovered following a bump to the head by a lawnmower in a film pillorying repression in the suburbs, starring Tracey Ullman and Chris Isaak in a 1950s-looking film.	2004
Falling Angels	Exposes the falsehood of security of the fifties and sixties Canadian, coming of age of three daughters, Saskatchewan alcoholism, underage sex, homosexuality; based on the novel by Barbara Gowdy.	2007
Five on the Black Hand Side	Barbers shop chauvinism, Harlem.	1973
Ghost World	Set in a suburban neighbourhood and based on a comic book; looks at frustration of suburban living and the taboo of a teenage girl in an intimate relationship with an older man.	2001
The Hillz	California: sex and drugs.	2005
I'm Losing You	Mortality, adultery, AIDS, and deceit, based on book by Bruce Wagner.	1998
The Joneses	The expresssion 'keeping up with the Joneses' taken to its logical conclusion in an indictment of American consumerism as we witness the seemingly perfect American family located in a perfect suburban neighbourhood as mere agents of product placement. Big budget with David Duchovny and Demi Moore.	2009
Life of the Party	Alcoholism dashes suburban dreams.	2005

Table 4.1 Continued

Title	Theme	Year
Lifelines	A day in the life of the Bernstein family who all have issues and are in therapy.	2009
Lymelife	1970s-set suburban rites of passage, Long Island.	2008
Masters of Horror: Season 2, Episode 2. . . . *Family*	John Landis-directed new neighbours discover psychotic murderer next door, Blugeoned bodies television.	2006
Me and You and Everyone We Know	Quirky story of suburban romance.	2005
Reckless Indifference	After suburban drug deal goes wrong an examination of the controversial California statute that mandates life imprisonment for those who commit murder during the commission of another felony takes place.	2000
Risky Business	While the cat's away (i.e. parents go holidaying vacation) the mice will play – cue teen sex comedy hi-jinks for suburban Chicago teenager (played by Tom Cruise) and his associates.	1983
The Safety of Objects	Intersecting tales of four suburban families, based on short stories, begins with aerial shot of suburban landscape.	2001
Serial Mom	Outwardly perfect Baltimore housewife takes revenge on neighbours who transgress suburban codes, for example flytipping, not wearing seatbelts, etc. and becomes a murder suspect. Directed by John Waters.	1994
Society	Beverly Hills Mansion, body horror lurks behind not all that it seems as central character; Bill uncovers cannibalism and vampirism behind the veneer of his daily suburban serenity.	1989
Smile	Film about suburban California Young American Miss Pageant behind which lurks suburban dysfunctional themes of depression, alcoholism and sexual frustration.	1975
Zero Day	Two troubled adolescents chronicle events that ultimately lead up to Columbine-like shootings terrifying assault on their school suicide bomber video.	2003

has helped illuminate much of the suburban history present in film with its multitude of freely available stream-able clips. DVD re-releases have also helped bring suburban film to successive generations, usually accompanied by extensive DVD features including retrospective documentaries to contextualize the films themselves. Of course suburbia was always more complex than stereotypical perceptions had it. Recent years have seen a growing number of films presenting dysfunction in suburbia and departing from the old accepted 'happy families' template (see Table 4.1) to the extent that in years to come perhaps to see a functioning harmonious picture of suburban existence might be a welcome novelty.

Notes

1   One assumes that this refers to the Barking campus of University of East London, since then in disuse now that the Docklands campus has been developed.

2   In the words of Betty Friedan: 'But on an April morning in 1959, I heard a mother of four, having coffee with four other mothers in a suburban development fifteen miles from New York, say in a tone of quiet desperation, 'the problem'. And the others knew, without words, that she was not talking about a problem with her husband, or her children, or her home. Suddenly they realized they all shared the same problem, the problem that has no name' http://web.viu.ca/davies/H323Vietnam/Friedan_FeminineMystique.1963.htm.

3   Both as seen as an 'extra feature' of the DVD release.

5

Suburbia on the Box

Whenever some blowhard starts talking about the anonymity of the suburbs or the mindlessness of the television generation . . . we know that inside everyone of those identical boxes, with its Dodge parked out front and its white bread on the table and its TV set glowing blue in the falling dusk, there are . . . families bound together in the pain and the struggle of love.

(Closing speech of Kevin Arnold, *The Wonder Years* episode 1, 1989)

This chapter addresses the subject of how suburbia is pictured on television: both underwent a growth period in the twentieth century. Indeed at the same time as marketing campaigns for new suburban housing the television was, alongside the labour-saving devices of refrigerator and washing machine, one of the luxuries that was dangled at new suburban dwellers to furnish their home with after the shackles of post-war austerity were being shaken off. Spigel (2001b:388) has looked at early print advertisements for television sets and finds that these offered and fed into 'utopian visions and middle-class anxieties about the future of family life and in particular, the future of gender and generational relations in the home'. The ideal lifestyle presented in many examples depicts families around the box which is positioned hearth-like as the focal point of the room emitting a rosy glow. From Queen Elizabeth II's coronation when whole British streets seeking a sighting of this hitherto unprecedented spectacle would cram into the homes of those, at the time rare, families who possessed a set, to its present near-universal penetration (with albeit fragmented viewing habits) via the era of mass audiences and prime time, television has attained a ubiquity and attendant promise of escapism to a far greater degree than the more discerning and arguably stratified or at least more specialized publics for literature, cinema and music.

When assessing how suburbia is portrayed on television, different trends can be discerned in the United Kingdom and United States. The trajectory of British television on all channels cannot be separated from the guiding principle of public service broadcasting and the ethos of the founding father of the BBC Lord Reith to 'inform, educate and entertain'. This was criticized from the commercial sector by Rupert Murdoch who claimed in 1989 that 'This public service television system has had, in my view, debilitating effects on British society, by producing a television output which is so often obsessed with class, dominated by anti-commercial attitudes and with a tendency to hark back to the past' (quoted in Holland 2000:18). Generating advertising revenue has always been a US concern. Other considerations are common to both, for example balancing high-quality outlet with remaining popular or the continuing viability of the prime-time popular storytelling medium as it struggles to compete for attention among the proliferating numbers of reality television and lifestyle shows. Certain stylistic conventions apply particularly to commercial television such as the staging of mini-cliffhangers to not lose the audience during the break for advertisements. Channel 4 arrived in 1982 with the explicit stated aim of social commentary providing 'gritty' drama, for example *Brookside* and hard-hitting documentary. More recently a number of remakes and revisitings of previous 'classics' have been screened with a suburban central theme on the small and big screen. During the twenty-first century it seems that on more than one occasion in recent years BBC output has been criticized as 'too white and middle class', for example the corporation's 2005 annual report which referred to *Keeping up Appearances*, *Fawlty Towers*, *My Family* and the classic suburban comedy *The Good Life*. As suggested in the previous two chapters the line between small and big screen has sometimes blurred with spin-off television series from what were films or vice versa, for example *The Brady Bunch, Sex and the City, Bless this House* or *Please Don't Eat the Daisies*, or between screen and page in films and television programmes that had been books.

Critics of suburbs decry them for their shallow value system of materialism and their boring uniformity yet how interchangeable are suburbs and are television programmes about them meant to uphold or question the status quo? In the United States the suburbs of New York have featured disproportionately, mirroring the heavy skewing of United Kingdom leaning towards London suburbia. There are also examples of less definable suburban territory. *The Wonder Years* (1989–93) was a warm coming-of-age drama series which never revealed its setting. Todd Solondz, well known as director of films of geographical suburban dysfunction has cited it as key to his artistic development stating 'The catalyst [for *Welcome To the Dollhouse*] was when I saw an episode of *The Wonder Years*, and I was struck at how little it resembled my memory or understanding of childhood. And when I thought more, I couldn't think of any American films that dealt in any serious way with childhood . . . there are European films like *The 400 Blows*, *Los Olvidados* and *Shoeshine*, but little else. In any films about American kids they were either cute like a little doll or evil demons.'[1] The show is being lambasted for its lack of risk taking and comfortable setting. Indeed it was unlike contemporaneous programmes which offered a variation of the usual domestically blissful white family suburban sitcom premise, for example *The Cosby Show* (1984–92) about the successful middle-class black Huxtable family, *Family Ties* (1982–9) in which the teenage son is a right-wing yuppie driving his ex-hippie parents to despair and the *Fresh Prince of Bel-Air* (1990–6) in which a streetwise Philadephia kid played by Will Smith escapes the ghetto for life with rich relatives in the exclusive Los Angeles suburb of Bel Air, home to The Playboy Mansion of *Playboy* magazine founder Hugh Hefner among others. Yet according to the *New York Times, The Wonder Years* was resistive at its origin in being 'a response to urbanites' superior attitude' (Strickland 1996). Like the later *Desperate Housewives* the show used an off-screen narrator (the chief character Kevin as a grown-up reminiscing back) to open and close episodes, who delivered the quote at the top of this chapter. The words hint at the idealism at the show's core which suggests a muted admiration for the passing of a bygone era. Certainly this plea for normality or hymn to the average is unlike the quote of Marc Cherry creator of *Desperate Housewives*: 'I love the values of the suburbs, loved my family, our neighbours. It's just that stuff happens. I don't romanticize that life at all . . . I remember the husbands leaving with their suitcases and my parents saying, "You're not allowed to ask them what's going on." I remember the custody battles. The full range of human experience was there.'[2] The *Wonder Years* original director wished Long Island to be the situation as he had grown up there but this was vetoed as potentially limiting its appeal. Robert Thompson, associate professor of television and film at the Newhouse School of Communications at Syracuse University has stated (Stickland 1996) of the location: 'Something about that postwar, newly created universe just reeked of Levittown, but to have it suspended in geography was a good esthetic decision. It created a universal representation of any suburb without all the baggage of a particular place.' This lack of specificity was designed to give the universal theme of childhood an everytown universal setting unlike say the British sitcoms *Terry and June* and the *Good Life* closely identified with Purley and Surbiton respectively or even *The Fresh Prince of Bel-Air* which had its setting in the title.

Its executive producer has stated 'Everybody felt *The Wonder Years* was set in their home street' (Strickland 1996). While television allows us to be voyeur it also can be comforting and reassuring – there is room for both tropes.

Even in an age when the media is exponentially increasing in form and size, the cathode ray tube and its LCD flat screen equivalent still have unparalleled power in shaping attitudes and exposing viewers to ideas and images. The rise of television encouraged a national shared culture. Television in this sense can act as leveller, it can enable access to a spectacle like a royal wedding, sporting event or historical moment. There is no need as John Lennon once did to differentiate between those in the boxes and those in the 'cheap seats'. Television can reflect, reinforce and challenge dominant norms or even create new ones. Certainly in the days of networked programming and a smaller number of channels (until 1982 there were only three in the United Kingdom) family life adapted to its schedules as television adopted suburbia making the suburban family both audience and subject matter of much television output. In both the United States and United Kingdom, post-war advances in living standards and local planning policy created in a rapidly suburbanizing population a thirst for accompanying consumer durables. Television was probably the most significant among these new labour saving acquisitions – although academic treatise have been written on the iconic status of the washing machine (Redfern 2003) and of Tupperware (Clarke 1997) in defining suburban living. The rise of television meant less time spent in cinemas, restaurants and watching or participating in sport and an increased domestication or privatization of the leisure sphere. Arguably however we are seeing a fall in its influence as a mass audience medium as one household may have several television sets or access programmes via other devices such as computers, smart phones and tablets via catch-up digital services allowing viewers to watch programmes free of their original scheduling shattering the old assumption of audiences sitting down together in family viewing.[3]

No laughing matter? Suburban sitcom

In some ways the sitcom as written extensively about by Mills (2005) is the *de facto* setting for portrayals of suburbia on television. Clapson (1998) even usefully provides a table of different British titles. Dean (2009) has written 'The snobbery, eccentricity, small-mindedness and proximity to larger, more dynamic, towns all lend suburbia an air of entrapment and plain daftness that make it ripe for comedy.' The suburbanization of the United States was also reflected in early situation comedies with titles such as *Father Knows Best* which placed a value system of traditional gender relations, traditionalism, small-c conservative (i.e. not Conservative Party) values and the importance of family and suburban ideals at their core. Some immortalized the very journey that their viewers were making rather than setting up 'the suburbs' as the situation for the comedy: in 1957 the celebrity couple of Lucy and Ricky Ricardo (who the sitcom vehicle *I Love Lucy* was conceived around) made the move in the storyline from their city base of Manhattan to Westport, Connecticut, an hour's commute away. The drama serial *Mad Men* which first aired in 2007 depicts the same era, but with less of an idealized picture and instead if not exactly modern sensibilities of some adult themes. Adultery, hard-drinking and heavy smoking seem to be a constant presence in the series, set in the pressurized environment of a New York advertising agency. We get occasional glimpses of the outside world – Don Draper's rural upbringing and the way that Betty Draper, a former model who we usually only ever see in a domestic setting, occasionally mentions her previous life in Manhattan, followed by 'I don't miss it' said more to convince herself. The show has paid great attention to period detail in its costumes, props and sets and contains moments of history: we see the election of Kennedy, death of Marilyn Monroe. Although humour is at times present the show is probably best described as a period drama. Unusually for a television programme the characters do watch television but this appears to be either something that the children do, only to be chided by their parents at bedtime or more usually a device or historical anchor for present-day viewers to get a sense of situating where in time the episodes are located, for example the 1960 Presidential campaign or 1962 Kennedy assassination.

For a number of years a veritable litany of UK situation comedies have portrayed the suburbs as entirely white, middle class and conservative. Indeed the BBC's own internal processes have highlighted the Corporation's failure to reflect contemporary Britain in its programme roster ('Governors say comedy output is still too white, middle-class and cosy', *The Guardian*, 13 July 2005). The situation comedy genre reinforces how the dullards of suburbia have all too often been the object of ridicule. Matters usually centre on the intact nuclear family unit which is usually always presented as a desirable ideal. *Terry and June* lived behind net curtains in Purley. The show has recently enjoyed a revival with the BBC dusting off its 1982 Christmas special to re-show in December 2010 and ITV2 re-running entire series of the show. The series can be located in a long tradition of British comedy narrating insularity and narrow-mindedness. Rojek (2007:155), for example writes: 'Victor Meldrew, from the popular BBC comedy

One Foot in the Grave, is the grumpy, choleric, suburban successor to Fawlty', referring to John Cleese central character the waspish Basil Fawlty in 1970s hotel sitcom *Fawlty Towers*. The sitcom genre has mainly tended to reinforce small-c conservative values of what constitutes the suburban lifestyle, but there are also exceptions to these predictable portrayals: the sitcom has sometimes thrown a curveball, teasing its viewers periodically by offering from time to time a break from the norm. Ahead-of-their-time eco-warriors the Goods of the *Good Life* experimented with sustainable living in Surbiton, South London bordering Surrey, described by Wagg (1998:19) as 'signifier of semi-detached suburban conformity'. By abandoning the rat race they had rejected society's dominant norms, or at least adapted them, to follow an alternative family structure.

The suburbs may not have traditionally been the scene of open revolt, when taken in a collective sense they have never been particularly 'angry' places in cultural cartography, but simmering resentment at the suburbanite's lot has been portrayed repeatedly in sitcoms. Here suburbs play host to the interfering busybody/put-upon 'angry of suburbia' who writes outraged letters into the *Radio Times* in a Mary Whitehouse-esque way. This character is often present in the British suburban sitcom. Rojek (2007:156) muses: 'What is it about life in Britain that makes the characteristics of anger and repression recognizably "British"?' Certainly there seems to be a malcontented, dissatisfied bent to the nosey suburban neighbour behind their twitching net curtains, waiting to oppose the next planning application, their pen (or keyboard) ready to fire off an another missive expressing their disgust as is their right in complaining culture. Youthful suburban frustration can be seen in the teenage fumblings of Channel 4's *The Inbetweeners* (2008–11) that also became a successful film (2011) which unlike the wholesome *Wonder Years* showed failed sexual experimentation, unrequited love and drunkeness.

Manifold examples exist: Reginald Perrin who lives a life of repetition including an identical daily commute and 'ravioli followed by ravioli' or Peter Barnes of *A Sharp Intake of Breath*. Also named by Rojek alongside Victor Meldrew the retired husband of the 1980s/1990s *Keeping Up Appearances* is Martin from *Ever Decreasing Circles* from slightly earlier, played by Richard Briers who passed away in 2013 having become almost embodiment of suburban everyman in different tv 1980s and 1970s sitcoms.

In Briers' earlier show, the now iconic 1970s series, the *Good Life* his character was an optimistic one; Tom Good, taking the old adage 'life begins at 40' had chucked in his mindless, meaningless, repetitive soul-destroying job in order to live off the land in his suburban lair with ever-supportive wife Barbara who does not work either. The *Good Life* presents a situation where the expected template we have come to associate with suburban living – laughs frequently derived from a long-suffering couple and their ungrateful children – is subverted. This can be seen clearly in the contrasting portrayal of the idealistic Goods who are counterposed with their more conventionally suburban middle-class next-door neighbours Margot and Jerry Leadbetter, caricatured as social climbers who are fully paid up members of the rat race and associative social life offered by suburbia. She is doyenne of the local operatic society and he is a frustrated employee at the same workplace where Tom previously worked at before rejecting this role for his new-found life. Even the name of the programme *The Good Life* seems significant as it conjures up the promise of a better world. So too are the lead couple's names: the Goods living up to being virtuous as contrasted with the allegorically named Leadbetters who literally see their mission in life as to 'lead better'. Neither couples have children which is usually a defining characteristic of suburban settlement. In an interview on the BBC documentary *Comedy Connections* the show's first producer explained that this decision was taken as the programme would not have worked with them. From 1988 to 1997 the US sitcom *Roseanne* also showed a suburban household scrimping and saving but the couple in the programme were blue and 'pink collar' workers (Betti 1995),[4] Roseanne and Dan Conner, who had three unruly kids. Family fiscal belt tightening was a running theme of the show: economies were enforced by their economic situation rather than playing at rejecting the trappings of middle-class life as a lifestyle choice in the way that the Goods were. Lippert (1997:22) has called the Conners 'the poster family for the diminishing expectations crowd . . . the economy size embodiments of the working class the last gasp of un-Gapped America'. Mention of class here is interesting as in the United States the pervasive ideology of the American dream has rendered the term largely redundant with 'blue collar' being a more widespread term. The series was the product of an earlier economic recession.

On an internet forum discussing whether *Roseanne* is 'Most Realistic Sitcom Ever' a poster named Rodgers01 weighs in 'The vast majority of sitcoms are incredibly unrealistic: a shoe salesman can afford a huge house in the suburbs? (*Married with Children*); 20-somethings can afford to live it up in big apartments in Manhattan? (*Friends* and God knows how many knock-offs). Suburban families are photogenic and polite and cheerful? (just about every family sitcom ever made).'[5] *Roseanne* is contrastingly celebrated for its conveying of more recognizable traits of suburban living than idealized examples which are itemized as 'the surly kids, the money troubles, the messy house, the neighbors [*sic*]. The parents were fat; one of the kids was a trouble-maker and semi-goth; one was bright but whiny'. Suburban disorder is rarely seen onscreen just as characters rarely themselves watch television. *Roseanne* is not the only sitcom to portray suburban disfunctionality with wisecracking philosophy. While the literally larger than life figures of the physically weighty Conners and their rebellious offspring made them appear almost as cartoon characters.

The Simpsons is a cartoon suburban family of a similar working-class stock where characters sometimes say the unsayable. It began in 1989 and its first series was rated alongside the fall of the Berlin Wall as a significant event in a *Time* magazine retrospective of that year. The show took the familiar familial but added several postmodern twists. Poniewozik (2009) remarked how it was 'a show about everything. Through insufferably wholesome next-door neighbor Ned Flanders, the show became about religion. Through fatuous local news anchor Kent Brockman, it became about the media. Through Springfield's venal Mayor Quimby, it became about politics . . . No institution was safe: there was a jaded reverend, a doughnut-gobbling police chief, an ambulance-chasing lawyer and a stoner school-bus driver.' It is the dialogue that the motley cast of characters speak which rewrites the suburban rulebook. Framing devices include school where the staff from the clueless principal to layabout janitor are imbecilic, *The Itchy and Scratchy Show*, a cat and mouse cartoon of extreme violence and the nuclear power plant where Homer works kow-towing to a corrupt boss with obsequious henchman in tow, symbolizing impending environmental catatrophe. In 'Eight Misbehavin', the seventh episode of the eleventh season (1998) Homer watches a black and white film that parodies *Rebel without a Cause* in which Jimmy repudiates his parents' suburban values. After Homer learns that the childless grocery store owners Apu and Manjula are trying to conceive he congratulates them and exclaims 'Kids are the best, Apu. You can teach them to hate the things you hate. And they practically raise themselves, what with the Internet and all.' This outrageously feckless attitude is what no other respectable suburban television character would ever dare to say is a running character trait. In the 2000 episode *Insane Clown Poppy* (season 12, episode 3) when Krusty the clown discovers he has an illegitimate daughter conceived during the first Gulf war Homer lectures 'Fatherhood isn't easy. Like motherhood. But I wouldn't trade it for anything.' In the episode 'Take My Wife, Sleaze' episode 8 of season 11 (1999) when Marge is kidnapped by a gang of hells angels she tries to persuade them to mend their violent ways and promote to them 'the dream of a good job, a loving family, and a home in the suburbs'. The words are almost identical to the opening proposition of Betty Friedan in her still much cited work *The Feminine*

Mystique (2010:60) revisited Chapter 6 which talks of 'what every . . . American girl wanted – to get married, have four children and live in a nice house in a nice suburb'. Again despite all the taboo breaking of the programme in portraying working class family imperfection the suburban ideal is seen as something to aspire to, imperfections and all in the *Simpsons* own case.

In a lather: Suburban soaps

In soap opera narrative storylines continue from one episode to the next, they are usually structured around dramatic hooks reeling in viewers and compelling them to tune in next time to see how this cliffhanger will resolve itself. Whereas situation comedy can centre on one family or given situation, soap opera is usually set in a geographic locale be it Weatherfield, the Salford home of *Coronation Street*, the fictional E20 postcode of *East-Enders* or *Beverly Hills 902010*. Soaps are a televisual format that prides itself on reflecting real life: the United Kingdom's longest running examples *Coronation Street* (1958–present) and *East Enders* (1985–present) are both located in fictional surrounds – Weatherfield in Greater Manchester and Walford in London. Both locations are largely self-contained. The United Kingdom's most prominent home-grown popular soap set in suburbia was *Brookside* which took place on a Liverpool new-build housing estate and ran on the newly formed Channel 4 (1982–2003).[6] The show contained some moments of postmodern interweaving of other texts, for example the *Magic Rabbits* show-within-a-show, often watched by the characters if they were housebound in the day, in which pink fluffy bunnies of the Duracell advert variety would be seen wiggling about to high-pitched electronically processed uptempo background music. *Brookside* itself had been intended to be titled *Meadowcroft*, a name evoking the pastoral dimension of suburbia but when this name was vetoed by Channel 4 for having too close a similarity with the station's *Meadowlark* programme, *Brookside* was settled on. 'Meadowcroft Park' became a fictitious soap opera within this soap (Kibble-White 2002:13) typifying postmodernism. These imaginary programmes operate in the same way as the *Simpsons*'s running *Itchy and Scratchy Show*, which exists to parody television violence. Such examples are rare as usually in most suburban television shows the characters do not spend their time in front of the box. As Monaco (2000:514) puts it, 'The single most irresistible fact about the television families with whom we spend most of our time is that they don't watch television. If they did we'd be as boring as they are; we'd turn them off as quickly as we do ourselves.' *Brookside*'s pioneering jerky hand-held cameras and left-leaning political stance exemplified Channel 4's initial amateurism and edgy remit. The willingness to feature a younger largely untrained and untried cast and tackle hitherto televisual taboos departed from that the Coronation Street norm that had dictated British soap since 1960 and arguably set the template for *East Enders* launched three years later on BBC1. Both had modern sensibilities compared to the comparative nostalgia of 'Corrie' – as Britain's oldest soap is affectionately known. Whereas *Coronation Street* had never particularly tapped into the permissive society instead opting for older cast members and established community structures (principally the pub) *Brookside* ran on issue-led storylines which included rape, lesbianism and a hostage-taking siege to name but three with a nightclub as an alternative setting to the housebound action. Founder Phil Redmond has commented (Kibble White 2002:7) that the programme's mission statement was 'to tell many different stories from varied viewpoints: stories of people on the way up and people on the way down; stories from across the class, gender and age ranges, and often providing different perspectives on the same subject'. Unemployment had equally hit both Paul Collins, a middle-aged middle-class ex-executive and school-leaver Damon Grant, son of a union official whose family living opposite saw moving to 'the close' as having 'made it' off their former council estate. Redmond embodied the prevailing Thatcherite logic of enterprise culture by setting up his own production company and purchasing the entire street in the realization that this would be cheaper than traditional set and props design/manufacture/maintenance. It was 1980s in spirit for dealing with the crises of de-industrialization and emasculated trade union power (in the character Bobby Grant). The built environment of new-build boxy houses serenely facing a green belied the modern in-yer-face hard hitting content and production techniques.

One of the 1980s most successful examples of suburban soap opera of recent years aired on British television was geographically located as far from blighty as it was possible to be. The Australian show *Neighbours* ran on BBC1 from 1986, at its height in two daily screenings, before moving on to the smaller-audience terrestrial broadcaster Channel 5. Although the programme no longer enjoys the popularity it once did its continuing effects are widespread and were seen the way that the actress Kylie Minogue who played the apprentice mechanic Charlene went on to become almost pop royalty in the United Kingdom, a national treasure in her adopted nation. Stratton and Ang (1994:6) have remarked 'As the decline of the British empire became an increasingly unavoidable fact in the daily experience of the British themselves, recently emphasized by the prolonged recession/depression in the post-Thatcher era, the ex-colony Down Under has become a focus for fantasies of a better life. The success of *Neighbours* can be understood in this light.' The plot centred on three generations of the Daniels family in the suburb of Erinsborough (itself an anagram of the word 'Neighbours'). Familiar situations were presented to a British audience with a sunny backdrop that was comparatively rare in the United Kingdom's own soap operas. Stratton and Ang (1994:6) quote Stephen Croft's identifying of 'good neighbourliness and wholesome, traditional, suburban values . . . moral certainties of hard work, decency and compassion' as explaining the show's appeal. They do not see this as representative of turn of the century Australia. Perhaps the declining audiences for the show illustrate changing attitudes as reality shows and talent competitions seem to have become increasingly popular in both the United Kingdom and United States. During its 1988–9 heyday (when Kylie Minogue and Jason Donovan starred), *Neighbours* was able to command an audience of 14 million UK viewers. By 2008 this had shrunk to 2.4 million prompting its sale to Channel 5. Initial ratings after the switch were relatively high for this minority channel. Shifting formats reflecting changing tastes are evident in the reality programme *A Place Down Under* (2004) in which families relocating from their (typically suburban) UK surrounds to Australia were followed coming to terms with climate and local life-forms (including insects).

Genre-bending

The Simpsons itself unlike the hi-tech CGI (computer-generated image) animation that followed from Dreamworks and Pixar in its wake, centred around (with apologies to Damon Gough) the 'badly drawn boy' of Bart Simpson and family. All are bright yellow, perhaps explained by the proximity of the family dwelling to a nuclear reactor where Homer the father is employed. Kutnowski (2008:599) has commented that the programme captures 'the physical, behavioural, and psychological profiles of the five family members plus the suburban American culture that surrounds them in the town of Springfield'. Although the opening titles were cut short in later series, commenting on the theme music Kutnowski (2008:601–3) finds that this changes in order to fit characters: for 'idiotic Homer' we hear a tuba 'dissonant, loud and crudely simplistic in rhythmic terms . . . which reinforced his anti-hero features' whereas for Marge it is 'gentle legato in the strings . . . [reflecting] the fearful challenges of daily life – juggling groceries in one hand and child in another . . . this activist-hippie turned mother figure is presented almost as a saintly vision.' It was not for nothing that President George George H Bush expressed the desire that America be more like *the Waltons* and less like *the Simpsons.*[7] The claim was the same sort of cultural canutism that John Major was guilty of in the same decade. Harking back to *the Waltons* (1971–81) was a reference to a Hicksville small-town agrarian clan in a show set in the 1940s which presented viewers a mythical golden age where wholesome family values permeated. In *The Simpsons* suburban life is far from polite and passive, it is complicated. The family constantly fight with one another (lazy Bart versus vegetarian intellectual Lisa or any combination of the kids against their parents who themselves are often warring against each other) and subsequently make up. There are ethnic minority characters present which were not there in earlier suburban portrayals, for example Apu the Indian grocery store owner one of a new US media stereotype (also seen for example in the film *SubUrbia*).

At the start of its sixth series *The Guardian*'s television listing (Skegg et al. 2010) conveyed a sense of boredom at what *Desperate Housewives* had become: 'Dear Wisteria Lane resident, sorry you were out, but your order of 1x family-with-a-dark-secret has been left with your neighbour . . . They're still furiously pumping the plot dispenser, but there's hardly anything left.' Yet when it began in 2004 the programme was seen as genuinely genre-straddling; a drama following a weekly instalment and cliffhanger soap-opera format also including off-camera narration, comic moments of absurdity, elements of horror/suspense and plot devices such as twists and critical-trigger happenings that lead to chains of events and unintended consequences. Associated press (2004) describes the show as 'comically dark'. The Facebook group 'Addicted to *Desperate Housewives*' describes it as 'A primetime soap with a truly contemporary take on the happily ever after, *Desperate Housewives* takes a darkly comedic look at suburbia.' Channel 4 (undated) describes the programme's subject matter as 'exploring the complicated reality behind the apparent domestic bliss of a group of housewives in a fictitious American suburb'. This description highlights the dual nature of the show. A constant theme of the programme, which ran to eight series before ending in 2012, is that all is not what it seems. The book's official companion volume (Anon 2005) restates on its back flyleaf a comment made by the character Bree Vanderkamp in the first episode 'Ah, But Underneath': 'It's the age old question: how much do we really want to know about our neighbours?' The dichotomy between public lives and private worlds is apparent from the start and unusually it is the men who are under-written as characters. From the outset the show is narrated beyond the grave by a central character who commits suicide in episode 1 as a voice-off. As the Channel 4 summary of the first episode explains 'One day, in her perfect house, in the loveliest of suburbs, Mary Alice ended it all. From her unique vantage point beyond the grave, Mary Alice can now reveal the secrets behind the closed doors of her friends and neighbours . . .' It is this character who we never see as a fully fledged cast-member who narrates the homilies through which the show hangs together. The first series is a murder mystery but subsequent series throw up new central themes with series 7 of 2010 revisiting this murder.

Desperate Housewives has been subject of a media studies book-length dissection from Akass and McCabe (2006) containing 16 essays on different aspects of it. The show has also featured as a case study in the media studies textbook of Devereux (2007). Despite a cast of beautiful women leading comfortable lifestyles on a fairy-tale like set on which the sun seems to always shine, the programme contains macabre elements, uncovering some dark themes: loneliness, drug dependency, isolation and boredom as well as one-up-manship, or rather *woman*ship. None of the cast seems to have achieved happiness despite their privileged lifestyles. Material possessions cannot compensate for stifling boredom and money can't buy them love. The show's creator Marc Cherry, a gay Republican, has been quoted as defending the genre and denying that it is satirical: 'Satire sounds like you're making fun of something. And the truth is I'm not making fun of the suburbs. I love the suburbs' (ABC 2004). In the 'teaser' at the start of every show there is a moral from Mary Alice. Constructing a list of these could almost serve as a handbook for suburban living. Conflict and Keeping up with the Jones are recurring issues. In 'Running to Stand Still' originally aired in 2004 (season 1, episode 6), 'Suburbia is a battleground, an arena for all forms of domestic combat. Husbands clash with wives, parents cross swords with children, but the bloodiest battles often involve women and their mothers-in-law.' In 'You Could Drive a Person Crazy', the twenty-fifth episode from series 2, the opener is 'Beautiful lawns, spacious homes, happy families. These are the hallmarks of suburbia. But if you look beneath the veneer of gracious living . . . you will see a battle raging, a battle for control. You see the combatants everywhere, engaged in their routine skirmishes . . . fighting fiercely to have dominion over the world around them, all the while knowing . . . it's a battle they will lose.' The idea of the unending quest to keep up with the Jones or even power-struggles within the household are hinted at here. The suburbs are home to unequal relations between couples and scene of intergenerational strife. The elderly characters are often stereotypical battle-axes, for example Mrs McCluskey and we sense their desperation through isolation. Outer tranquillity belies inner turbulence.

As seen in the previous chapter, the shattered illusion of suburban serenity with an undercurrent of humour has been seen in cinema productions of the 1990s including *Edwards Scissorhands*, *Blue Velvet* and *American Beauty*. Particularly in its first series *Desperate Housewives* echoes these with its dreamy visuals conflicting with dark subject matter. The episode 'You'll Never Get Away from Me', series 2 and episode 3 (2005), closes with the voice-over of Mary Alice intoning: 'Yes, each new day in suburbia brings with it a new set of lies. The worst are the ones we tell ourselves right before we fall asleep. We whisper them in the dark, telling ourselves we're happy . . . Yes, each night before we fall asleep we lie to ourselves in a desperate, desperate hope that come morning . . . it will all be true.' Another television series that followed this principle was *The Sopranos* set in New Jersey, dealing with a mafia boss and his secret double life of suburban calm respectability by the proceeds of crime. De Stefano (2007:142) remarks on this mismatch: 'Relocating the mob narrative from urban mean streets and social-clubs also links *The Sopranos* to other pop-culture works about suburban *malaise*.' He concludes: 'The pertinent pop-culture referents for suburbia have changed, as now *The Stepford Wives* has been supplanted by *The Sopranos*' (De Stefano 2007:143). The programme ended its run in 2007 but ever since the same notion that all is not what it seems in suburbia has been repeated in other US comedy series depicting happy families with a twist. The suburban theme was explicit enough to be used in the opening credits of the series *Weeds* in which a widowed mother resorts to pot dealing (although not drug-taking) to fund her two sons middle-class upkeep. In *Breaking Bad* a mild-mannered suburban chemistry teacher and one-time science whizz becomes increasingly machiavellian crystal-meth-maker to fund his family's complex medical treatment needs. There is then an impulse of suburban anxiety from which escape is sought by illegal means and/or chemically but also spiritually in suburban drama. For the sister of Peggy Olsen in *Mad Men* and *Desperate Housewives*' Gabrielle, the confession box of the Catholic church serves as an outlet for pent-up suburban frustration guilt. In the *Sopranos* Betty Friedan's 'problem with no name' applies to men too (Tony Soprano) who take anti-depressants like Prozac and Zoloff.

The emergent 'reality tv' at the turn of the decade fused drama and suspense with old style documentary positioning the viewer ostensibly 'fly on the wall' observing the general public rather than professional actors. In a sense the mundane is elevated to the level of the Victorian freakshow which audiences lap up. This further forum for the presentation of suburbia exemplifies the observation that 'Television wants to go beyond the role of witness, beyond upholding definition. It wants nothing less than to give the viewer the feeling that he or she is "there"'

(Dyan and Katz 1987:184). Numerous echoes of the past and intertextuality have pervaded reality televsion in retreads of earlier formats – befittingly given the historic body of work that exists in television history. When Channel 4 dusted down the pioneering 1970s BBC series *The Family* for a 2009 version, the original white working-class Reading bus-driver and his brood were substituted by an extended Sikh family in Maidenhead, which now effectively is a suburb of London despite lying outside it. In 2010 the BBC series *Giles and Sue Live the Good Life* was screened with presenters Giles Coren and Sue Perkins testing the original self-sufficient suburban dream adding a celebrity dimension to an earlier series ITV *The Real Good Life* commented on by Thomas (2008) as an example of ambivalent consumerism within mainstream media. The fact that celebrities were enlisted for this second *Good Life* experiment shows how the famous have pervaded this genre. In the old documentary journalists were relatively absent or passive, maybe just voicing over the action. The prominence and visibility of the presenters in reality shows such as *Giles and Sue Live the Good Life* show how they have moved centre-stage. Experimenting with sustainability indicates how once comfortable suburbia was seen to feeling the economic pinch with shows such as *Make Do and Mend* and *Superscrimpers* tapping into a vein of thrift culture. This meta genre promising close up, unscripted action and access to witness private moments of intimacy is ostensibly factual in nature, although the participants of such shows often complain of unfair editing that has left them portrayed in a bad light. Dicks (2004:22) remarks that these are 'game-shows which place the quotidian idiosyncrasies of other people (who are, simultaneously, like us and not like us), under the camera's microscopic eye . . . we gain sight of a contrast between their lives and our own, which in turn allows us to see our own lives as "other"'. The everyday becomes spectacle, sometimes putting people into situations outside their usual daily routine and normal comfort zone and we are all voyeurs. Many initial UK examples were located in the moment of positive economic growth-fed interest in the sense of well-being bred by rising property prices. The humble suburban house was an asset for financial gain and a canvas for designing on. Home improvement programmes in the space of a decade have ranged from interior décor (*Changing Rooms, House Invaders, Home Front*) and DIY tasks (DIY SOS) to wholesale structural remodelling (*Grand Designs*) to house-price value aggregation (*House Doctor, Property Ladder* and *Location, Location, Location*) including at auction (*Homes under the Hammer*). Even the domestic chore of dusting and polishing was turned into entertainment in Channel 4's *How Clean is Your House?* Suburbs were often the settings for these programmes although they were often naturalistic settings, that is 'real' peoples' houses not commissioned sets. Rather than relying on a series of storylines to communicate a narrative, the genre of reality usually takes the documentary form as its template although we are invited assume that the suburban cast members are not hamming it up as they are members of the public supposedly 'warts 'n'all' and 'acting natural'. The shows are comparatively inexpensive to produce as they require no expensive sets or star actors. In Patrick Keiller's film *London* of 1994 the narrator states 'It seems everyday we were served with a new reminder of the absurdity of our circumstances.' Reality television provides endless examples.

Changing depictions of ethnic suburbia

In the United States Latinos and Italians are examples of ethnic diversity that do not feature in as significant numbers on the UK cultural landscape. *The Sopranos* (1999–2007) has attracted attention from inside and outside academia including several scholarly articles and book-length accounts.[8] There is an inherent duality in the Italian catholic family at the show's centre headed up by a patriarch figure who on the surface lives a peaceable life in plush New Jersey surroundings working in waste disposal whereas actually this is a front for his true calling as a mafia boss which has paid for a luxury lifestyle with its ill-gotten gains. Tony Soporano craves suburban respectability and longs for the family values experienced by his own father who despite less material trappings had a stronger value system. 'In a lot of ways he had it better than me', Tony muses, 'he had his people, they had pride, today whadda we have?' Tony is however in the words of the 1988 film 'married to the mob' evoking numerous *Godfather* or other gangster movies. His wife Carmela enjoys living in a large house with a swimming pool but turns a blind eye to how these trappings of success have been financed, she comforts herself with the attentions of the family priest to compensate for her sense of Catholic guilt. Their angsty teenage daughter Meadow longs to get out of her suburban surroundings right from episode one; this character is cut from a similar cloth as the sarcastic daughter of *Roseanne* Darlene or *Daria* (the droll animated MTV teen who began as a character on *Beavis and Butthead* before getting her own show from 1997 to 2002). In the very first episode Carmela Soporano wants mother and daughter to 'drive into New York' to have tea and scones at the Palace Hotel, only to be rebuffed. On expressing dismay that this is an annual tradition that was supposed to continue long after Meadow eventually marries, her daughter snaps back 'Hopefully I won't be living anywhere round here by then.' Meadow's caustic riposte contrasts with a name that suggests

pastoral innocence. Family dysfunction extends across the generations: Tony
tries to have his own mother the widowed Livia rehoused in what he calls a
'retirement community' but she does not want to rot away in a 'nursing home'
as she sees it. The violence witnessed also contrasts with outward suburban
perfection. A fight to settle an old score spills out into a car chase and punch-up
occurs, a Czech rival waste merchant has his brains blown out and a restaurant
is blown up: this is all during the first episode. The programme takes the form
of day in the life of Tony as (selectively) related to his psychiatrist Dr Melfi, also
of Italian heritage. Tony, although sceptical of the benefits of psychoanalysis,
remarks that his parents would have liked for him to marry an achiever like
her – a generation behind him she represents ethnic embourgeoisement through
graft, an education embodying the American dream.

The ethnic deficit of *Desperate Housewives* is largely realized by the Latino
Solis family (Merskin 2007). According to Ricardo Antonio Chavaria the actor
of Carlos the attraction of the part was that it was the Latino family that were 'the
richest family on the block [b]ut they don't beat you over the head with the fact
the Solises are Latino. They could have been any race' (Anon 2005). Gabrielle
sometimes refers to her time as a New York catwalk model, the same 'could've
been' character that we often see in portrayals of suburban women who showed
great promise before settling down to a humdrum suburban life, for example
April in *Revolutionary Road* and Betty Draper of *Mad Men*. Nonetheless in
series 7 Mexican illegal immigration became a storyline, corresponding with
the fourth element of Román's (2000–1:39–40) typology of the modes in which
Latinos are seen onscreen.[9] This arguably falls foul of burden of representation
arguments by presenting a rather clichéd portrayal. Despite Marc Cherry's stated
aim from 2005 'I wanted the Solises to be Latino because it was important to
me that not all the families in the show be white', black characters have only
featured since rather fleetingly: series two saw the Applewhites enter, seemingly
a single mother and her teenage son, although it later transpires that another
son is kept incarcerated in their Wisteria Lane basement as part of a family
secret. The family lasted a single series, leaving an all white cast again. In season
3 Gabrielle marries the town mayor Victor Lang only to overhear Victor tell his
father on the wedding night that the only reason they wed was so he could win
the Latino vote in his run for state Governor. In *Mad Men* no black characters
are seen in the first series apart from the lift operative and Drapers' home help
Carla who is a completely undeveloped character with no hint at any life or her
own until series 3 when we learn of her regular church-going (in contrast to her
employers) and see her visibly upset at the death of President Kennedy whose

civil rights programme she had invested hope into. The show has featured gay characters (Salvatore who is also Italian from the suitably creative/effeminate art department rather than engaged in hard-nosed business) as has *Desperate Housewives* with a make gay couple in later series to a limited extent redressing the balance after earlier criticism of the show as 'desperately straight' (Chambers 2006). In the *Mad Men* episode 'Candle in the Wind' of series 2 we hear Don and Roger casually remark and express surprise that a rival agency has hired 'a black guy'. The character Paul Kinsey has a black girlfriend who Sally Draper confuses as his maid. Black characters are not seen as comedy material as they have been in other series but they do not seem to be present on their own terms and do not seem to be part of the genteel suburban landscape of manicured lawns and station-wagons as envisaged by American suburban shows. With many declaring that Obama's election symbolized the move to a 'post-racial' America the invisibility of black America may be unsustainable and while the blogosphere has raged with posts from those decrying the lack of black characters who have parts that are more than extras in the programme there is speculation that series 5 (not yet aired at the time of writing) will reverse this state of affairs with *Mad Men*'s first substantial black character imminent.

Conclusion

This chapter has looked at a set of representations of suburbia onscreen on the 'idiot box' of the television. The examples cited demonstrate a series of particular cultural constructions of the suburb each connected to specific representations of national identity, place and space which are all rooted in their context. To some extent they have reflected my own viewing habits and which American shows have been exported to the United Kingdom. Needless to say the case-study source material is not exhaustive. What has been outlined is highly subjective, in keeping with Williams' outline of structures of feeling. Watching *Desperate Housewives* from suburban West London I will take away similar and different conclusions from say a viewer on Long Island or anywhere else that the programme has been exported to. This is consistent with the way structures of feeling are culturally determined and bound up with the values of the contexts they emerge from and are subjectively experienced. According to Williams they 'can fail to be fully understood by living people in close contact with it' (1977:49), but they are still 'very deep and very wide' (1977:48). At the same time many of the examples cited could be described as polysemic texts of multiple overlapping and interlocking messages and meanings. Each of them can be read as a text but they are not self-contained, the point of emergence is also an 'event'. They can be analysed for their audience effects or according to production values.

Fictitious mass-media depictions have contributed to the images of places as well as communities in the popular imagination. In the 1980s the Liverpool-set BBC sitcom *Bread* by longstanding Liverpudlian sitcom author Carla Lane played out the trials and tribulations of a working-class Irish-Catholic descended scouse family of assorted ne'er do-wells ducking and diving in recession-hit Thatcherite times in a densely populated corner of the city on a weekly basis – in some respect contributing to the city's image of failure. The series was criticized by Liverpudlians at the time for its over-concentration on negative stereotypes such as dole-cheats and the cardboard cutout characterization, for example the no-nonsense mother presented as a matriarch figure who ran the household. The BBC's realist comedy-drama *Boys from the Blackstuff* (1982) scripted by playwright Alan Bleasdale also helped to create a cultural construction of the same city but was seen as a 'quality' production likened to the classical work *Ulysses* and has had been academically analysed for its 'hard-hitting' portrayal of life on the dole (Paterson 1987). For the 1990s we can substitute *The Royle Family* or *Shameless* – both portraying slothful, indolent Mancunians. Vesna Goldsworthy (quoted in Dines 2009) has also argued that it is from 1970s sitcom that many negative stereotypes about suburbia derive with the genre's unrelentingly beige and brown-coloured sets.

There is evidence that the cultural contours are shifting. With therapists, confessionals and anti-depressants recognizably present the new realism of suburban US television portrayals we see in *Desperate Housewives* and *The Sopranos* to name but two show family life as imperfect and suburbia a place that is, as the title if the 2002 film has it, far from heaven. The same themes pervade screen representations of earlier times written in the present day, for example *Mad Men*. In the United Kingdom the theme of suburban rampage as seen in the latter and films like *Falling Down* was seen in Channel 5's satirical series *Suburban Shootout*. In 2011 the in-house journal of middle-class middle England *The Daily Telegraph* reported 'BBC to introduce more working class comedy' (Gammell 2011) in a story outlining a direction from the top of the corporation to try to counterbalance the glut of series that revolve around 'affluent suburban families'. Of the programmes cited the semi-improvised *Outnumbered* is set in a suburban London home (filmed in Wandsworth) to a family of five. In 'A family Day Out', episode 1 of series 3 (2010), the clan and maternal grandmother take a trip across London on a sightseeing bus, thus are pictured as tourists in their own city, a reminder that not all suburbanites journey to the city centre for work or use its resources daily. The mother and grandmother discuss familiar suburban parental concerns (how to get into a good secondary school: bribery? moving to a better catchment area? feigning religiosity?). The youngest son Ben meanwhile plays 'spot the chav' [pejorative term for lower class youth] theorised by Jones (2011) from atop the upper deck of the open-topped vehicle. The class superiority of the family vis-a-vis the uncouth city population is clear.

Suburbia on television often has a 'them' and 'us' theme to it. From the 1950s onwards when United States shows such as *Ozzie and Harriet* or *Leave it to Beaver* still aired throughout the 1970s when the United Kingdom showed *Terry and June* and the *Good Life*, television has relentlessly depicted comfortable and spacious middle-class living conditions of harmonious middle-class suburban families even if the reality for many of the viewers would have been cramped and possibly broken homes. Class mobility has been subtle: for example, the shift from *The Likely Lads* (1964–6) the tale of Newcastle factory workers Bob and Terry to *Whatever Happened to the Likely Lads?* (1973–4) in which the social climbing of Bob via engagement, white-collar job and move to suburbia is evident. Channel 4 was also groundbreaking, for example for the mixed suburban estate *Brookside* and also screening the US shows *Roseanne* and the *Sopranos* showcasing the uncouth and corrupt. However for the most part despite the differentiated nature of suburbia it is largely the historical middle-class variant we have seen time and again onscreen. There have also been other notable omissions in some of these programmes: racial and ethnic difference has tended to be marginalized or in early examples seen only from the perspective of 'majority' white culture, for example the sitcoms *Mixed Blessings*, *Love Thy Neighbour* and *Mind Your Language* (set in an English for Speakers of Other Languages class). Here we see a more subtle type of racially coded imagery in stereotyping rather than outright racist statements on screen, although the three were also framed from the viewpoint of the white majority audience and some of the content of these programmes sail dangerously close to the wind. Of *Mixed Blessings* the BFI (undated) remarks of the racial taunts '"coon", "sambo" and "honky" recurring with distressing regularity, to the apparent hilarity of the studio audience.' As Bowes (1990:136) puts it, 'The closer the black families came to fitting into [dominant white] culture and society the less of a threat they appeared to present.' In the same way on *Desperate Housewives* gayness has frequently been a laughing matter (e.g. Carlos unwittingly becoming a gay basher when assaulting a homosexual television repairman he suspects of having an affair with Gabrielle or the day that the new gay couple move in during series 4) seen through the prism of straightness, despite the show having a gay executive producer in Marc Cherry.

Recurring themes can be traced in the programmes under discussion. In the United States the suburbs in television shows often seem to service the ultimate urban setting of New York. The UK examples discussed have been resolutely London-focused with their settings in Purely, Surbiton, etc. and more recent examples have followed this trend, for example *The Inbetweeners*, a Channel 4 sitcom about sexually frustrated teenagers in a London suburb and *Friday Night Dinner*, a Jewish-themed North London suburban situation comedy. In 2011 when it was announced that the *Inbetweeners*, a title that refers to both the luminal status between childhood and adulthood and geographical positioning of the central characters, was to be remade in the United States where it was felt its suburban ethic would make it perfectly suited (*OK* 2011). Just as the suburbs themselves have not stayed still, there has been progress from the cultural myopia of early suburban portrayals as resolutely ethnically white. Indeed mixed race is the fastest ethnic category on the United Kingdom and is projected to be the largest single group in due course (Wohland et al. 2001).[10] Malik (2002:74) has rightly warned: 'British broadcasting can no longer sustain itself, on a local or global basis, if it continues to model itself on a simple homogenised nation-state paradigm. The increasing number of "mixed-race" and hyphenated identities means that audiences are becoming more and more ethnically and culturally diverse, placing new pressures on the medium (including Black programmes) to move away from its prevailing White versus not White binary logic.' Apart from the questionable term of 'Black programmes' this statement has important implications. The cumulative effect of BBC statements about their lack of diversity and the furore over *Midsomer Murders* in 2011 (e.g. Brooker 2011) make it feel a long time ago that programmes where black people were the butt of the jokes were accepted mainstream favourites as Hornby (2008) reminds us:

> Remember that sit com *Love Thy Neighbour* about a white couple finding themselves living next-door to a black family, with 'hilarious' consequences? Bill Bryson's foggy memory of the period, as he recollects in *Notes From A Small Island*, is coming to England and finding us all giggling at something called 'My Neighbour is A Darkie'. Its intrinsic racism was considered fine at the time and it got worryingly high ratings in the 1970s. Now, of course, it is looked back on with horror.

It seems reality shows have been quicker to incorporate mixed-race cast members than scripted drama (particularly *Big Brother* line-ups). Audiences are increasingly drawn from this demographic so television has a duty to reflect this. Media literacy dictates that the viewing public are far more knowing than their comparative unsophisticated 1970s counterparts. To view earlier television programmes alongside contemporary counterparts one can sense shifting production styles, for example the contemporary reality show with its rapid delivery, fast cut editing and constant reminders of what is to come in the remaining content renders it precursor to the documentary even from the 1990s as comparatively languid in pace.

The power of television in the post-war era cannot be underestimated. Its outreach is near-universal and it is able to bring subjects from being 'out there' into people's front rooms and thus social acceptability and vice versa. There are many examples that have not allowed a discussion of in this chapter due to lack of space. Children's television, for example is a genre that academia has been relatively silent on. Here too suburban values have been historically reinforced in drama series. Of recent UK offerings *The Sarah Jane Adventures*, a spin-off from the long-running BBC science fiction series *Doctor Who*, was based in Ealing. Part of the show's attraction was that such storylines of time travel and aliens could be unleashed in such an unlikely setting as a strait-laced, upstanding and ostensibly boring location. *The Guardian* columnist Ditum (2010) stated: 'It makes sense that children would feel comfortable with the character, investigating intergalactic menaces from a comfortable suburban house.' Although this West London suburb was once home of Ealing studios which gave its name to Ealing comedy, the redoubtably British genre of old stiff upper lip values, the children of *The Sarah Jane Adventures* who formed the main nucleus/gang of time-travelling investigators included a black Caribbean boy and an Asian girl befitting contemporary Ealing's multi-ethnicity. Two of the three (and in series one all three) were from single-parent families, also an increasingly common feature of the suburban landscape countering the old assumptions of suburbia equating with nuclear families (see Chapter 6). As well as junior drama and cartoons since the 1990s the genre of 'adult animation' has flowered. The best-known example screened internationally but set in the US suburb 'Springfield' is the *Simpsons* (to be looked at further in Chapter 6) which has been described as 'animated sitcom' (Mills 2005). The format was continued further with *South Park* (edgy for the liberal swearing coming out of children's mouths), *Family Guy* the slacker chronicle *Beavis and Butthead* and the more ethnically attuned *Boondocks*: all aimed at the adult-viewing public with late night slots to match. Having started life as a newspaper strip cartoon the *Boondocks* was about young black brothers who live in suburbia with their grandfather rather like the earlier *Fresh Prince of Bel-Air*. Their anxiety about losing their Afro-American side results in programme content parodying blaxploitation culture by referring to gangsters, pimps and hoes with the word 'niggaz' used repeatedly which might make viewers uncomfortable. *Monkey Dust* and *Crapstone Villas* with their wry commentary on the foibles of life in turn of the century Britain were the nearest that the United Kingdom got to this genre.

With increasing media platforms fighting for the consumer's attention it seems that soundbites are ever shortening and within programmes are constant reminders of what is yet to come in order to keep audiences there. Messages are increasingly spelt out for audiences rather than to let them read between the lines as in earlier times. This can be seen in the way captions are onscreen through reality programmes or at its most extreme in *Desperate Housewives* with its narration throughout (Feeney 2005). Suburbia has variously been represented as conformist, bland and mediocre or as a place for experimental living or as a location on television that harbours hidden secrets. Crucially just as there is no singular suburbia this chapter has shown that there is no portrayal of the suburbs that can claim to be definitive or completely authoritative. Both television and suburbia were criticized at their outset for instilling suffocating passivity into those subjected to them and duping the public into unquestioningly accepting unchallenging blandness in everyday life and new ways of watching television with interactive catch-up services and reacting via other media such as the digital playgrounds of blogs, Facebook and twitter mean that the future allows viewers to move beyond pure observers to more active control, filtering and responding to what they watch. Critics of the suburbs saw them as, for those who could afford them, exclusive enclaves in which to flee from the unruly city with its pressures of ethnic mix, built-up landscape, post-industrial economy and fragmenting society. Yet in the twenty-first century it is now the suburbs that are characterized by these same issues that early advertising hinted, if not promised, that the suburban-dweller could leave behind. It would be facile to claim that those in the suburbs took the problems of the city with them or that those problems followed them when the 'suburbanizing out' model does not necessarily follow. Suburbs are constituted of multiple ways of life; they always were. Many of those currently living in the suburbs were not necessarily city dwellers moving out in self-improvement, many would love to be closer in to the city but cannot afford to be. As we move to a post-mass audience era the series of representations described then offer a solid set of reflections which between them say much about the transformations in suburbia in the United Kingdom and United States in the television age. We now turn to an application of these by considering women's portrays onscreen, on the page and in pop.

Notes

1   Undated interview at: http://toddsolondz.com/welcome.html.

2   Associated Press (2004) Suburbia sizzles in 'Housewives': Creator says he doesn't romanticize suburbs at: http://today.msnbc.msn.com/id/6133690/ns/today-entertainment/.

3   There are still occasional spikes, for example the Royal Wedding of April 2011 was reckoned to have commanded an audience of 25 million in the United Kingdom and a much wider (and less easily calculable) worldwide figures.

4   She has been bartender, telemarketer and shampoo girl.

5   http://boards.straightdope.com/sdmb/archive/index.php/t-347864.html.

6   It is not the only example; Channel 5's *Family Affairs* ran from 1997 to 2005 purporting to be in Charnham, an invented West London suburb. *Hollyoaks* of the same production team as *Brookside* takes its title from a fictional *suburb* of Hollyoaks affluent Chesire city Chester in north-west England.

7   The quote attributed to Bush 'We're going to keep trying to strengthen the American family; to make them more like the Waltons and less like the Simpsons' was cited as reason number one in an article by Freguson (2003) entitled '300 reasons why we love *The Simpsons*'.

8   Examples include Regina Barreca, ed., *A Sitdown with the Sopranos: Watching Italian American Culture on TV's Most Talked-About Series* (New York: Palgrave Macmillan, 2002), David Bishop, *Bright Lights, Baked Ziti: The Unofficial, Unauthorised Guide to The Sopranos* (London: Virgin Books, 2001), David Chase, *The Sopranos Scriptbook* (London: Channel 4 Books, 2001), Glen O. Gabbard, *The Psychology of the Sopranos: Love, Death, and Betrayal in America's Favorite Gangster Family* (New York: Basic Books, 2002), *The New York Times on the Sopranos*, introduction by Stephen Holden (New York: ibooks, 2000), Allen Rucker, *The Sopranos: A Family History* (London: Channel 4 Books, 2000), Allen Rucker (Recipes by Michele Scicolone), *The Sopranos Family Cook Book as Compiled by Artie Bucco* (London: Hodder and Stoughton, 2002) and David R. Simon, *Tony Soprano's America: The Criminal Side of the American Dream* (Boulder, CO and Oxford: Westview, 2002). Also journal articles and academic contributions include: P. Keeton (2002) '*The Sopranos* and Genre Transformation: Ideological Negotiation in the Gangster Film', *Atlantic Journal of Communication*, 10(2), pp. 131–48; C. Vincent (2008) 'Paying Respect to *The Sopranos*:A Psychosocial Analysis'; D. Lavery McFarland (ed.) (2002), *This Thing of Ours: Investigating the Sopranos* (New York: Columbia University Press).

9   These are: (1) the hot-blooded sexy character, (2) the gangster (3) the snazzy entertainer and (4) the (often illegal) immigrant.

10   Also see United Kingdom in 2051 to be 'significantly more diverse', Leeds University Press release on 13 July 2010 at: www.leeds.ac.uk/news/article/853/uk_in_2051_to_be_significantly_more_diverse.

6

Women on the Edge? Representations of the Post-War Suburban Woman in Popular Culture to the Present Day

Each suburban wife struggles with it alone. As she made the beds, shopped for groceries, matched slipcover material, ate peanut butter sandwiches with her children, chauffeured Cub Scouts and Brownies, lay beside her husband at night – she was afraid to ask even of herself the silent question – 'Is this all?'
(Betty Friedan, *The Feminine Mystique* 1963/2010:1)

It's bad enough having to live amongst all these damn little suburban types . . . without letting ourselves get hurt by every little half-assed – what'd you say?
(April Wheeler after her disastrous in an amateur drama production
(Yates 1961:24))

As the chapters up until now have demonstrated, 'suburbia' is not only a topological construction but also connotes a set of attitudes, mores and values. It is 'safe' space. In the popular imagination, it exists as gendered space: where a code of good housekeeping prevails as women tend to the nest (i.e. household and children), while their men are out in the big bad city earning a living. Suburbs were seen as a space of 'ideal home . . . for women and children first' (Pile et al. 2000:31). Clapson (2003:125) notes the feminine suburbs have tended to be pitted against the macho-thrusting city for they 'signify domesticity, repose, closeness to nature, lack of seriousness, mindlessness, and safety'. Chambers (2001:78) has spoken of how the advertising campaigns for home electrics in the leisure and domestic spheres represented a utopian American suburbia in which the family was sacrosanct.' The stereotypical suburban daily routine established in 1950s-set suburban television shows sees besuited males kiss goodbye to their wives and kids en route to the daily commute to office leaving her to cheerfully perform household chores, for example baking sometimes with a housemaid/cook. The weekend consists of car washing and barbecues. Cast members are almost always all white whether the broadcast be sitcom or soap opera – a genre named after its original function of selling washing powder to housewives via daytime broadcast drama (Brunsdon 1997). Ethnic minorities, single mothers and divorcees were largely absent. This chapter turns away from considering popular culture in typological fashion to the theme of suburban women across types and in particular the character of the suburban housewife in popular culture. It considers key feminist sociological work *The Feminine Mystique* by feminist author Betty Friedan and tests some of its claims in exploring of changing representations of women and the suburb.

John Updike revisited the Rhode Island suburb Eastwick first introduced to us in his post-Vietnam seventies-set book *Witches of Eastwick* of 1984 in his last ever novel *The Widows of Eastwick* published shortly before his death in 2009. The women of the post-9/11 version of the town are described by Updike (2008:139) as: 'toned-up young mothers driving their overweight boys in overweight S.U.V.s to hockey practice 20 miles away, the young fathers castrated namby-pambies helping itty-bitty wifey with the housekeeping, spending all Saturday fussing around the lovely *home*. It's the '50s all over again, without the Russians as an excuse'. It seems as if everything has come full circle cancelling out progress of feminism that had allowed three divorcees to enter a world of suburban sorcery in the original story. The suggestion is that the cars may be people carriers instead of station wagons but the notion of keeping up appearances is still paramount. The three slip into their old ways when they return to Eastwick after all going their separate ways on remarriage. Even though they have been away, suburban habits die hard. They tut-tut at one house for being an 'eyesore' and 'dragging the neighbourhood down . . . ruining . . . property prices' (178–9). More dramatic is the nightmarish cautionary tale *Safe* (1995) exposing us to future fears on a global scale although set in the 1980s. The film closely follows the trajectory of a well-heeled if somewhat characterless suburban housewife who finds her comfortable lifestyle turned upside down when she starts experiencing medically unexplained illnesses and allergies which is seen in the film as symptomatic of an intolerance of twenty-first-century living and its chemical after-effects. The familiar portrayal of the unfulfilled contemporary post-war suburban housewife that persists in contemporary representations can be traced back to the novel *Madame Bovary* which constructs marriage as social norm and adultery as violation of the usual moral code that is commonly associated with suburban normality. The early examples arguably helped set the template for the 'what goes on behind closed doors/ net curtains?' curiosity that has informed much suburban-set popular culture ever since.

The problem with no name: The post-war suburban housewife and classic portrayals

By offering a critique of the patriarchal system whereby girls were socialized into accepting marriage and motherhood as their natural gender role with any deviation considered improper, Betty Friedan's (1963) *The Feminine Mystique* became pivotal to the emerging second wave feminist movement. It suggested empty promise behind the prevailing ideal of 'the suburban housewife . . . [as] the dream image of the young American woman' (1963/2010:3) requiring them to ferry their children to and from school, be expert at baking and master domestic technology designed to make life easier. The book was based on a survey of 28 women graduates. For Friedan, 'the chains that bind . . . are not easily seen and not easily shaken off' (1963/2010:15). Freidan called this suburban state of affairs 'the problem with no name', and indeed at the time of her writing, feminism was in its infancy and sexism not a commonly understood term as today. It is claimed, 'Many suburban housewives are taking tranquillizers like cough drops' (Friedan 1963/2010:19), and in the study's sample of educated housewives in their thirties and forties, 18 were taking such drugs, 16 were undergoing psychological treatment and 'several' had attempted suicide. The revelations were all the more shocking as in the United States the suburban environment had been sold as idyllic and equated with the 'American Dream', other pillars of which were patriotism/ national pride, Christianity, self-reliance, domesticity, fear of big government, Cold War-fuelled anti-communism and opposition to social agitation.

Although many critics of suburbia see them as trapping women in futile lives of dull domesticity, suburban living was aided and abetted by the rise of consumer durables and the entree of many families into the car-owning classes, leading Britain's aristocrat prime minister Harold Macmillan to declare in the run-up to his successful 1959 election campaign 'you've never had it so good'. According to Jackson (1985), US suburban development was fertile particularly under President Eisenhower with favourable local planning policy, rising home ownership (from 40 per cent of the population at the start of the Second World War to 60 per cent by 1960) and gross national product (GNP) that grew by 250 per cent from 1945 to 1960. Many early suburban-themed cultural products appear to have an undercurrent of moralism at their core. Indeed Richard Hoggart's landmark lament to the passing of the richness of organic culture *The Uses of Literacy* (1958) named 'canned and packed provision' as a nail in the coffin of organic working-class culture which was being replaced by mass-produced models making the ritual of the family gathering around a meal cooked from scratch to eat together now a rarity. For Ritzer (2004:56), this has declined further with the spread of the microwave oven reducing food preparation time to 'minutes, seconds even' and rendering the most culinary inept children capable of whipping up ready meals. Of course tinned foods and microwaves are not just confined to suburbs but their impact was felt in suburban households among housewives in the same way as the Rolling Stones' sentiments in tale of housewifely depression *Mother's Little Helper* which referred to prescription drugs rather than her eagerly attentive offspring mucking in with chores: 'Cooking fresh food for her husband's just a drag/ so she buys an instant cake and she buys a frozen steak/ and goes running for the shelter of her mother's little helper.' The implication was similar to Freidan's questioning 'is this all?' suggesting a lack of fulfilment despite the state of affairs where advances in living standards and labour-saving devices provided all mod cons. The newfound spoils of consumer capitalism included the washing machine (Redfern 2003) and Tupperware (Clarke 1997), but television was probably the most significant among these new acquisitions in defining suburban living leading to an increased domestication or privatization of the leisure sphere.

Pile et al. (2000:31) have described how suburbs were intended to be 'places where women could take control of their lives, rather than their being inescapable prisons'. However, there is evidence that many original inhabitants found that their suburban surrounds did not live up to their initial promise. In series 1 of *Mad Men*, Betty Draper tells her psychiatrist, 'We thought it'd be a nightmare to raise kids in Manhattan so we moved to Ossining. Suddenly I really felt so old.' The solution for women who dared to express any disquiet at their lot in life was usually diagnosis of mental illness, hence both Betty and April Wheeler in the novel *Revolutionary Road* (Yates 1961) are persuaded by their husbands to receive therapy as they come of terms with trading formerly carefree youthful existence for adult responsibilities including children and suburbia. The Wheelers constantly justify the latter as a necessary sacrifice and a compromise between their former bohemian existence and the 'real' country side which would be too difficult with young children. The estate agent promises, 'Simple, clean lines, good lawns, marvelous for children' (Yates 1961:29). The couple try to convince themselves, 'The gathering disorder of their lives might still be sorted out and made to fit these rooms, among these trees' (Yates 1961:30). The UK physician Dr Stephen Taylor (1938, 1958) in a pre-war *Lancet* article identified the condition of 'suburban neurosis' borne out of frustration, loneliness, boredom and false values which he later revisited applying the term equally to new towns.

Physical symptoms included backache, weight loss, loss of breath and insomnia from this depressive anxiety-related illness. The condition is directly referred to in the now cult 1970 film *Diary of a Mad Housewife* set on suburban Long Island which began as an unhappy marriage/rebellion novel (Kaufman 1967).

Friedan's famous 'is this all?' passage above voicing realization that suburbia was not all it was cracked up to be is echoed in the novel *Little Children* (Perrotta 2004:29) in a passage that takes place at the playground among the smug mums:

> Underlying Mary Ann's every utterance was an obnoxious sense of certainty, of personal completeness, as if she'd gotten everything she'd ever wanted in the best of all possible worlds. *This?* Sarah wanted to ask. *This is what you wanted? This playground? That SUV? Your stupid spandex shorts? Your weekly roll in the hay? Those well-behaved children who cower at the sound of your voice?*

Sarah used to be a someone, having studied feminism at college when she was in a lesbian relationship, but now she is trapped in a loveless marriage to an older underwear-fetishist man who seeks kicks in internet porn, and her own identity is consequently fading as she must consort with snobbish status-seeking women that she would not normally have anything in common with apart from their children. Indeed at the start of *The Feminine Mystique*, the suburban homes that stifle are described by Friedan (1963/2010:244) as 'comfortable concentration camps' in which 'American women are not, of course, being readied for mass extermination, but they are suffering a slow death of mind and spirit'. The book's profits were donated to the National Organization of Women, the pressure group that she founded. These feelings of being trapped have been heard time and time again by suburban women in fiction but are more prevalent in more recent fictitious accounts than historic ones where suburban life is often akin to an out-of-body experience. At the start of *Little Children* in both book (Perrotta 2004) and film versions, Sarah tells herself that she is an anthropologist conducting a study into suburban mums allowing herself to step outside her ascribed role. In the 1940s, Mrs Brown in the *Hours* tells herself as her husband clumsily blows out the candles on his birthday cake spraying it with spit, 'She herself is trapped here forever, posing as a wife . . . in these rooms, with nowhere else to go. She must please; she must continue' (Cunningham 1998:205). Eventual suicide is the fate of the character of Mary Alice who appears as off-screen narrator of *Desperate Housewives* and of April in *Revolutionary Road*, although Laura Brown does not meet this fate, but by abandoning her children and leaving them to live in another country in some ways commits a worse sin.

Pop music's teasing references to suburban women, such as those of The Rolling Stones' 'Mother's Little Helper' on 1960s housewives pill-popping propensity have largely been produced by men. The Jagger family roots in the London commuter hinterland of Kent are evoked by Philip Norman (2002:27) alongside typical suburban clichés, for example 'Their small house in Denver Road, Dartford, was scoured by Eva into a spotless state the equal of any neighbour's. Joe and Eva's whole life was dictated by consideration of what those ever vigilant neighbours might think.' We are also told of 'Their mother's house-proud fastidiousness' (Norman 2002:27).[1] More indirectly, while 'I Want To Break Free', the 1984 comeback single from Queen does not have lyrics that particularly deal with the concerns of housewives, the video depicting the band in drag in a suburban sitting room (with Freddie Mercury doing the dusting) suggests that it is from a cycle of domestic drudgery that the protagonist wishes to be liberated. Similarly, the lyrics of the Pet Shop Boys' 'Suburbia' do not particularly refer to the condition of women (apart from possibly 'Mother's got "mother's hairdo to be done"'), but the song's live rendition during the band's 1991 tour was accompanied by a slickly choreographed dance routine featuring women vacuuming (Zuberi 2001). Men onstage mowing grass in synchronicity in identical chinos and open-necked shirts would have served the same purpose but were not on display presumably as they would not be eye candy in the same way although there is a scene of lawns being sprinkled with hoses in the first pilot episode of the 2011 ABC comedy *Suburgatory* from the United States shown on E4 in the United Kingdom. Joni Mitchell's 1976 album 'The Hissing of Summer Lawns' returns to the theme of the downside of suburban existence for women who end viewed as objects in its lyrics. In 'Harry's House/Centerpiece', a frazzled mother can be heard admonishing 'Get down off of there, I said get down off of there!' to her children, inviting the comparison with to freeing oneself from the repetitive cycle of suburban conformity. On the track 'Harry's House', a disillusioned wife is uncomfortably trapped in comfortable suburbia with offspring, while her materialistic husband who views her as an object to service his needs is away on a business trip:

Battalions of paper-minded males
Talking commodities and sales
While at home their paper wives
And paper kids
Paper the walls to keep their gut reactions hid.

'9 To 5' sung by Dolly Parton and 'Manic Monday' written by Prince, then popularized by The Bangles, both also capture dissatisfaction with the working routine, although this is waged labour rather than unpaid domestic work in the house. In sum, most reflections on suburbia in song and in interviews with song-writers seem to be about the male protagonist's restless desire to escape the suburban surrounds that their parents had chosen which they had no decision-making stake in.[2]

Television can reflect, reinforce and challenge dominant norms or even create new ones. As we have seen the television set itself was a vehicle for promoting and propagating suburban family lifestyles; often placed at the centre of the sitting room akin to a hearth radiating out or serving the function once reserved for the piano in communal gatherings. Certainly in the days of networked programming and a smaller number of channels (until 1982, there were only 3 in the United Kingdom), family life adapted to its schedules as television adopted suburbia making the suburban family both audience and subject matter of much television output. The suburbanization of the United States was also reflected in wholesome programmes with titles such as *Father Knows Best* and the much cited and YouTubed *Leave It to Beaver* which followed an all-American value system of traditional gender relations, traditionalism, small-c conservative values and the importance of family and suburban ideals at their core. A clip from the latter for example shows the father taking charge of the barbecue and explaining to his son that woman's place is in the kitchen where she has domestic appliances at her dispersal, whereas it is mens work to cook outdoors with fire as this is 'rugged' and requires the skills of a 'caveman'.[3] Some of these series immortalized the very journey that their viewers were making, rather than setting up 'the suburbs' as the situation for the comedy: in 1957, the celebrity couple of Lucy and Ricky Ricardo of the sitcom *I Love Lucy* made the move in the storyline from their city base of Manhattan to Westport, Connecticut, an hour's commute away, thereby playing out the inherently US suburban imperative of seeking out freedom beyond the frontier and taming the wilderness, as mentioned in the opening chapter. Although this has been seen as a masculine desire, Pfeil (1995:172) writes, 'the emphasis on wildness . . . manly individualist spirit which resists both the suffocatingly blandishments of womanly domestication and homogenizing, rationalizing tendencies of industrial society', in suburbanization to have the dutiful wife and family at the side of the primeval, neo-colonial male was almost a requirement, and as we have seen critics saw that her fate was to become trapped in what Weber might have called an iron cage of rationalized suburban existence.

The personification of the ideal woman on-screen can be seen in cultural referents to actual or imagined examples who personify domestic prowess as attentive child-rearers and expert cooks. *Desperate Housewives'* (2005–12) uber-perfect housewife Bree Van der Kamp has been repeatedly likened on blogs to Martha Stewart, the US figure who became a brand for her television and cookbook empire with herself centrally positioned as the original 'domestic goddess'. Betty Friedan disapprovingly refers to Stewart in her 1997 rewritten introduction to *The Feminine Mystique*, even through her full commercial potential was realized after Friedan's death in 2006. Bree's character is presented from the first very episode as concerned neighbour and champion baker when she arrives with freshly baked muffins at the wake of Mary Alice for her grieving husband and son, but stipulates rather icily that she will need the baskets returning. In the first episode, her son pillories her, likening her to the robotic cold-hearted characters from 1975 film *The Stepford Wives* and her husband fails to defend her, showing to what extent she is taken for granted:

> *Andrew*: Mom, I'm not the one with the problem, all right. You're the one who's acting like she's running for Mayor of Stepford.
>
> *Bree*: [turning to her husband for support] Rex, seeing that you're the head of this household I would really appreciate it if you said something.
>
> *Rex*: Pass the salt?

In later series, Bree begins a catering firm taking on the role of businesswoman. Similarly in *Mildred Pierce*, originally a novel (Cain 1941), then an Oscar-winning 1945 film noir and eventually a 2011 HBO mini-series, baking is the film's main motif and the way that the central character (who has been played by Joan Crawford and Kate Winslett) lifts herself out of penniless single motherhood to become a successful restaurateur while her lover Monty is a loafer. Role reversal, that is deviation from expected gender norms is rare in these portrayals. In Perrotta (2004:144), Todd has become a student supported by his wife contrary to his original expectations: '[When] she got accepted into film school, he figured that she was just killing time until they could begin a conventional middle-class life in the suburbs: i.e., he'd work his ass off every day. . . [with her] picking up the kids at day care.' The reality has not lived up to this. When he runs away with lover Sarah, he has nightmares about checking products on a conveyor belt at the quality control in a factory, hinting at a desire to step out of line or freeing himself from the shackles that are expectations of suburban perfection. As Sarah waits at the end of book for Todd, so that they can make their final flight from the imprisoning suburb, she fantasizes about being breadwinner: 'Todd could stay home, ferry the kids back and forth to school and music lessons and soccer practice, take care of the cooking and the housework if that was what he preferred' (Perrotta 2004:338). Todd in the event does not turn up, injured in a skateboard accident and paralysed by inability to leave his wife.

Revolting moms

On-screen depictions of suburbia as haven for the housewife seem to show a collapse of the suburban dream as having occurred over time. *The Man in the Gray Flannel Suit*'s Tom Rath and *Mad Men*'s Don Draper have extracurricular sexual exploits on the CVs and work in the high-pressured environment advertising on Madison Avenue of which their dutiful wives, both named Betty, are only dimly aware. In both cases, their unhappiness precludes us from using the expression 'blissfully' unaware to describe their condition. Their husbands keep them and their (increasingly rebellious) children in the style they are accustomed to, but they both seem to yearn for more. Betty Draper is a one-time model and anthropology major turned mother of three who develops a nervous condition necessitating psychiatry sessions. At times she appears to accept her fate, telling Henry who becomes her second husband in an early meeting that although Ossining was not her first choice after living in Manhattan, 'it's grown on me'. At others, she voices what we sense are her inner feelings in an echo of Betty Rath. After returning from a business trip to Italy in series 2, after Don's question to her 'what's wrong?' she rails shrilly, 'What's wrong? I hate this place, I hate our friends. I hate this town'. By the end of the series, the couple are divorcing. We see her in season 1 episode 11 fantasizing about the door-to-door salesman in rhythm to the juddering vibrations of the washing machine – consumer durable taking on sex-aid properties. In episode 9 of series 1 'Shoot', troubled by their birdsong, Betty both administers revenge on her pigeon-training neighbour who earlier threatened to shoot the Draper family dog and vents her multiple frustrations by taking a gun and gunning down the pigeons, one by one. The accompanying extra features of the series 2 DVD includes a documentary on the changing status of women which refers liberally to Betty Friedan. In the film *The Man in the Gray Flannel Suit*, Betty Rath describes the family house in Connecticut as 'a graveyard' and the cause of her unhappiness. Based on the Sloan Wilson novel, this was a rare cinema treatment at the time for showing the 'dark' side of suburbia. Of novels negative of the suburban way of life that were contemporaries, *The Crack in the Picture Window* was not filmed, while Yates's

Revolutionary Road (1961/2001) only made it to cinematic version four decades later and *Mr Blandings Builds His Dream House* and *Please Don't Eat the Daises* were feel-good comedies reinforcing expected usual gender roles.

As the situation comedy got more adventurous, programme makers had to go further than making 'the trials and tribulations of a family in the suburbs' the situation alone. There needed to be a twist present too: *The Brady Bunch* were a reconstituted clan drawn from two earlier fractured families (having each lost a parent) producing a total of six children, with Alice a maid to attend to them. In *Bewitched*, the housewife at the show's centre possessed powers of sorcery. Even later, cartoons saw more and more of a departure from the original formula of suburban family plus dog, but even these reinforced the usual nuclear familial set-up: the *Jetsons* were a suburban family in space and the *Flintstones* were a *prima facie* standard-issue television 1970s family unit (commuting breadwinner Fred, wife Betty and cute baby Pebbles), except they lived in a cave and this was the Stone Age. Aimed at children, the cartoon allows disbelief to be further suspended as in the social satire of the *Simpsons* which began a trend towards adult animation followed by *Family Guy, King of the Hill* and *American Dad*. The *Simpsons* episode 'Little Big Mom' (episode 10 of the series 11: 9 January 2000) addresses how difficult the actual job of housewife is. Marge is hospitalized leaving Lisa to assume her role in taking charge. After unsuccessfully attempting to get the rest of the family to help her with the physically exhausting tasks of housework, a chaotic situation descends with unwashed plates. Overnight the ghost of Lucille Ball appears at Lisa's bedside to teach her how to get revenge on Bart and Homer who have been slobbing around playing out general sitcom male buffoonery taking her for granted watching endless reruns of *I Love Lucy* (the show she starred in). The role of the men is to enjoy the fruits of the women's labour. As with Mr Cheever in *Leave It to Beaver*, men are expected to do 'rugged' gardening, DIY and light the barbecue, but the interior of the home is the woman's domain where it is the space to nurture the kids. The alpha-male Neanderthal Bart and Homer Simpson are poor role models of even these limited household tasks. In this way, the show pokes fun at and challenges accepted gendered normative behaviours. Musically, punk thumbed its nose at conventional rock structure, and prominent women in the scene included Siouxsie Sioux who was far removed from the dolly birds of previous pop in the urgency of her delivery and refusal to conform to traditional gender roles. The rejection of a life of submissive domesticity can be heard in the track 'Suburban Relapse', the story of an adult female/housewife who 'snaps one' day while doing the dishes and throws consumer goods at her neighbours.

While a woman's place was squarely in the home according to traditional gender relations shown in early portrayals of suburbia on television (in the role as housewife and mother), the rise of the working woman signalled a change ushering in more modern values of equality alongside declining deference to authority including a range of institutions: the church, monarchy, political leaders and the patriarchal family. Dissenting visions of the suburban housewife were hinted at for some years, although it took until the 1970s and the 1980s for them to filter through to television series. The sarcastic wise-cracking and physically weighty rotund *Roseanne* also contradicted earlier all-American versions of the suburban housewife and the wholesome hearth. Like the *Cosby Show*, the series derived its title from an already popular comedian rather than the family in the story: Roseanne Barr as lead was far removed from the suburban beauties with compliant kids of earlier shows. Indeed in Western society to be fat is to be uncouth and slovenly suggesting a poor junk food diet as opposed to in Third World nations where to be overweight can connote wealth and being well fed. Betti (1995:132) has commented, 'Roseanne is rude, insubordinate, and rarely a passive victim, on either class or gender grounds. The show routinely provides a fantasy response to working-class women's attempts to sustain self-control in a world where they have little control'. In *Rosanne*, rather, the suburban affluence we are used to seeing time and time again where characters in series inhabit spotlessly clean homes, economic hardship formed a backdrop to the series with a family also arguably lacking cultural capital, for example by living in a catalogue-furnished house that is often a mess. The nearest UK equivalent was *Butterflies* (1978–83) showing the general domestic ineptitude of demure suburban housewife Ria played by Wendy Craig (Andrews 1998). Unlike Roseanne, the earnings of her dentist husband played by sitcom regular Geoffrey Palmer allowed her to not have to work leaving her and her two teenage sons to fire dry asides about, or just despair at, her unpaid labour within the home for example cooking. The audience was invited to sympathize with Ria's reveries of escaping quotidian reality and being swept away by a stereotypically tall, dark and handsome stranger (Leonard) for whom extramarital activities were suggested using fantasy dream sequences but were never realized. The butterfly's wings were clipped: conventional expectations of the suburban housewife to be ideal homemaker remained intact and had only teasingly been undermined but not seriously subverted.

Boredom or suburban *ennui* is a consistent theme that can be seen repeatedly in portrayals of women in suburbia. Of Virginia Woolf in the book *Hours*, we are told that she recognizes living in suburban Richmond is a better and safer alternative to London given her history of depressive illness 'and yet she is dying this way, she is gently dying on a bed of roses' (Cunningham 1998:169). In the commentary that begins, the *Desperate Housewives* episode 'Suspicious Minds' (season 1, episode 9) narrator Mary Alice intones: 'Gabrielle was waiting for her next great idea . . . Before she knew it, she had jumped off the runway [catwalk] and moved to the suburbs. Her most recent great idea was borne out of her boredom with her new life. That's how she came to start an affair with her teenage gardener, which was cut short by a tragic accident.' This same divide of the generations is also present in the *Graduate* where again the sexual prowess of a young man provides escapism for a suburban housewife (and vice versa). This rebellion is a specifically youthful middle class, one against parental value systems not inequality. *Desperate Housewives* off-screen narration (which has been condemned as 'preachy and dull' by Feeney 2005) frames episode 7 from series 1 'Anything You Can Do'. Proceedings begin with a shot of the novel *Madame Bovary* by Gustave Flaubert lying on a table at Bree's house, the latest subject of study for the Wisteria Lane Book Club. Mary Alice's voice-over comments on this ritual as there are intercut shots of the characters trials and tribulations:

> *Mary Alice*: We found the problems of literary characters so absorbing . . . the way they dealt with adversity . . . [Lynette swallows some of the twins AHDD tablets] . . . conducted illicit affairs . . . [Gabrielle and John pass one another with a hint of a frisson between them] – '. . .endured domestic dramas . . . ' [Rex leaves the house with wife Bree looking frustrated behind him] . . . and planned romantic conquests. [Susan circles a date in her calendar that reads 'Date with Mike!'] But since my death, my friends had lost their interest in fiction. Their own problems had become absorbing enough.

The book – set *en province* a French expression of all that is not Paris – is mentioned in the novel *Revolutionary Road*. In Flaubert's plot the eponymous heroine conducts a series of affairs to escape the boredom of her vacuous provincial existence and loveless marriage to a dullard. This parallels Gabrielle's situation in *Desperate Housewives* – here in *Revolutionary Road* and in *Madame Bovary* itself possibilities are presented as limited and suburbia/life *en province* stifles dreams.

Creator Mark Cherry has repeatedly cited the 2002 case of Andrea Yates, a Texan housewife who drowned her five children as an inspiration for the series. He has stated that the catalyst or 'light-bulb moment' when he heard his own mother had expressed some sympathy for Yates's actions: 'it was shocking to find out that she indeed had moments of great desperation . . . And I realized if my mother had moments like this, every woman who is in the suburban jungle has. And that's where I got the idea to write about four housewives.'[4] At times, the characters harbour underlying resentment at their role as homemaker. When one-time high-flying executive turned mum Lynette Scavo meets a former colleague in the supermarket by chance towards the end of series 1, she is asked how she likes full-time motherhood. The question is of course heavily loaded. Accordingly, she replies with the socially acceptable answer, 'It's the best job in the world!' with a weak smile that belies her supreme exhaustion at having four unruly kids. To give a more accurate or balanced answer might invite suspicions of being a 'bad mother' after all. The episode comes close to saying the unsayable and the viewer to hearing anti-motherhood sentiments voiced. McCabe and Akass (2006:12) talk of 'the cardinal television rule that women should not express dissatisfaction with housewifery and motherhood'. The title of the first chapter of Perrotta's novel *Little Children* (2004) is 'Bad mommy' which can be used as shorthand for the fictitious characters that think the unthinkable in their dissatisfaction with their caring role. At the start of the book, opprobrium from the fellow mothers at the playground is upon Sarah for forgetting to bring a snack for her 3-year-old Lucy, but her transgressions go further as she embarks on an affair with a handsome stay-at-home dad who frequents the same circuit of daytime toddler haunts. We also learn of her lesbian past. To counterbalance her 'bad mommy' role, Hatten (2007) brands Todd her lover a 'boy-man' who is exponent of 'retrograde masculinity'. He has failed at his breadwinning responsibilities leaving his wife to do the earning, and his main outlet for enjoyment is either the camaraderie of the follow jocks in his amateur baseball team or watching local teenagers skateboard: another youthful passion of his that he yearns for. Sarah's 'bad mommy' status is sealed when Todd's wife begins winning him back with her adeptness at sex, something that the comparatively amateur Sarah is not as skilled in. He ends up crippled with inertia, not quite able to follow through the plan of running away together with Sarah and literally injured in a skateboard accident the day of the planned escape – again underlining what a boy-man he is.

The idea of liberation is a common one that occurs in fictional portrayals of suburban housewives be it real, imagined or thwarted. In *The Widows of Eastwick*, Updike's final novel, the accusation is made that the hard-won gains of the 1960s have been squandered (Updike 2008:160) '*This generation*, Alexandra thought. They watched us rebel against our pious upbringings and in reaction have reverted to the old sentimentalities, family and home and such tyrannies'. Indeed she goes as far as to justify the witchcraft that she practiced with two other friends before leaving Eastwick in the 1970s as an escape from suburban housewife routine mapped out for them at the time. She lectures her dowdy daughter Macy who has ended up as full-time homemaker with two kids and a conventional husband, 'Girls your age just can't realize how few opportunities there were for women when I was young. Our job was to make babies and buy American consumer goods. If we fell off the marriage bandwagon, there was nothing much left for us but to ride a broomstick . . . it was *power*. Everybody needs power. Otherwise the world eats you up' (Updike 2008:160–1). In *Little Children* (Perrotta 2004:89), as Sarah dresses more and more flirtatiously, adopting a red bikini bought from the internet to attract Todd at the town poolside, she rationalizes her actions as those that the enlightened Madonna would have no qualm with: 'Madonna didn't say, *Oh no, I couldn't possibly wear those cones on my chest. Oh no, I couldn't pose as a nude hitchhiker*. She just said yes to everything. *Cowboy hats – sure! Sex with Jesus – why not? Motherhood – that's cool, too*. When one role got old, she just moved on to the next one. That was a form of liberation in itself.'

In the film *The Man in the Gray Flannel Suit* (1956), Tom has more depth than any of the female characters who are comparatively one-dimensional, for example his hectoring wife Betsy and the childrens' shrill nanny. Tom's brief wartime fling is presented as understandable given the pressure he was under, whereas wife's freak-out is futile. She speeds off in the family car but has to be bailed out by her husband from the local police station after running out of fuel. In the *Graduate*, Ben's affair with the older Mrs Robinson is widely seen as not only a tale of the children of suburbia for whom the promise that lured their parents in has become empty but it is also illustrative of her own lack of fulfilment as an unhappily married woman who practices rebellion in being open about her alcoholism and being of an overtly sexual neediness. The confrontation towards the end with Mr Robinson makes clear that prevailing ideas positioned suburban wives as existing to be attentive to her husband, rather than having any character or desires in her own right.

New formats and retreads

The rise of suburban-set reality television revolving around the single family unit was satirized in *The Simpsons* episode 'Homer Simpson, This Is Your Wife' from series 17 which first aired in the United States on 26 March 2006, featuring a guest appearance from Ricky Gervais as 'Charles' adopting the same voice and job description as in his portrayal of David Brent of popular United Kingdom and later Americanized series *The Office*. When Homer announces his plan to take part in a *Wife Shop* show, Lisa exclaims, 'I don't understand dad. Our family has so many flaws, why do we have to share them with the world?' Quick as a flash Homer shoots back, 'Because we get to go on tv'. The episode was the highest ever rated *Simpsons* in the United Kingdom of 2.8 million after heavy promotion by Sky television. A familiar reality television format is the placing of people in situations outside their regular comfort zone, for example, the *Wife Swap* programme that the *Simpsons* episode parodied or *Big Brother* placing strangers to live in a house together. In the United Kingdom, the late contestant Jade Goody had a remarkable rise and fall, becoming a star in her own right before death from cervical cancer in 2009, while benefit claimant *Wife Swap* star Lizzy Bardsley who was later sentenced for benefit fraud for not declaring her media appearance fees and was found guilty of child cruelty. Mirroring *Desperate Housewives* have been the well-known US series *The Real Housewives of New Jersey* filmed in the environs of New York as well as similar shows set in Orange County, New York City, Atlanta, Beverly Hills, Miami (United States) and Vancouver, Canada (United Kingdom). *The Real Housewives of New Jersey* in particular has a title sequence and name obviously derivative of its ABC near-namesake. In the United Kingdom have been the semi-scripted docu-soaps *The Only Way is Essex* and *Desperate Scousewives*. Another vein of reality programmes frequently with domestic life and homemaking at their core which have a self-help imperative at their core where 'expert help' is called in to improve people's unmanageable situations. There is frequent reinforcing traditional gender roles: in *Changing Rooms* it is a woman who presides over transformations of family homes presenting participants with the results after they have been redecorated (either comforting them if the final result is not according to their taste or popping open the champagne when it meets with the householders' seal of approval). By contrast, it is the men who do the physical work. A woman superficially dresses the home for resale to maximize profit in *House Doctor*. Domestic chores of dusting and polishing are performed by two women on *How Clean Is Your House?* And parenting experts are always women, Dr Tanya Byron in *The House of the Tiny Tearaways* and in *Supernanny*, Jo Frost. Reality television is some ways the small-screen's answer to cinema verité. Despite the relative newness of the reality show, subjects under the microscope are also at times rather old-fashioned.

The remakes of earlier outings of suburban housewifery usually have zeitgeist-chasing details in their rewrites. The 2005 film *Bewitched* was derived from a long-running US sitcom (1964–72) in which a suburban housewife who with a twitch of her nose becomes skilled in witchcraft. This character, Samantha, has married a mortal and has a meddling mother who sets the template for interfering in-laws. In its Big Screen update four decades on however the story turned into one about the making of a remake of a 1960s show. The opportunity for an intertexual satire on recycling culture and/or an indictment of the star system was somehow missed, and the suburban sets looked fairly generic as if they had been seen hundreds of times earlier (which they probably were). The 2005 *Bewitched* star Nicole Kidman also played the leading part in 2004's update of Bryan Forbes 1975 *Stepford Wives* from Frank Oz. The central plot remains in which a wife realizes that something is amiss with the idyllic suburb of Stepford she has moved to with her family. The town's women lead lives of such bland perfection that they appear to be devoid of any character. The film's originating book by Ira Levin was inspired by Betty Friedan (1963/2010:248–9) who had predicted: 'The comfortable concentration camp that American women have walked into . . . denies women's adult identity . . . away from individual identity to become an anonymous biological robot in a docile mass.' The remake includes the sinister men's club who reprogram the women into docile, cupcake-baking, robotic clones who are sexually compliant, and lack all personality. There are some variations from the original though: including a gay couple. The main exception to the expected rules of wifely conduct is the independent-spirited, chaotically untidy, wise-cracking Bobbie who Joanna teams up with (as in the earlier version) to get to the bottom of what on the DVD commentary calls the 'insane quest for perfection' of Stepford. By 2004, Bobbie has been given the surname Markovitz (Bette Midler) and is Jewish in a nod to multiculturalism but there are still no black characters. Even such twists, for example the detail that Joanna has had a breakdown after having been fired from her high-powered job in television, could not prevent the film being critically panned. It seems that irony can easily backfire in this type of remake given the all-knowing media-literate nature of the modern audience.

Revisionism and postmodernism are also present in the rewriting of earlier eras in popular culture. In the time-travel film *Pleasantville*, which starts off shot in monochrome the twins' 1950s mother home-cooks their meals including waffles laden with syrup which their modern palettes find too heavy in cholesterol content to bear, and she and the 1950s father sleep in separate beds. At the instigation of the sexually liberated 1990s sister, the whole town seemingly discover recreational sex, neighbourhood housewives begin answering back to their husbands using as their weapons the iron or husband's dinner as bargaining tools and the town is awakened to the idea of art and literature. Gradually, Technicolor engulfs Pleasantville despite the efforts of the old guard to cling on to how it was. In the present, the dutiful son David ends up having to comfort his (single) mother who has had to change her plans due to the unreliability of his father who has failed to respect the access arrangements again. This is a generational reversal: unlike the all-knowing happily married parents of earlier screen families, it is the son who provides emotional stability to his parents who we see as having difficulty keeping life together. In *Far From Heaven*, another retro look at the 1950s, Cathy is initially presented as a conventional housewife, but as the plot develops, she emerges as more enlightened than her peers who see a fundamental incompatibility between other cultures: her best friend displays homophobic tendencies in commenting how she likes her 'men to be all men', while it feels like the whole neighbourhood stares disapprovingly when Cathy and black companion Raymond accompany one another out. The viewer is presented with the dilemma of which is more transgressive: the husband's homosexuality or the wife's befriending a black man? Homosexuality is present in all of the three parallel plots of the *Hours* referred to on p. 36: Mrs Brown makes a pass at her neighbour in the 1940s, and in the contemporary section of the story, Clarissa lives in a lesbian partnership and even 'Richard told her, thirty years ago. That under her private-girl veneer lay all the makings of a good suburban housewife' (Cunningham 1998:16), and her one-time lover who makes this observation is gay. In addition to this is the story of Virginia Woolf. While a largely affectionate glance at 1970s suburban values emerges from the 1995 gently mocking film *The Brady Bunch* which was marketed with the strapline 'They're back to save America from the '90s' (i.e. greed of corporate developers), the 1990s penned books *The Ice Storm* and *The Virgin Suicides* which later both became films suggest between them that there was more to suburbia in the so-called decade that taste forgot than simply light fluffy good-naturedness including sexual swinger parties, child neglect and depression.

In Friedan's study, making ones own bread was a marker of how 'good' a housewife would be. Indeed, in the remake of *Stepford Wives* (2004), cake baking recurs as an ideal standard for women to aspire to. Dave chides Bobbie for her inability to make cupcakes when he says through a freshly baked mouthful, 'Why can't you make stuff like this?' Bobbie retorts: 'Why don't you?', to which Dave shoots back, 'Because I have a penis'. Postmodern pastiche is heavily laid on in the scene where Joanna throws herself into baking which seems uncharacteristic which her two allies who are respectively Jewish and gay remark on:

> *Bobbie*:   You kind of look like Betty Crocker.
> *Joanna*:   I know.
> *Roger*:   At Betty Ford.

Betty Croker is a brand-name for baking products personified by a smiling woman adorning the packets who has been updated over the years but was not based on reality. As the Roy Rosenzweig Center for History and New Media (n.d.) state, 'One of the best-known women of the interwar years – *Betty Crocker* – never existed.' The character has become a byword for home-baking but was contrived to incorporate the last name of a retired company executive William Crocker, with the first name 'Betty', which was thought of as 'warm and friendly'. Betty Ford is the widow of former US president Gerald Ford who after a period as an alcoholic later gave her name to the Betty Ford alcohol treatment centre and drug rehabilitation clinic for families suffering from narcotic and chemical dependency. In the film *Hours*, Laura Brown played by Julianne Moore in part realizes the failure of her suburban existence when the cake she bakes for her husband's birthday goes wrong which she later redeems with a second successful cake. Friedan (1963/2010:15) claimed that juggling 'the enormous demands of . . . wife, mistress, mother, nurse, consumer, cook, chauffer; expert on interior decoration, child care, appliance repair, furniture refinishing, nutrition and education' resulted in women's identity that is submerged by this mass of mindless, meaningless, repetitive and soul-destroying routine. In *Little Children*, when hatching a plan to escape her loveless marriage and routinized drudgery with Todd, Sarah daydreams of leaving behind the usual list of domestic chores: 'they'd have nothing to do but eat, sleep and make love whenever they wanted to, free from the banal responsibilities of childcare, the ceaseless petty time pressures of family. The sweetness of the prospect was almost too much . . . to contemplate' (Perrotta 2004:297).

It seems that certainly for the three Betties, Friedan, Rath and Draper, the reality of being a suburban housewife did not live up to the promise of the prospectus. Betty Crocker's ever-smiling unquestioning expression appears to have more in common with the women of early suburban television series who were contented homemakers rather than these unsatisfied examples who raise questions about the bland representations we are more used to. Her features no longer appear in the instant cake and pancake mixes now readily available at UK supermarkets. Instead there is an authenticity-affirming signature in white lettering on a stylized cartoonish red spoon bowl as the current logo. 'Betty Ford' is barely remembered as a person anymore but the two words are synonymous with breakdown and rehab, two things that most depictions of suburbia only teasingly hint at as stoic women carry on. Advanced capitalism has meant that some of the certainties of the traditional suburban set-up have faded: under present economic circumstances and for some years now in many major UK cities, two incomes would be needed to purchase a home. The now normality of the dual-earner household means that the wife cannot be consigned to a life of suburban *malheur* and the husband parcelled off to the city as two incomes would be needed to service most suburban mortgages, for example in London. Cohabitation, what was once quaintly called 'living in sin' has lost its stigma and divorce/partnership break-ups help to keep the property market moving – helping avoid near-stagnation of transactions in the recent downturn. Later examples of representations of women in suburban context show that women's lives do not have to be determined (by patriarchal power structures) but can also be determining (of their circumstances), a state of affairs that has been helped by legislative advance, for example the UK Equal Pay Act of 1976.

Discussion and conclusion

The suburbs have been the backdrop to musical, film and television products straddling a range of genres between them with women often central in these portrayals. Just as suburbia and mass-produced popular culture have come of age, so has feminism now spanning three decades of demands. The ways of receiving music, television and films have changed with self-scheduling, possible via web resources, music downloading and television catch-up services. By taking a range of case-study material with diverse depictions, this chapter has attempted to counteract the view envisaged by Thorns (1973:118) when he declared, 'The society of the suburb . . . is, for the most part, female dominated and narrow and insular in its outlook'. Indeed many of the examples cited could be described as polysemic texts of multiple overlapping and interlocking messages and meanings. They can be analysed on many levels, for example their audience effects or according to production values. Each of them can be read as a text but they are not self-contained, the point of emergence is also an 'event'. For Kutnowski (2008:603), in being a comedy 'these gags ultimately address the dysfunctional life of the *Simpsons*, and portray an updated, naturalistic, disenchanted version of the American Dream that offers an alternative to decades of television shows portraying suburban family life as something neat and stable'. The same could apply to *Desperate Housewives, American Beauty* or the UK's *Outnumbered* in which the strains of modern middle-class parenting are presented. Even children's shows accept that what were once pejoratively called 'broken homes' are not now uncommon: CBBC's *Sarah Jane Adventures* briefly touched on in the previous chapter centred on a single mother and time traveller combating aliens with her adopted son and his friends from her attic in suburban Ealing. Some of the women's lifestyles we see, for example the decision to stop work when one has small children, is frequently forged by necessity, not choice; although public policy is finally and frustratingly slowly playing catch-up with legislation on nursery entitlement and flexible working.

Ordinarily, one would assume that the portrayal of women in 1960s popular culture as compliant housewives to be tame by modern standards but contemporary examples of cultural depictions of earlier eras reimagine these periods with modern sensibilities: *Mad Men*'s 1960s is written from 2007 onwards, so it does not shy away from unwanted pregnancy and extramarital affairs. The US television series and 1957 film *Peyton Place*, although set in a small town rather a suburb *per se*, helped speed up the portrayal of suburbia as an ideal haven for the compliant wife as seen for example witnessed in the sunny disposition of Doris Day in *Please Don't Eat the Daisies* to the dark secrets behind in women's lives of *Mad Men* or *Desperate Housewives*. Luckett (1999) claims that *Peyton Place* was groundbreaking for showing female sexuality *outside* marriage and defining women's identity and selfhood in the process, even if the programme was criticized for eroding moral standards. Of course what is acceptable over time changes. In *Mad Men*, the fact that the cast almost all smoke seems to be the most immediately shocking aspect to the twenty-first-century viewer. When Peggy, the secretary who rises to the level of copywriter, goes on the pill, the doctor who prescribes it smokes throughout the appointment while raising doubts about authorizing the medication as she is not married. When Betty is expecting her third child Eugene (accidentally conceived), she smokes throughout the pregnancy. In series 2, Don's mistress Bobbie Barrett tells the dowdy Peggy: 'no one will tell you this, but you can't be a man. Don't even try. Be a woman – powerful business when done correctly.' By series 3, Peggy's transformation from conformist secretarial staff to powerful corporate woman is sealed when she moves to Manhattan (the city) because of the stress of commuting from the suburbs (Brooklyn). In *Far From Heaven*, the *mise en scene* is 1950s but a woman negotiating race and homosexuality would never have been seen in a popular film of the time: modern-day sensibilities interpret a previous age. Context of the era of a media text's cultural production is intrinsic to it, as the past undergoes continual rewriting as it ends up reflecting present times. Similarly, representations become more daring over time: *Desperate Housewives'* subversion of the age-old US soccer mom cliché was later bettered by *Weeds* in which a widow in the sterility of the suburbs becomes involved in the murky underworld of drug-dealing after being forced to provide single-handedly for two sons. The 'cover' for this illicit income stream is a bakery that outwardly conveys the veneer of suburban respectability. The first episode of season 1 shows the hypocrisy of her trying to ban carbonated drinks from the school canteen as they are harmful to children while she supplies gear to their parents.

Some of these examples suggest that it is not just women who are stultifying in suburbia but that masculinity is in crisis too. Both mature student Todd and the disgraced cop Larry in *Little Children* busy themselves with sports and involvement in a committee to oppose the local resettlement of a convicted sex offender to compensate for their failure to live up to the usual bringing-home-the-bacon role of suburban males and inability to keep together their respective marriages. Todd also embarks on an affair as it makes him feel like a teenager rather than suburban head of household with attendant responsibilities. In the 2004 pilot episode of *Desperate Housewives*, Rex delivers a speech cataloguing Bree's faults despite her outward perfection: 'I want a divorce. I just can't live in this detergent commercial anymore. I'm sick of the bizarre way your hair doesn't move. I'm sick of you making our bed in the morning before I've even used the bathroom. You're this plastic suburban housewife with her pearls and her spatula who says things like "we owe the Hendersons a dinner." Where's the woman I fell in love with? Who used to burn the toast and drink milk out of the carton? And laugh? I need her. Not this cold perfect thing you've become.' In subsequent episodes, both of the couple attend marriage guidance counselling, suggesting that they both accept some responsibility for the relationship breakdown. Rex is dead by the series' end, although he does come back to narrate one later episode in ghost form. He expresses disdain for suburban values in his monologue which gives a male perspective of Wisteria Lane intoning:

Take a drive down any street in suburbia . . . know what you're going to see? A bunch of guys wearing the same expression, it's a look that says 'oh crap, my dreams are never going to come true' . . . yeah, the suburbs are filled with a lot of men who have given up hope. Of course every once in a while you do come across some lucky SOB who's dreams have all come true. You know how to spot them? They're the ones who can't stop smiling. Don't you just hate those guys?[5]

This world-weary tone seems to demonstrate that men too can suffer from suburban melancholy, though most portrayals of this condition are focused on women often having a breakdown while the men are out in the city being breadwinner, for example, *Revolutionary Road* which ultimately is a tale of suburban self-destruction.

The examples cited demonstrate a series of particular cultural constructions of the suburb each connected to specific representations of national identity, place and space which are all rooted in their context. Suburbia has variously been represented as conformist, bland and mediocre or as a place for experimental living or as a location that harbours hidden secrets. Much has changed since *Feminine Mystique* in 1963: contraception, abortion and divorce have made women less biologically determined. The age of marriage and that women have their first child has been delayed and the two are not both simultaneously needed at once. Women are not now simply defined through their partners being reliant on their husband's salary, the reverse situation is also possible and also households of single women or single parents of either gender. The gains of earlier generations in the United Kingdom arguably peaked with the New Labour government's equalities bill continuing in the governments' recognition of the state's role in childcare and extending maternity and paternity pay. All of these developments have changed suburban society. Rising divorce rates have helped to keep the property market from total stagnation at the 'downsizer' end of the spectrum. Liberal feminists would claim that the success of the advances made by the womens movement can be seen in the way that many demands that were once the site of extreme struggle are now a given. Radical feminists by contrast would conclude that there is a long way to go when pay remains stubbornly unequal and there are so few women in leading stock exchange company boardrooms, the argument known as the glass ceiling. Some point to post-feminism and the so-called 'third wave' of feminism as undermining the hard fought gains of the women's movement that Friedan paved the way for. In her article on the subject, Mc Robbie (2004:259) worries that feminism's advances are undermined by the tendency towards 'laddism' and mass-produced garments with slogans advertising porn aimed at very young girls. Women's studies and feminism are now integral to sociology syllabi, so have become part of the accepted academic canon as have media representations, making us more aware of stereotypes with their tendency to overlap with prejudice and the labelling of deviance.[6] Crucially, just as there is no singular feminism or agreed definition of suburbia, this chapter has shown that there is no single portrayal of women in the suburbs that can claim to be definitive or completely authoritative. However, the series of representations can be described as a set of reflections of the transformations in suburbia in the United Kingdom and United States in the post-war era in which the situation of the suburban woman and family life has changed on a number of fronts.

Women in the twenty-first century are not chained to the kitchen sink as earlier clichés dictated. Gentrification of the inner city has seen the middle classes take up residence in such areas away from the suburbs they grew up in. McRobbie (2004:261) states that education for women has 'loosened the ties of tradition and community for women, making it possible for them to earn an independent living without shame or danger', citing the case of Bridget Jones, the *Independent* column character that became a hit film showing an outwardly emancipated woman who is still plagued by self-doubt, although perhaps this can in part be explained by the fact that the story was loosely based on Jane Austen's *Pride and Prejudice* which revolved around the theme of marriage. Friedan's research subjects (and characters such as Sarah in *Little Children* and *Mad Men*'s Betty Draper) were college educated however and had problems accepting life with a role reduced to breeder and maintaining a spotlessly clean household. In Friedan's introduction from 1997 to the reprinted edition of *The Feminine Mystique*, she concedes that the situation has improved for women citing the role model of Hilary Clinton. Friedan (1963/2010:20) claims, 'women are no longer the passive victims they once felt themselves to be'. She does express regret that family mealtime has declined. In an era where women feel time pressured and society is ever atomized, this decline has continued. Although Jagger and Richards decried the frozen steak, even that may look like a relatively labour-intensive food preparation method in the twenty-first century. Ritzer sees food zapped and nuked in the microwave as symptomatic of altering the family ritual of sitting down together to eat. He claims that 'the spread of microwave cooking as well as the wide variety of foods available in that form, makes it possible for family members to eat at different times and places' (Ritzer 2004:111). Media representations often show that 'having it all' is not all that it is cracked up to be. 'Marrying well' (as we heard the Southall-raised Carole Middleton criticized for doing in the lead-up to the Royal Wedding) is something the characters of *Footballers Wives* have all done as well as having it all, but in the storylines they are still fundamentally unhappy. More positive past imagery can be seen in *Made in Dagenham* where confident women sewing machinists win an egalitarian battle if not the war.

Much suburban drama is peopled by one-dimensional characters in utterly predictable situations, but the examples raised have shown a diversity of practice and gone some way to illustrate the subtle shifts that have occurred in the way that women have been depicted in suburban settings from the late twentieth century to the present day. A very particular discourse of femininity with categorically defined gender roles where the woman/wife was a domestic foil fulfilling the main familial functions while the man/husband performed the role of protector and provider historically played a key role in defining how suburbia was culturally constituted from the 1950s onwards. Much of what these early portrayals depicted is now lost; even in the 1970s, programmes such as *Terry and June* seemed to be showing us a disappearing world, that if not quite sepia-tinted was one coloured seemingly in one of 50 shades of beige. This is not a cause for mourning, it is an undeniable fact and the diversity of contemporary suburbia is one of its most positive attributes. Past pictures are of use mostly for historical use now: today's suburb is complex, dynamic and in an era of economic downturn contrasts with received notions of suburbia as equating with simplicity, security and safety, life there is sometimes precarious. Many city tendencies are present in the present-day suburb including population churn that makes it more than just the stomping ground of neurotic, bored, pill-popping housewives. What the future may hold for women in an economic downtown where those who expected to enjoy rising living standards with improving on the material living conditions of their parents as a given and buying into the property-owning democracy of suburban dream as a birthright when they may have their hopes dashed remains to be seen. Popular culture needs to chart these changes, the 'better' examples, however these are defined, can offer a powerful mirror to complement social scientific empirical data. More work from women writers would be welcome: working-mother guilt is rarer in popular culture than bored housewife, yet it is a feeling very acutely felt by many suburban women, particularly those working round the clock to pay the mortgage and keep up the suburban lifestyle and whose children are asleep by the time she gets home.

There are also multiple references to outside events in these films and series. In *Mad Men* season 1 episode 3, an illicit, well-thumbed copy of the banned racy novel *Lady Chatterley's Lover* is passed around by the office girls from Joan via Marge of the switchboard to Peggy. In the first series of *Desperate Housewives*, Bree Van der Kamp ends up telling her therapist Dr Albert Goldfine her views on Freud:

> He grew up in the late 1800s. There were no appliances back then. His mother had to do everything by hand, just backbreaking work from sun-up to sun-down, not

to mention the countless other sacrifices she probably had to make to take care of her family. And what does he do? He grows up and becomes famous, peddling a theory that the problems of most adults can be traced back to something awful their mother has done. She must have felt so betrayed. He saw how hard she worked. He saw what she did for him. Did he even ever think to say thank you? I doubt it.

Bree here speaks up for the unsung role of Freud's mother as housewife. Indignation and rage also states that the women of the suburbs are capable of. In *Revolutionary Road* (Yates 1961), wifely anger is tempered with her familial responsibilities. After an epic argument with Frank towards the end of the book she resumes the dusting. In J. G. Ballard's *Millennium People* we encounter a mother of two from Kingston at an animal rights protest and of whom we are told, 'Angela stared across the road with narrowed eyes and all a suburbanite's unlimited capacity for moral outrage' (Ballard 2003:36). Meanwhile, the novel *Madame Bovary* seems to be a favourite of the suburban book clubs: being a choice for discussion both in the film *Little Children* and the first season of *Desperate Housewives*. Here the reading is used as a device to suggest under-the-surface sexual tensions and draw the viewers attention to infidelity that lies beneath conventional exteriors of suburban propriety and decorum. However, the coming of the dual-earner society has given women financial independence free of the spousal shadow and in turn freed suburbs from their stereotypical role as cosy, indeed suffocating, confined spaces that trap women into their expected gender role as breeder and homemaker. Whereas suburbia was once seen as comfort zone of predictable stability, it has since the recession become at times highly unstable and prone to multiple anxieties covering financial and emotional dimensions. The suburbs are increasingly diverse ethnically and in terms of family formation, being home to singleton households, reconstituted families, single-parent families as well as couples and nuclear families which may contain married, unmarried or civil-partnered couplings within them. Perhaps the tried and tested titles under discussion at suburbia's fictitious housewives book clubs are in need of revision as are portrayals of women themselves, the updated *Feminine Mystique* (Friedan 1963/2010) with new introduction might be a candidate.

Betty Friedan's seminal 1963 book *The Feminine Mystique* propelled second-wave feminism from academic obscurity to the best-seller lists of popular reading matter. Can the overall representational tableau vivant that emerges from the examples discussed above add up to something that is larger than the sum of its parts which can be coded in terms of the politics of the women's movement? Obviously, given the different genres dealt with and varying stances within each one, a mixed picture emerges. Way back before Mumsnet, there have long been associations with women and suburbia and by extension the family. There are also anxieties about what all of these three things are mutating into: gender, location and family all might once have been described as structuring structures but have undergone rapid transition and continue to do so. The church too has declined in importance over the past century. In its place, there are fears of modern society and its wider effects. There is for example a worry of twenty-first-century children as overprotected and living a chauffeured, caged and commercialized existence. Portrayals of the fairer sex in the suburbs in films in particular have increasingly shown female discontent at comfortable, even emotionally numbing, suburban surroundings resulting in mental breakdown, suicide, vengeance and 'playing away' in marital infidelity, the notion of women on the verge of a nervous breakdown. Yet the daily lived reality of most suburban women – juggling work with caring for children and ageing parents – is far from the representation. It is about 'getting on' with it. One could argue from a Marxist perspective that the history of women's representations in popular culture is one of compromise and limitation imposed upon them by the logic of late capitalism. The recession has undermined some of the certainties that the Fordist settlement was founded on leading to fears surrounding the accessibility of the American Dream and the UK ideal that an Englishman's home is his castle. Some of these themes will be returned to in this book's final chapter. Sharp (2006:12) has referred to 'our culture's deep ambivalence and contradictory attitudes towards housewifery and the homemaker'. This seems to have been forcibly depicted as trivial and/or unsatisfying. Yet the post-industrial suburbs are increasingly under pressure calling into question their comfortable status. This confused stance, oscillating with sometimes sympathizing with the suburban female condition but more often seeing it as a source of laughs, only mirrors confused treatments of suburbia at large.

The suburbs have been variously seen as the territory of (i) idyllic family dreamhouses, (ii) horror-laden land of dark undercurrent and (iii) stomping ground for adolescent angst. Linking these portrayals has been the insistence on the norm of nuclear family revolving around the woman of the house left behind while the man is breadwinning in the big bad city. In this traditionally feminine space we have seen depictions of wifely suffering from suburban anomie when reality does not live up to the promise. Yet suburbs do not stand still. The dual earner economy that requires two salaries even to buy modest property in once unremarkable suburbs thereby necessitating couples working round the clock, add up to a state of affairs whereby in many ways suburbia has gone from paradise to pressure cooker. Lone parent mothers too in suburbia also face the reality of what is termed the 'triple shift' combining paid employment as well as the expectation to perform housework and childcare which are both hugely time-consuming and totally unremunerated. The arrival of ethnic groups into the suburban mix is another shift into suburbia's presumed traditional form. This is turned to in the next chapter which shifts the focus to Asian suburban London.

Notes

1   The song is broadly empathetic of housewives conditions. Nonetheless, other songs of theirs of the same decade were less easy to sympathize with for their denigration of females, for example, the outright misogyny of 'Under My Thumb'.

2   Other examples of songs looking at 'women and suburban sadness' identified by Clapson (125) are Siouxsie and the Banshees' 'Suburban Relapse', Suede's 'The Power' and Marianne Faithful's 'The Ballad of Lucy Jordan', two of the three were performed by women and the third by Suede came from a group whose early appeal rested on lead-singer Brett Anderson's pronounced androgyny and links with the gay scene.

3   'Before Woman's Lib . . .' at www.youtube.com/watch?v=Pq_9wu-KjTk.

4   This anecdote is both quoted in the DVD extra features of the first series and also at B. Weinraub (2004) 'How Desperate Women Saved Desperate Writer' 23 October 2011 in *New York Times* at: www.nytimes.com/2004/10/23/arts/television/23cher.html?_r=1&ref=bernardweinraub.

5   The episode 'My Husband the Pig' (series 3, episode 16, originally aired 3 April 2007) which is narrated by Brie's then-dead ex-husband Rex from beyond the grave.

6   Although one wonders with the combination of current savage cuts being inflicted on the higher education sector in the United Kingdom and the trebling of fees for students whether the discipline of womens studies can survive in its current form. Indeed there has already been a cutting back of such courses, see McRobbie (2008).

7

Darkness on the Edge of Town:
Mapping 'Asian' London in Popular Culture

At the time, minority programming had a genre of its own. It was only made for those audiences. Asian people being funny wasn't on the radar.

(Anil Gupta, *Goodness Gracious Me* producer (Hundal 2005))

Guru's greatest strength is its heartfelt refusal to pander to a (white) audience's expectations of cornershop-owning Asian Britain. Many characters might easily be substituted for other races without undermining the storyline – yes, young Indians also swear, smoke, drink and screw.

(Review of film *Guru in Seven*, *Empire* magazine (Caterall 1998))

This chapter traces South Asian diaspora in post-colonial suburbia through popular culture. It focuses on this demographically young population, so effectively is about UK-based South Asian youth culture. The 'town' it takes for consideration is arguably not just a town but the super-diverse megacity of London, the United Kingdom's capital. The word 'Asian' itself is fraught with complexity. In UK parlance, it normally means populations with origins in the subcontinent or ex-British India. Yet it connotes a plurality of communities. Describing west London and its overspill alone, Malkani (2006:12) through the character Jas explains in slang style that 'the Sikh boys . . . ran Southall . . . the Muslim boys ran Slough. Hounslow's more a mix of Sikhs, Muslims an Hindus, so the brown-on-browns tended to be just one-on-ones stead a thirty desis fighting side by side'. The comment appears to be alluding to a divide and rule principle that had meant less unity within the old Asian-bloc category. Within these faith groups are Pakistanis, Bangladeshis and Indians to name but three. The word 'desi' is often taken by these groups to refer to 'of the homeland' e.g. a second generation Asian might express a longing to return to their parents home 'to eat some desi (home-cooked) food'. As a result of global crises such as the 9/11 terrorist incidences the term 'Muslim' has become increasingly perceived to be a problem category by the host community as they themselves become aware of the vast internal diversity in linguistic, faith and national terms masked by the word 'Asian' and all the othering implied by it. Religion as referred to by Malkani's character Jas is the biggest fault line in the light of global events including 9/11 and the 2005 London bombings of 7/7 in which Muslims were implicated. The chapter looks at popular cultural production and reception as well as the interplay of orientalism with a firmly occidental setting: suburban London which in itself is often considered inferior to 'London proper'. The subject has specific resonance to my own circumstances as someone who both lives and works in outer London confounding the received wisdom of the suburb as an exclusively residential area sustained by the city centre which acts as business district with transport routes radiating out from it.

Situating London's suburbia and the place of Asians within it

In his exhaustive study of London titled simply that, Peter Ackroyd (2000:279) refers to the purpose of suburban movement as 'to escape the sheer proximity of other people and other voices . . . the principle of exclusion . . . surrounded and protected from the depredations of the city'. There is a principle known as 'white flight' that is seen as one of the motivating factors behind relocation to the suburbs. It is an unspoken constituent part of the suburban allure that part of what was being escaped was ethnic populations. Frey (1979:426) has stated that in the US post-war movement of suburbanization, 'evidence . . . suggests that racially motivated movement patterns and discriminatory housing practices, when superimposed upon market forces of the period, served to exacerbate the selective mobility of whites to the suburbs'. Yet contradictions abound in thinking about the metropolis of London in relation to the usual received notions of suburbia in design and ethos as all about wanting to hark back to a mythical golden imagined age of English purity as seen in its retro street names implying placidity, for example 'dells', 'wayes' etc., and architecture, for example the neo-classical, sub-baronial or mock Tudor building styles. Contemporary London, as the 2005 winning bid for the highly successful Olympic games of 2012 stressed, is about the world in one city with its polyglot population of multiple creeds, colours and sexual orientations who call it home. It is awash with contradictions, sometimes constructed as happy multicultural melting pot but at the same time is home to rampant neo-liberalism including the city of

London where unregulated financial trading with little accountability and no responsibility to migrant workers created the global economic meltdown (Massey 2007). The design of its underground stations, particularly when tube lines were extended out to the suburban hinterlands, were fashioned as distinctly futuristic accompanied by advertising stressing the new labour-saving homes speculatively springing up with them. Crucially, the same largely interwar suburban houses are now prized locations for the population of the post-colonial Asian settlement who now buy and sell them on the open market. Furthermore, London contains suburbs that stray from the stereotypical template of white suburb such as Southall which has been a long-standing area with connections to the Punjab (Gillespie 1995; Brah 1999; Nasser 2004). In past decades, Wembley and Harrow have become increasingly 'Asian' with Gujeratis favouring these areas for residential settlement. Even the assumption that suburban residential dwellings are for single nuclear family units is not automatically the case in Asian suburbia where several generations under one household is not necessarily uncommon.

In the popular culture discussed in this chapter certain locations are more prevalent than others. Back in 1939, the hero of the Orwell novel *Coming Up For Air* discussed in Chapter 2 George Bowling escapes his suburban daily surroundings for a journey back to the countryside of his childhood. The journey takes in

> outer London . . . the Uxbridge Road as far as Southall. Miles and miles of ugly houses, with people living dull, decent lives inside them. And beyond it London stretching on and on, streets, squares, back-alleys, tenements, blocks of flats, fried-fish shops, picture-houses on and on for twenty miles, and all the eight million people with their little private lives which they don't want to have altered. (Orwell 1939:214)

Nirpal Daliwal (2007) states: 'Sandwiched between the leafy bourgeois west London environ of Ealing and Heathrow, Southall is recognised throughout the world as "Little India", a place akin more to Mumbai than a British suburb.' Yet this characterization misses the point. Southall, in many ways, *is* a thoroughly contemporary British suburb displaying (perhaps in a more extreme fashion than elsewhere) the characteristic of diversity that is a defining feature of UK suburbia attached to the big multicultural cities of today. Tim Lott like Daliwal has negative recollections of growing up in Southall captured in his memoir which details a nightmare world of narrow-minded post-war suburban England (although Lott's account has attracted criticism from Avtar Brah 1999). Furthermore Southall today is markedly different in character now than Lott's retrospective 1960s/1970s youthful memories of repression and a close-knit community. Southall has become home to numerous newer groups in post-millennial times. In 1993, McAuley stated of it, 'walking down these streets you will see few except Asian faces', but if he were to take a trip there today, he would doubtless see Polish and Somalis too. Their shops and specialist businesses which can include DVD and book stores help give the lie to suburbs as cultural deserts. It always numbered Afro-Caribbeans as remembered by Kwame Kwei-Armah on his documentary, *The House I Grew Up in*, broadcast in 2009 on BBC Radio 4 which described 1970s Southall when Asians were moving in, white families were moving out and the Afro-Caribbean community were left marginalized. Many of the black and Asian pioneering Southall settlers of the 1950s onwards have moved on and their children choose to set up independent residence elsewhere. Brick Lane is another (inner London) area associated with migration at large. Previous arrivals such as the French Hugenots and East London Jews suburbanized out but Bangladeshis are the most prevalent group now among a multitude of others – so much so that in 2002 one of the council wards had its name extended to 'Spitalfields and Banglatown'. Sandhu (2003a) talks about the cacophony of different sounds making up the soundtrack to the area, a veritable aural assault:

> Some amped-up desi beats CD that a carload of teenagers are nodding their heads to, the cries of a dosser who has been set on by a gang on an idle summer's day, a heated argument at an intersection between a Turkish and a Somali driver, a police helicopter roaring overhead in the middle of the night – everything rears up and assaults your ears, forcing you to learn about the neighbourhood and deal with newness in a way that is utterly unfamiliar to Asians who grow up in more sedate, affluent areas.

However this implied suburban tranquillity is a rarity in the multi-ethnic megacity where previously sleepy shopping parades are infused with vendors of exotic produce playing the sounds of their homelands in their shops, for example Burlington Road in the New Malden district of Kingston in South West London of which one blog poster commented disapprovingly (New Malden People 2011):

> it's become a very messy and untidy road. the shops don't look enticing, and with such a large choice of Sri Lankan and Korean supermarkets to choose from, it would be nice to balance it out with perhaps . . . Just somewhere to get a pack of sausages and yorkshire puddings when you forget them on a Sunday!

Southall and Brick Lane have more in common than their relative geographical positionings respectively at the edge of the city and nuzzling its core may suggest and the evidence of diversity has made itself felt on many suburban streets.

The attention commanded by Asian youth in academia and the media has waxed and waned over the years. The 1970s arguably represented a peak in Britain for youth culture studies, during this period the CCCS (Birmigham University's Centre for Contemporary Cultural Studies) was prolific in output but Asian youth were not uppermost in their analyses. Indeed articles addressing Asians could appear with phrases like 'paki-bashing' in their titles (see Pearson 1976). In terms of mainstream visibility, television has been the most powerful medium at bringing British Asians from 'out there' to the nation's front rooms. Sardar (2008:232) has written that the early specialist Asian-aimed programmes were aimed principally at persuading Asian women to learn English in keeping with the BBC's Reithian public service remit. Certainly their target audience was not Asian youth. We can also draw a distinction between representations of Asians in Asia and those domiciled in the United Kingdom. Sardar (2008:250–1) reels off a list of colonial era dramatizations of British-ruled India including the *Jewel in the Crown*, *Passage to India* and *The Far Pavillions* before concluding that such nostalgia-infused offerings 'authored a vision of all things Indian which in insidious ways controls contemporary attitudes to the settled communities of British Asians'. Certainly these scenes of heat and dust were unrecognizable to most everyday second-generation Asians living in the United Kingdom. Asian youth could instead be sighted often in defensive roles, for example as the quivering victims of school-bully Gripper Stebson suffering behind the bike-sheds racism on the 1980s BBC childrens drama set in a fictitious comprehensive school *Grange Hill* (1978–2008). The programme's location was never explicitly stated although early series were recognizably set in suburban London with production moving from 2003 onwards to Liverpool. At other times in one-off television plays and drama series such as *King of the Ghetto* (a series about British Bangladeshi tensions in 1986) and *Shalom Salaam* (1989 series about a taboo Muslim/Jewish love affair) the inner city seemed to be a more staple setting for Asians on television; the latter featured Bradford in West Yorkshire, a well-known area of Pakistani migration which has attracted a fair share of hand-wringing from academics and think-tanks (Alam and Husband 2005; Hussain and Bagguley 2005). In the United Kingdom, 1997 was almost a peak in media interest in Asian youth as a new 'Asian underground' club scene emerged from some of the more fashionable spots of central London; however, the term 'Asian' itself has unravelled somewhat since. When, long before 9–11, in summer 2001 northern English towns witnessed riotous friction between British-born

Asians, extreme right-wing sympathizers and the police, Hindus were quick to claim that these clashes were not 'Asian riots' as the police labelled them but were Muslim riots as those concerned were of Pakistani and Bangladeshi origins (Huq 2003). Reasons were manifold, including the principal driver of structural disadvantage coupled with racist provocation. Subsequent years have seen the rise of a politicized Islam led by charismatic imams and followed by youth who are asserting religious identities that their parents frequently downplayed. Minority communities once seen as passive and quiescent have increasingly flexed their muscle. The government has been keen to downplay any link between domestic events and foreign policy but the United Kingdom's joining with the United States in the invasion of Iraq in 2003 did not help New Labour's image among Muslims, leading to the loss of Labour suburban parliamentary seats such as Hornsey and Wood Green and Manchester Withington from the party in 2005, and the inaction over Israel's bombing of Gaza might have possibly served to reinforce resentment. The coalition government has since assuming office have not reversed Labour's a cross-departmental initiative entitled 'Preventing Violent Extremism' which ostensibly is designed at countering international terrorism but tellingly provides funding for Muslim groups providing that they are from the 'right' persuasion.

On-screen – Asians on television

In the *Good Life* episode 'The Guru of Surbiton' (1975) from series 2, a number of themes surface including student radicalism, community activism and ethnicity. The good-hearted couple Tom and Barbara Good take in an earnest long-haired student couple who seem to talk in the language of counter-hegemonic resistance to help with harvesting crops grown in their garden and other chores. The students then attempt to buy up the house next door in order to start a hippy commune. Margot, Gerry and the Goods set up a committee to resist the move and block the purchase by any means possible, a plan that Tom eventually backs out of in a delayed reaction of disgust at the lifestyle-policing implications that resistance to the plans entails. In the end, the students withdraw their offer, and Tom and Barbara wish them well with some friendly advice to not take themselves so seriously. In the final scene, Margot pops over to declare that 'you and your hippy friends', as she calls the Goods disparagingly, have driven Gerry and her out of Surbiton. She explains how they are to move to Cobham (deeper into Surrey) as a solution only to be told to her palpable relief by Tom and Barbara that the commune is off. Tom then starts informing them of the new couple who have decided to buy the house instead to Margot's increasingly delighted approval as the description continues: they are a banker, his wife who doesn't work apart from 'the odd charity dos' and two children at boarding school. Margot asks of their name so she can 'drop a notelet through' by way of a welcome. She gets the shock of her life and shouts out for Gerry in horror when she's told it is Mr and Mrs Aziz Mohammad Ibbin Khan. From the mirth and merriment that ensues, one can only assume that this scaremongering was a joke. Cue canned laughter and the closing titles. Here the possibility of immigrant Muslims next door is very much a threat not an opportunity. We see a clear case of othering leaving us to wonder which is worse: trustafarian hippy students who are white or a family who are to all intents and purposes the embodiment of respectability save for the fact that they are not white. It is a shame that this storyline was never developed – the family were never seen but instead were used as a comic device for cheap laughs. The show was recorded in an era when sightings of Asians on television could be described as somewhat sporadic, for example in news footage of the militant unionized women in saris striking at the Grunwick film processing plant during the mid-1970s industrial dispute or consigned to Asian slots with separate programmes such as the 1960s–80s Hindi language broadcasts of Sunday morning aimed at a pan-Asian audience of immigrant parents with presenters who looked like uncles and aunties deep in discussion interspersed with performances of classical Indian music.

By the second decade of the new millennium, Asians had become markedly more visible in mainstream media, particularly as presenters of the national and regional news bulletins. Anti-racism had ceased to be a fringe/loony Left concern and as part of the New Labour settlement became more of an accepted part of daily conduct which contributed to visibility of Asians in public life. The 2009 series of Channel 4's reality show *The Family* centred on an extended family of five Sikhs living in Berkshire with Heathrow airport looming large as an employer. The series was in a prime slot centring on a family of three generations under the same roof rather than them just playing bit parts – a departure from previous portrayals of Asians. As already seen, depictions oscillated between the stern aunties and uncles presenting Hindi-language programming tucked away in specialist slots, dramas on BBC 2, usually about the tyranny of arranged marriage or alternatively the terrified playground victims of school-bully Gripper on *Grange Hill*. The *impasse* was broken with the advent of Channel 4 with its attention to minority programming, for example the airing of Hanif Kureishi's film *My Beautiful Launderette*, initially created by Film4 for the cinema and the magazine show *Eastern Eye* presented in the English language, unlike the BBC equivalent at the time. The phrase 'artistic licence' in which realism can be tempered with dramatic effect can operate as a cultural cop-out, an unofficially sanctioned caveat to justify artistic products lacking in the credibility stakes. In the cultural climate of twenty-first-century Britain, artistic licence is present alongside another vexed question: 'the burden of representation' which is concerned with the messages and meanings majority audiences take away from cultural products dealing with minority subject matter. This can make characters in Asian drama sometimes seem like cardboard cut-outs created only to prove a point. In the feverish times we live in, cultural sensitivities are heightened with 'Muslim', now a category apart from the 'Asian' bloc category.

The television sketch show *Goodness Gracious Me* takes the story up from the *Good Life* to see what happens when Asians *do* move to the suburbs showing different aspects of Asian Britain through a range of characters in comedy sketches. The programme enjoyed a successful run from 1998–2000. When it toured as a stage show in 1999, the accompanying press release commented on its 'success and universal appeal; at a time when Indian culture is having a big influence on music, fashion and now comedy . . . [it] has broken the mould of "ethnic comedy"'. Among staple characters were two rival aspiring middle-class families who appeared together weekly at awkward social gatherings revolving around golf and barbecues where they aimed to outdo each other. This itself is unremarkable in a suburban comedy of manners style. However, the anglicised foursome are both terrified of the revelation of their Indian backgrounds. The Kapoors always insist that the correct pronunciation of their name was 'Cooper' headed by the patriarch Dinesh Kapoor who called himself 'Denis Cooper' while the Rabindranaths preferred to be known as the Robinsons with mother Veena insisting that she be known as Vanessa. Both pairs were shown as extreme suburban social climbers desperate to fit in and to be seen as more British than the British. In the first series, the sketch in which they are introduced sets up the situation via a visit by the Rabindranaths to the Kapoors in their newfound surroundings of suburban Chigwell, which we interpret has meant a move 'up' in the world, although we are not told exactly from whence they came it is elsewhere in London. The mention of the son of the Coopers/Kapoors son going off to 'discover himself' on a gap year in India as well as the offer to serve Indian tonic water are sneered at by the Robinsons/Rabindranaths. Matters climax when, in what is clearly a racist incident, a brick is unexpectedly thrown by persons unknown through the front door. It is interpreted as 'a present' with a note attached. On closer inspection, the note rubber banded round it reads: 'Pakis go home.' There is a pause inviting a moment of suspense. Things are unfrozen and the canned laughter roars on again as we hear the words uttered in unison from all four present: 'quite right too'. Opinion polls have repeatedly shown that the chief issues that concern suburb dwellers and the related demographic known as 'middle England' are fear of crime and immigration (Reeves 2007). This sketch suggests that this applies as much to Asian suburbanites as it does to more 'standard' white residents of suburbia. In a later episode at a family barbecue, union jack aprons are worn all round. This shows cultural convergence around at the appropriation of once Far Right imagery by Indians and the neutering of this formerly shocking symbolism by New Labour as part of the cool Britannia project. It would be erroneous to assume that minority electors are 'soft' on immigration issues. Indeed an opinion poll conducted for the BBC during the 2005 general election found that some 60 per cent of British Asian voters (of Indian, Pakistani and Bangladeshi origin) replied that there are already too many immigrants in the United Kingdom.[1] The sentiment is counter-intuitive to that which one would expect from Asians but might find favour with David Cameron (and Angela Merkel), given recent speeches.

The children of the *Goodness Gracious Me* foursome, the next generation, we glean are more enlightened in their attitudes. The Coopers'/Kapoors' son is initially mentioned in passing as on a gap year in India before later appearing in the series. This sketch suggests that preservation of suburban racial purity applies as much to these Asian suburbanites as it does to more 'standard' white residents of suburbia – as long as they can pull the ladder up behind them after getting in themselves. In another role-reversing sketch, rich young gap-year Indians came on a coach excursion to see the beggars and street hawkers of London (the latter being a road-side *Evening Standard* stall-holding seller). At the end of their trip, one of the young Indian backpackers decides to stay behind and follow in the footsteps of some pioneering wayfarers of the 1960s, as he'd found his spiritual home. The punchline of the sketch turns out to be 'Hounslow', the suburban west London borough that has benefited from nearby Heathrow airport and Asian migration for the past four decades. In some ways, *Goodness Gracious Me* and the successor show *The Kumars at Number 42*[2] continued the historic television tradition that had persisted for many years whereby ethnic characters only really featured in situation comedy when they become the situation rather than characters in their own right who happen to incidentally be of minority ethnicity. In earlier times, the character Alf Garnett was a mainstay of BBC schedules since the pre-politically correct 1960s uttering foul-mouthed racist tirades both in *Till Death Us Do Part* (1966–75) and its follow-up *In Sickness and in Health* (1985–92), although black and Asians did not feature much in the programmes. Conversely the Asian-writing team making *Goodness Gracious Me* and *The Kumars at Number 42* effectively made them agents of representation as well as the represented. The suburban idiom triumphed most markedly in the latter. The premise was of a spoilt kid with his own home television studio trying to present a celebrity chat show but being constantly interrupted by his overbearing family members – the venal money-making father, mother trying to marry him off and crude grandmother. Part of the appeal of the show was the way that sometime other-worldly internationally known A-listers (e.g. David Hasselhoff) or even refined national treasures like Stephen Fry were transplanted to the cosy confines of comfortable suburbia: an unfamiliar setting for them in the viewers' eyes. In the 1970s shows *Mixed Blessings* (situation comedy of an interracial marriage), *Love Thy Neighbour* (a black couple next door) or *Diff'rent Strokes* (US white city-slicker widower adopts the black sons of his deceased black housemaid elevating them from Harlem to a swish city apartment). By the 1980s and the 1990s, black characters got their own shows which tended to be inner-city based, for example Channel 4's *Desmonds* (comings and goings at a Peckham barbers) and *The Cosby Show* (veteran black comedian Bill Cosby playing a doctor/father of four kids married to a lawyer). The latter was the most pioneering by centring on the affluent black Huxtable family living in New York's exclusive Brooklyn Heights neighbourhood, but the title indicates that this was formulated as a vehicle for Cosby. It was only when *Goodness Gracious Me* and *The Kumars at Number 42* arrived that ethnic minorities were situated in suburbia in the United Kingdom. *The Boondocks* did the same thing for African Americans in the United States by animation, but in none of these examples were blacks and Asians present as 'another character', in each case their ethnicity conditioned the story.

Stranger than fiction

Hanif Kureishi's 1970s-set novel *The Bhudda of Suburbia*, arriving in 1990 after he wrote a string of plays is much celebrated as a work of suburban fiction unsettling received notions of class, sexuality, ethnicity and life on the periphery. Unlike the follow-up *The Black Album* (1995) or later short story/film *My Son The Fanatic* (1994/97), it is a largely secular story that does not explicitly deal with Islam. Muslim-born characters do not refrain from lewd practices, eating pork pies or 'drinking un-Islamic drinks' (Kureishi 1990:208). The novel is written in the first person. Its narrator and the nearest thing the book has to be a 'hero' is the pop-culture loving sixth-former and narrator Karim who makes a declaration of his identity at the outset stressing his suburban rather than Indian heritage: 'Englishman I am (though not proud of it), from the South London suburbs and going somewhere. Perhaps it was the odd mixture of continents and blood, of here and there, of belonging and not, that makes me restless and easily bored. Or perhaps it was being brought up in the suburbs that did it' (Kureishi 1990:3). The story is a coming-of-age tale of this central character who inhabits Bromley, the same south-east suburb where Kureishi was raised as were other cultural alumni including science-fiction writer H. G. Wells (after whom the coffee shop of the town's Allders department store was named), the leading punk movement known as the 'Bromley contingent' (see Chapter 3), and David Bowie, who produced the score to the television series of the book. By the end of the book, Charlie has swapped loon pants for punk which in one of the book's many questionings of role and manifestations of masquerade, Karim sees as inauthentic as the following exchange between the two of them illustrates:

'Why not, Karim, Why not, man?'

'It's not us'

'But we've got to change. What are you saying? We shouldn't keep up? That suburban boys like us always know where it's at?'

'It would be artificial' I said. 'We're not like them. We're not from the estates. We haven't been through what they have.' (132)

Perhaps also the fact that Karim views the music as 'pallid [and] vicious' (130) also explains his disapproval as his own preference has been for the bloated colourful world of psychedelia into which foreign influences are more readily accepted than the back to basics three chord and more straightforwardly superficially 'white' prescription of punk, notwithstanding strong ties between the music and Jamaican reggae. Although Karim sees punk as a social housing movement, a significant volume of punk from Bromley and suburbs like it was practised by those who were 'playing' and experimenting with roles that were more downwardly mobile than their actual origins in the semi-detacheds of the city's outskirts. Indeed the character Charlie, who Karim has homoerotic fumblings with at the start in the attic room while both their parents are downstairs at a suburban soirée, was allegedly based on real life punk-star Billy Idol who attended grammar school in Bromley and later Sussex University before dropping out and becoming a key member of the Bromley set as described in Chapter 3.

The titular Bhudda is Karim's father Haroon of Indian birth who is married to his dowdy English mother. There is a sense that he is an aristocrat manqué, dispossessed of his heritage. All this is played out at the same time as Britain too has lost an empire and is seeking a role in the world. When Karim and Charlie are caught in a stoned semi-embrace, Haroon is disgusted and responds 'with utter contempt . . . It must have been his upper-class background' (18). There are references to the servants he used to have at his beck and call and the sunny climes of Haroon's youth, juxtaposed with the reality of now: 'Dad had had an idyllic childhood, and as he told me of his adventures . . . I often wondered why he'd condemned his own son to a dreary suburb of London' (23). The poverty of rationing came as a shock and he ended up as a functionary in the civil service. 'His life, once a cool river of balmy distraction, of beaches and cricket . . . was now a cage of umbrellas and steely regularity. It was all trains and shitting sons, and the bursting of frozen pipes in January . . . the organization of love into suburban family life in a two-up-two-down semi detached in South London' (26). It seems Karim's English mother has also inherited the stories of patrilineal greatness: 'If Mum was irritated by Dad's aristocratic uselessness, she was also proud of his family. "They're higher than the Churchills", she said to people. "He went to school in a horse-drawn carriage." This ensured there would be no confusion between Dad and the swarms of Indian peasants who came to Britain in the 1950s and 1960s' (24). Here is a reversal of the white society as superior and this particular Asian, not all Asians, as subordinate. Although Haroon is Muslim, caste is a key organizing principle of Hindu Indian society where everyone has a rank that is not easily transcended. In the eyes of the English host population, when migrants arrived in England, all Asians were rendered the same. The reality of life with no servants meant fixed gender roles too dissolved in blighty – Karim's father was probably expected to do his share of childcare with no *ayah* [servant girl] to share the load.

Oswell (2000:80) claims: 'Kureishi's representation of suburbia is not the fixed uniformity of Edwardian Dumroamin's, but a feast of cultures: a mix of Asian and white English, late hippy, glam rock and punk, S/M and wife swapping. Karim's flight is from a suburb and family, which is hybrid. Karim is an actor and his performances draw on these particular suburban and familial resources. In this way Karim is a *flaneur*, strolling through the detritus of the city and suburbs thumbing his nose at convention.' The book shows generational differences in perceptions of suburbia. Bromley is seen as socially superior and a safe haven by Karim's 'Uncle Ted', a family friend who along with his wife Auntie Jean sides with his mother after his parents eventually split. When he and Karim pass through inner-London locations on the train together as they near its London terminus, Ted explains, 'That's where the niggers live' (43). For Karim however, the big smoke has associations with exoticism rather than the inner-city danger as seen in his description of 'the slums of Herne Hill and Brixton, places so compelling and unlike anything I was used to seeing . . . rows of disintegrating Victorian houses'. From a present-day perspective, most of these same dwellings in Pooterish suburbia would be very likely to have been fiercely gentrified since then and become highly desirable period properties in close enough proximity to the city for an easy and short commute. Although Oswell describes a hybrid world, we get the sense that for Karim, Bromley itself is a narrow-minded constricting location. In the private sphere, Haroon's memories of his lineage, imagined or real, predominate the family's self-positioning: By contrast in the public world, both he and Karim suffer various incidents of racism. At one of Haroon's séance-like gatherings, one guest asks if he has arrived by camel or magic carpet (12). When Karim almost falls off his bike in the street, a passer-by remarks, 'Get back in yer rickshaw'. One wonders if Ted had not known Karim personally whether he would have reacted in the same way. Of playground taunts, he opines, 'I was sick . . . of being affectionately called Shitface and Curryface . . . all my Dad thought about was me becoming a doctor. What world was he living in? Every day I considered myself lucky to get home without serious injury' (63). Here there is a pronounced mismatch between George Harrison-esque exoticization of a version of Asianness (Indians far off in India) and daily-lived experience (those who are in suburban London).

Although the book, which has inspired numerous academic analyses (e.g. Schoene 1998; Childs 2000; Oswell 2000; Maxey 2000; Nasta 2000), is formally divided into two, its structure could be divided into three: in the first part of the book, we get a fair amount of contextualization and scene-setting before the second section in which Karim comes into his own as an actor, and a process of self-discovery follows before finally the threads are tied together at the book's close. He is, by moving to inner London, in part reacting to his circumstances as is his father who begins a parallel career offering spiritual guidance to the locals. The popularity of Haroon's service spreads through word of mouth – 'They are looking forward to me all over Orpington' (21), he tells Karim; this newfound status and popularity compensating for his lowly pen-pushing status at the ministry. Through the keyhole as he accompanies his dad to happenings or listens in on rehearsals at home, Karim sees the irony in his reinvention: 'He was speaking slowly in a deeper voice than usual . . . hissing his s's and exaggerating his Indian accent. He'd spent years trying to be more of an Englishman, to be less risibly conspicuous, and now he was putting it back in spadeloads.' In this way, everyone is playing a role and perfomativity takes centre stage. The theatre is an apposite metaphor which recurs in the book. 'Chiselhurst [neighbouring suburb] had greenhouses, grand oaks and sprinklers on the lawn; men came in to do the garden. It was so impressive for people like us . . . Sunday visits to Auntie Jean we'd treat as a lower-class equivalent of the theatre' (29). Later on, the focus broadens as he runs away to join the theatre (literally) and experience new horizons provided by the lifeline of public transport to destinations such as West Kensington (125), taking the 28 bus to Notting Hill (206) or travelling by tube to squats in Brixton (238). There is a clear demarcation between the capital and its suburbs:

'In bed before I went to sleep I fantasized about London and what I'd do there when the city belonged to me' (121). A similar passage is to be found in *The Black Album* in which Shahid (1995:11) 'sat in the Kent countryside dreaming of how rough and mixed London would be, his brother Chili had loaned him *Mean Streets* and *Taxi Driver* as preparation'. Needless to say, he longs to escape the unmean streets of Sevenoaks. Both Karim and Shahid, like their creator Kureishi, have a fantasized imagined version of London partly as a result of initial feelings of being outsiders from it; their fascination has been shaped from having grown up at the capital's edge, or at its extremity. Kureishi's characters express sniffy disdain for suburbanites as uncultured. The observation 'Few of them had even books in their homes – not purchased, opened books, but only gardening guides, atlases, Readers Digests' is condescendingly made by Shahid of his neighbours in *The Black Album* (1995:35). Similarly, in *Bhudda,* we are told that in Bromley 'when people drowned they saw not their lives but their double glazing flashing before them' (23). Yet given that life in Bromley (with its arts venue, the Churchill theatre), Sevenoaks and London's outer reaches are all becoming more city-like, such observations are outmoded and condescending.

Karim's suburban angst solidifies, and he seeks extracurricular diversions as the story develops. He befriends Terry who is full of the call for revolutionary socialism. 'I wanted to tell him that the proletariat of the suburbs did have strong class feeling. It was virulent and hate-filled and directed entirely at the people beneath them' (149). It is his theatre period that should allow reinvention par excellence, but there he finds himself typecast. When he is told by his director 'We need someone from your own background . . . Someone black' (170), he can't think of anyone apart from a Nigerian classmate that he's lost touch with. By his own admission, Karim whose nickname 'Creamy' has connotations of pigmentation as well as sexual shades admits, 'truly, I was more beige than anything' (167). Unsatisfactorily, he lands the role of Mowgli in *The Jungle Book*, the qualification for which is ostensibly that he has seen the Disney cartoon. The choice is attacked by his favourite cousin Jamila as colluding with imperialism. Other characters he later develops are based on acquaintances including his uncle Anwar, proprietor of the ironically titled stereotypical corner shop 'Paradise Stores', and Changez, who has an arranged marriage to Jamila. After performing drama in America and seeing Charlie in his prime there who has long transcended 'the front page of the Bromley and Kentish Times', Karim boomerangs back to London. By the end, both of his parents have different partners. Surrounded by them, he sits down and feels a happy/sad/moving sentiment about his London existence. *The Black Album* (1995) contains the same central themes of escape and stoical ending experienced by Shahid as that of Karim five years earlier.

New directions in Asian fiction

While Kureishi has inspired a welter of academic literary criticism, his book was set in the 1970s and came out in 1990. More recently Gautam Malkani's (2006) *Londonistan* has offered a contemporary treatment taking Hounslow as its setting which is dubbed 'car park capital of the world'. The book is not to be confused with Melanie Phillips (2006) polemic *Londonistan* of the same year. Malkani's (2006) narrative style is memorable for its writing in a vernacular tongue of hybridized English incorporating Jamaican patois, text-speak and Hindi words as can be seen from this passage addressing the youth cultural ideal of not 'selling out' (in this case appropriate with the lifestyle of the majority white population) with a yearning of narrator Jas to escape his suburban surroundings:

> In't no desi needin to kiss the white man's butt these days, an you definitely don't need to actually act like a gora. Fuckin blanchod. din't matter what you called them. Coconuts, Bounty bars, Oreo biscuits or any other fuckin food that was white on the inside. Good desi boys who didn't ever cause no trouble. But how many a them'll still be here in Hounslow in ten years time, workin in Heathrow fuckin airport helping goras catch planes to places so they could turn their own skin brown? (Malkani 2006:23)

Throughout the book, Jas and his all-Asian peers negotiate and refer to various points of suburban west London including gentrifying river-side Brentford and Ealing Broadway station with its pinstriped commuting classes as they plan an elaborate and thoroughly modern heist involving mobile phones. They glide through the locational settings in various drive-by episodes using their parents' cars as they are nominal college sixth-formers and none has left the family home. The book contains some familiar Kureishi-esque themes (coming of age, masculinity, self-doubt), but is probably more remembered for the publishing hype surrounding it than its literary qualities – it attracted a record advance and even had a cinema-style trailer filmed as part of its publicity campaign. When central character Jas ventures out, it is to Kensington and Hyde Park Corner which we are reminded are each a straight ride down the Piccadilly line home. Various scams involving driving and mobile phones surface as well as forbidden interracial relations. First-person narrator Jas (2006:89) paints a picture of a landscape broken up with 'newsagents, halal kebab shops an [*sic*] minicab companies with Special Autumn Airport Fares'. Southall is referred to with reverence, for example the 'old days' of the rival gangs, the Holy Smokes and

Tooti Nungs which attracts the comment: 'Now those boys were the hardcore shit. I'm too young to be remembering much bout them' (Malkani 2006:84). At the beginning of the book, a white kid is subjected to the following accusation for calling Hardjit a 'paki' which illustrates the world of the boys beyond Hounslow (Malkani 2006:11):

> U cuss'd my sister an ma bredren. U cuss'd my dad, my uncle Deepak, u cuss'd
> my aunty Sheetal, my aunty Meera, ma cousins in Leicester, U cuss'd ma grandad
> in Jalandhar

The character is also inflamed by the insult 'paki' as he is not even from Pakistan in origin. When a gang fight is threatened, we are told that other lads from Southall and Slough may join in.

Around the same time, Nirpal Singh Dahliwal's *Tourism* (2006) came out narrating another first-person second-generation journey. In this instance, Puppy/Bhupinder frequents various central and inner-London hangouts with his friends who are a fashionable crowd but ultimately he cannot avoid coming back to see his mother in Southall when he is in need of money to bum some off her. There is a pronounced gulf between Puppy's mum's kitchen with its yellowing lino and the polished chrome minimalist surfaces in the flat of his journalist city-slicker girlfriend or the middle-class country home of the lawyer woman he lusts after. The book is graphic in its portraits of sexual encounters, masturbation and for the misogyny on display. We are told that Southall is 'petit bourgeois suburbia' inhabited by 'the Punjabi tribe' (40), while in Holland Park where girlfriend Sophie lives, 'It felt beautiful, stepping out if the house and into her car, exchanging nods with the couple who lives opposite, obvious millionaires who assumed I was one too' (52). In the 7.5 miles between the two locations on the same road the A4020 there is a wealth of difference from Southall's humdrum Edwardian and interwar semis to the imposing stucco-fronted dwellings of the super rich. Gentrifying inner East London cannot compete with this westerly wealthy species: 'They were a beloved elect: Europeans, Arabs, Americans and Jews; each saw other through a prism of money . . . Hackney's rich owned Land Rover Discoveries and Smeg fridge-freezers; Holland Park's owned *the world*' (53). Wealth seems to dictate his value system. On a return visit to collect post at the Hackney flat which is his official dwelling, he is reminded of his playground tormenters from schooldays on spying some trashy youth we are told: 'I hate poor white. No one is more stupid or useless. They made my life hell when I was a child' (115). While his brother has remained in Southall, dutifully running the family shop in his father's absence and is about to submit to arranged marriage, Puppy has got out after doing a college course. He suffers acute embarrassment every time he returns as can be seen from this description: 'For her disappointments we suffered a mother who looked like an animal. Walking with her through streets, down supermarket aisles, we felt ashamed, revolted and guilty for feeling so' (34). This sort of disavowal is common among the children of suburbia of all ethnicities who have made it to London Travelcard zone 2, but here we see a sense of it being multiplied for those who have entered a metropolitan jet set where they are accepted for being exotic but will never shake off their ethnic roots. At a later point, Puppy becomes tongue-tied among his city-slicker friends because of the sound of his own voice: 'It was an absurd jumble of accents: cockney enunciation overlaid with a quiet drone from the Punjab . . . I was taken aback by how particular I was, rooted in time and place: everything about me came from the Punjabi suburb of west London. I felt embarrassed. I realised how outlandish my presence was here' (189). It seems to be the opposite of the old cliché 'it's not where you're from it's where you're at'. Here we seem to be told, you can take the kid out of Southall but you can't take Southall out of the kid. Puppy feels like a tourist looking in on the lives of white privilege that he can never fully belong to.

Meanwhile Shukla (2010:121) offers the following description of more upmarket Asian suburbia where front lawns have been tarmacked into carports:

> The walk to Harrow was ten minutes of winding through rows of terraced two-storey houses, all with the same façade: grey pebble-dash, white PVC doors and gravelled driveways. I always wondered what Indians had against grass and gardening because there wasn't a tuft of green anywhere in sight.

The remark is interesting to read alongside the Southall resident of Indian origin quoted in Oates (2003:105) who claims: 'When I first came to this country I was shocked by the difference of the weather, grey buildings, grey sky and dull clothes.' Southall is often seen by commentators as 'colourful' for the celebratory public display of its high street at festival times,[3] but the privatized exteriors of the Asian suburban side-street domestic dwellings described by Shukla are functional and drab rather than the riot of colour reserved for the interiors of ostentation of its high-streets and public thoroughfares. Pebble-dashed and stone-clad exteriors are part of what Lott (1996) found so hateful about the Southall he grew up in. In Govinden's (2007) novel, set in Surrey narrated by a half Tamil half-Jewish sixth form boy casual violence appears to be liberally practiced.

Suburbia is often a place associated with childhood, that its metropolitan critics end up fleeing. It seems that masculinity is an abiding theme of this tranche of 'coming of age' suburban Asian novels. Chasing girls that are out of their league seems to be a central preoccupation for example for the first-person narrators of Shukla's *Coconut Unlimited* (2010) and Malkani's *Londonstani*. As well as describing the physical changes of puberty that the narrator and his mates are going through, Shukla (2010:95) confides in the reader: 'the truth of it was the band *was* to get girls' attention – but the attention of girls beyond the slim remit of Harrow, worldly (and preferably white) girls who liked hip-hop.' Elsewhere we are told, 'There was nothing for me here, something I mentally told myself every time I walked through Harrow. I had my sights set elsewhere, in London' (Shukla 2010:57). Daliwal (2006) displays deeply unpolitically correct misogyny in his narrator's graphic descriptions of sex that appears to have little connection to romantic love, a trait that has seen him likened by reviewers to novelist Michel Houellebecq (Charlton 2006; Saha 2006; Woolaston 2006). Certain titles are deemed more worthy of being considered as 'literature' than others who remain simply 'fiction'. Kureishi and Malkani have become the subject of academic articles and PhD thesis[4] while literary criticism of their female counterparts is by comparison muted with their work often not considered serious enough to rise above the more supposedly fluffy, insubstantial genre of 'chick-lit', for example the works of Meera Syal (1996; 1999) and Shyama Perera (1999; 2000; 2002). The multi-authored anthology of 21 stories promising to showcase new young British Asian writing edited by Bhanot (2011) in some degree aimed to reverse this and was greeted by mixed reviews.

Dhaliwal, Malkani and Kureishi are authors who have contributed to an increasing visibility of Asians on the British youth cultural landscape as well as in fiction contributing to an understanding of what we might term 'Asian (suburban) London'. In *Tourism*'s twenty-first century Southall, Asians are predominant on the landscape which is replete with 'pavements . . . full of people hawking Bollywood soundtracks while their asylum claims are processed' (Dhaliwal 2006:40–1), unlike the historical account of Bromley from *The Bhudda of Suburbia* where Karim is a rarity. Linked developments include the late 1990s emergence of the Asian underground club scene and the advent of series such as *Goodness Gracious Me* written and performed by young Asians. Novels by other second-generation hybrid writers such as Monica Ali's *Brick Lane* and Zadie Smith's *White Teeth* are also noteworthy, although these latter two were set in the inner London's Willesden and Tower Hamlets respectively. Malkani and Kureishi's tales from the outer reaches are more representative of demographic trends than usual inner-city = ethnic area clichés.

Suburban soundtrack case-study: Bhangra in Ilford

Contemporaneously with the mainstream cultural trend of Britpop was a parallel British Asian clubbing scene encompassing both bhangra music and the later style Asian underground. This helped to bring Asian youth away from the margins of youth culture. Among the sites of its practice were suburban clubs. The scene which is documented more fulsomely elsewhere including by myself (Huq 1996; 2003; 2006). It helped to bring visibility to a hitherto almost invisible community importantly in the suburbs as well as British cities. Sandhu (2003b:228) has written:

> Young Asians had no cultural ambassadors or role models. They lacked sporting heroes . . . Even more importantly they lacked an indigenous youth culture. They forged no musical alliances such as those between rude boy ska and skinhead stomp at the end of the 1960s or 1976's reggae-punk axis. It was these marriages encompassing fashion, music, sex and shared attitudes that helped to create the open-minded, pick'n'mix, urban British youth culture which flourishes to this day, through such style-magazine-designated epiphenomena as 'new Asian kool', 'bhangramuffin' and 'the future soundz of India', Asians have only recently entered.

Bhangra music had played a role in introducing Asian youth onto television screens and into Sunday supplements. Birmingham's Apache Indian fronted a 1995 television series for Channel 4 before the words 'reality' and 'television' had been yoked together in which the self-styled purveyor of bhangramuffin was seen criss-crossing India on a gruelling tour through India where he was garlanded at every turn and welcomed as quasi-royalty. The premise of the show is interesting as it begs the question of whether this music can be considered linearly or the story is more one of circuits of influences rather than one-way imports/exports. Yet it is still wedded to the seemingly unassimilable bhangra (although this icy status was starting to thaw somewhat) that had been a mainstay of the Asian wedding. In 1998, the single 'Brimful of Asha' by second-generation Punjabi Sikhs Cornershop from Wolverhampton made Number One in the UK charts; the first time such a feat had occurred for an 'out' Asian artist – I am not counting the East African Asian Freddie Mercury who denied his heritage throughout his life or Indian-born Cliff Richard in making this statement. The track 'Brimful of Asha' namechecked singers known to singer/songwriter Tjinder Singh through his parents' record collection, Asha Bhosle and Lata Mangeshekar and was celebrated by Radio 4 in a 30 minute retrospective documentary in January 2013[5]. By 2004, BBC2 had launched *the Asian magazine show DesiDNA* which the BBC website describes as 'Focusing on the new generation of Asians breaking the mould and seeking out the hottest in Asian clubs, fashion, music and lifestyle in the UK and abroad'.[6] The show was firmly aimed at young and fashionable audiences featuring trendy DJs as its presenters unlike the bifocaled uncles and aunties in cardigans who had been the staple of the corporation's earlier Asian output. The emphasis on club culture and fusion music implies fluidity and mixity and a general progressive/ celebratory/hedonistic ethic as opposed to the patriarchy of arranged marriages and the caste system that used to dominate Asian onscreen imagery. Here were second-generation Asians having fun rather than toiling over examinations – although it is worth making an aside that universities were key in the importance of bhangra as the first generation of students living away from home coincided with the birth of British bhangra. Since then Asian-originating music has fused with numerous other musical and commercial styles and scenes, for example Panjabi MC of the hip-hop scene or the 2003 hit 'Bhangra Nights' by Husan that became a hit after featuring in a television advertisement for French car manufacturer Peugot.

As well as a metropolitan nucleus Asian clubbing has been played out in suburban locations and venues such as Ilford since the early 1990s. The effect of Asian settlement on Ilford's character can be seen from the shops in Ilford Lane, the Bollywood Bowl venue towards the rear of the town hall is another sign of the Asian character that Ilford has taken on. It offers on-site Indian cuisine and the popular Nandos restaurant in the same parade has also tailored its product to meet the needs of local diners with halal chicken, demonstrating the flexibility of capitalist chains somewhat in contradiction to the standardizing critique of Ritzer (1993). Predating this venue offering a restaurant and bowling were bhangra (Punjabi/ UK fusion musical) concerts that took place at local venues. This transcript from an event organizer interviewed in 1994 for my PhD shows how the Ilford Island nightclub had been identified as a suitable location in the mid-1990s:

RH: Why Ilford then?

J: Out of experience there are at least 60 per cent of Asians in Waltham Forest, that's 32,240 – one of the largest Asian populations in the country. All the kids were going west. Luckily we got this venue when we did. I know that Le Palais [in Hammersmith, west London], the Hippodrome [central London] and Kudos [Watford] are out of bounds. The three major promotion companies all have exclusive contracts.

RH: How many people are here tonight?

J: I'd say 6–700 at a glance. I've noticed strange quirks about the shows here. Normally at Bhangra is people in their early twenties, college kids. Here in East London there's not much [*sic*] places to go. I've seen people's Aunts and families here. At the other end there's the eight to nine year old generation.

The location of Ilford, to London's suburban east but not lying in profound, Essex has long been a place for suburbanization from London's East End including Jewish communities. Bangladeshis and Pakistanis are now making the same Eastward journey that Wilmott and Young (1957) traced in the classic book *Family and Kinship in East London* and subsequent studies (1963; 1967).

Other venues in the town now include the Coliseum, primarily a banqueting hall on Ilford High Street hired out for weddings which has hosted various bhangra happenings as has IF bar on Ilford Hill. The local Vue Cinema also includes Bollywood among its programming, offering instant escapism to ticket holders. In this way leisure, commerce and dining are all accommodating if not quite a purely cockney diaspora, a masala variant of it.

On-screen II – Asians on film

A different image of women and suburbia emerges from female writer/director Gurinder Chadha's films, where received ideas of Asian femininity are too on display. Helsby (2005:192–3) states, 'actor-led rather than star-led, social realism, heritage, nostalgia, literary adaptations, a quirky sense of humour, and class structure all contribute to an idea if Britishness in film'. Indeed Chadha has cited David Lean's *This Happy Breed* which contains various elements from this list as a major influence for its proto-typical realist intergenerational portrayal of suburban British family life.[7] Referring to his own childhood questioning of self-identity while growing up as a British Asian, Sukhdev Sandhu (2000) has claimed that Hanif Kureishi 'not only captured these anxieties, but offered for the first time a recognisable portrait of British Asian life. Previously we had made do with sitcoms such as *It Ain't Half Hot Mum* and *Mind Your Language*, in which Asians wore comical headwear and were the butts rather than the tellers of jokes'. Although Kureishi and Chadha deal with ostensibly the same subject (second-generation Asians), the differences in their work are manifold. The exoticism of *My Beautiful Launderette* could almost feel other-wordly to most humdrum suburban Asians like myself. Sandhu (2000) itemises the dramatis personae in a non-exhaustive list including 'pushers, tyrannical ex-foreign ministers, bogus mystics, brutalising landlords, togged-up likely lads, sex-hungry cripples [who] . . . exploit or augment their ethnicity at will'. Gurinder Chadha's characters are arguably more credible fully fledged and three-dimensionally written human beings than these caricatures. Chadha's films tend to revolve around strong female characters and are usually set in the suburbs – *It's a Wonderful Afterlife* is in Ealing and *Bend It Like Beckham* in Hounslow with the well-known Punjabi district Southall which borders these two areas identifiably present in both. The latter has been described by Donnell (2007:47) as 'both a feminist and a postcolonial triumph . . . [which] ends with a more celebratory and harmonious version of cosmopolitan conviviality than Stuart Hall or Paul Gilroy could have imagined', although there is criticism for the fact that the theme of queer sexuality is not directly addressed but only naggingly hinted at. Chadha managed to break out of the ethnic ghetto with *Beckham* which proved to be a mainstream box office success no doubt helped by a cameo appearance from the world-famous footballing personality featured in the title.

Gurinder Chadha's biography as a Southall-raised Punjabi is repeatedly stressed in profiles of her and interviews that she gives and her identity as a woman is also apparent in her directing: even the teen romance *Angus, Thongs and Perfect Snogging* (2008) was from the girls' perspective. Strong women are commonly present in her work. In both the midlands-based *Bhaji on the Beach* (1993) and *It's a Wonderful Afterlife* (2010) the main lead is female and works with women suffering from domestic violence. These characters are portrayed in assertive crusading-for-social-justice roles that contradicts old stereotypes of the Asian female as doe-eyed and submissive. Bollywood Indian film aesthetics are here, as in a short scene of East is East where daughter Meera lets herself go dancing in the backyard to Indian music, transposed into true Brit/English setting. This technique was perfected perfected with different scenery in Chadha's later *Bride and Prejudice* (2005) with its dazzling visuals and choreography. Most of this later film was filmed in country houses but there were some flashes of life behind the door of an Asian suburban London semi.

There are numerous overlaps between the phenomena discussed in this chapter. Before he was known as a novelist, Hanif Kureishi wrote the screenplay for *My Beautiful Launderette* (1982) which was followed-up with *Sammy and Rosie Get Laid* (1987) about a middle-class married couple on the edge of a heavily ethnic London inner-city war zone, who are in an interracial relationship with each other and extramarital affairs with others. Kureishi's 1991 film was entitled *London Kills Me*, demonstrating an ambivalent love/hate relationship towards the capital. In his films and books, characters often cavort around the metropolis, they are attracted to the centre having broken free of the shackles of suburbia; London is their playground. Despite its title *The Bhudda of Suburbia* (1992 novel and later television series) finds the chief character escaping to London from narrow-minded far-flung suburb of Bromley. A similar journey is undertaken in the follow-up *Black Album* (1994 novel). When he broached the subject of Islamic extremism in Bradford (*My Son the Fanatic*), the review in *Empire* magazine noted (Parkinson 1998): 'Kureishi is less at home in Yorkshire than in the London suburbs and tends to overdo the references to early 60s grim-up-North movies. He also presents caricatures of the immigrant wife, the prosperous restaurateur and the arrogant German businessman.' The accusation of cardboard cut-out characters is frequently applied to white-authored arts dealing with minority ethnic populations but here the person accused is (mixed) Asian themself. Both this statement and the quote at the beginning of this chapter alludes to stereotypical Asians in popular culture. One of the stereotypes that attaches itself to ethnic minorities at large is of them residing in the inner city, but statistical evidence backs up the movement of them away from these districts and towards the suburbs (Hinsliff 2008, Peach 1996) confirmed by the 2011 census (Huq 2013). Elsewhere, Peach (1994) has claimed that West Indians in Britain face an 'Irish future' (languishing in the ghetto) while Asians face a 'Jewish future' of suburbanization (although Bangladeshis excluded from this). This now seems rather outdated as both groups have diffused in population to outer London often along familiar arterial roads and transport links, for example from Brixton to Croydon or Tower Hamlets to Redbridge, which includes Ilford as mentioned above. In some respects, Asians are 'normalized' away from being simply exotic fare once they penetrate the sort of arenas that are mainstream and reach the average suburban viewer so at the time of writing both the big national UK soaps have Asian families – Sinita and Dev on *Coronation Street* and the Ahmeds of *EastEnders* on ITV and BBC respectively. All have acted outside the traditional expectations of Asians.

Different hierarchies exist between high and low culture and what is considered worthy of academic/seminar-room study and what is lowbrow trash. This tension which has existed since cultural studies began is now joined by a technological divide. In an age of instant archival availability of source material, some films are more easily available than others ensuring longevity while others have faded. The Channel 4 financed low-budget film *Wild West* (1992) had a similar starting point to the *Commitments* in its good-time tale of an amateur country and Western band with the added element of band members being of Pakistani origin and the film's setting being the west London suburb of Southall allowing for some stereotypical Asian uncle baddies thrown in for good measure. Released as it was in a pre-YouTube era, it has left very little digital footprint despite starring Naveen Andrews, later of hit US series *Lost*. A review at the time (Newman 1992) remarks that culture clash is a theme: 'the heroes' confusion of cultural identities – torn between Pakistan, Southall and Nashville – and a kind of defiant stupidity in their love of an unfashionable music form.' It concludes that the film does not however take itself too seriously offering the 'chance to have a giggle and to witness a complicated bit of modern Britain being allowed to enjoy itself on screen for a change'. The film then like *Goodness Gracious Me* in its own way helped to bring the element of humour into portrayals of British Asians and showed another side of suburbia than conventional understandings of it. Similarly, the London-set low-budget film second-generation Asian *Alfie*-like film *Guru in Seven* (1998) also has largely disappeared without trace although lead actor Nitin Ganatra later became one of television's most notable Asian faces as the father of the Ahmed family in BBC1's soap opera *EastEnders* (2007–present). The review that begins this chapter was written at the height of Asian visibility in mainstream British media claiming (Caterall 1998): 'Given the current vogue for all things curry-flavoured (from Cornershop to Kundun to Kureishi) [this] laughably low-budget affair might appear a hurried, zeitgeist-riding cash-in, with even less money than sense. Except it packs more energy, brio and honest-to-goodness spunk than many of the other more lavish products currently clogging the multiplexes.' Interest in British Asians in mainstream popular culture has arguably faded since although Bollywood itself is a regular box office success in venues such as the multiplexes in suburban and exurban locations across the United Kingdom such as the Feltham Cineworld or Trafford Centre in Manchester which each devote a number of screens to this genre. At the same time 'suburban dysfunction' as a recognizable strain of film seems to be solidifying; it is now a category on the Netflix on-demand film streaming service.[8]

Discussion and conclusion

This chapter has shifted in scope from those earlier taking not just one cultural form in its examination but instead looking across novels, musical and on-screen representations. Oates' (2003) respondent quoted above on p. 176 complained that on initial arrival to Southall in the 1960s from India the greyness of the area struck them. Today Southall is well known as a west London suburb of Punjabi-Sikh migration, often described in tourist guides as 'colourful' for its shopping parades of silks of all hues and proliferation of restaurants. A fuller exploration of 'Asian London' had time and space allowed could have looked less obvious examples and at the built environment. The work of Nasser (2003, 2004, 2006) has shown how for example Asians are constantly adapting their environment. Using the examples of Southall and Bradford, she has found that loft and back extensions to Edwardian and Victorian houses are common to accommodate growing families and that many places of worship have been hewn from what were houses co-opted into sacred use before purpose built or simply larger premises have been found. The chapter has been selective in its choice of media forms to consider and media forms to analyse.

Sport is another popular cultural category through which the changing face of Britain has become apparent, peaking with the London 2012 Olympics. The boxer Amir Khan of Pakistani origin, although not from suburban London did hail from Bolton, Lancashire, which has in some respects been swallowed up by the Greater Manchester sprawl to become a Mancunian suburb. Burdsey (2007:623) remarks that his professional ascent constructed him 'as the "acceptable" or desirable face of British Islam'. Second-generation British Asian theatre too has flourished with plays such as the lavish West End *Bombay Dreams* (2002) or smaller community theatre affairs such as *Deranged Marriage, Desi Soulmate, Balti Kings, Papa Was a Bus Conductor* And *Unsuitable Girls* which outer-London venues like west London's Watermans Arts Centre and Theatre Royal Stratford East have been vocal in promoting. There has been a tendency towards adaptations transposing well-known tales to or shifting between genre for example the Bollywood version of *Wuthering Heights*, a stage version of Bollywood film *Hum Aapke Hain Koun* as *Fourteen Songs, Two Weddings and a Funeral* and a stage play of Hanif Kureishi's novel *The Black Album*. Tapping into the reality-show vogue was the production *Britain's Got Bhangra* in 2009. From the same year the play *Shades* won writer Alia Bano an *Evening Standard* award for its story of a single Muslim London woman's quest for love, a further example in mapping Asian suburban London removing Asian females from the 'family' role that they are usually viewed in.

As outlined above, religion has become more pronounced as faith identities are no longer shied away from. The far right English Defence League have been provocative in their choice of locations to stage marches. As well as areas known for Muslim populations such as Tower Hamlets and Luton, they have selected Harrow as a destination, although their 2010 attempt stalled. The *Harrow Times* (Royston 2010) reported: 'An Islamaphobic group has reportedly called off a planned Harrow demonstration due to the start of its founder's trial.' New cases add themselves continually to the list of fictitious works representing the lived realities of Asian suburbia. Importantly these examples showing us multiple versions of both of these terms for example complimenting work set in the established settlement of Southall is newer work looking at Gujerati youth in Harrow (Shukla

2010) and those of Sri Lankan descent in Surrey (Govinden 2007). Two decades ago, Peach (1996:233) remarked: 'Indians in London have an outer- rather than an inner-city distribution' noting also an outward residential shift of the Caribbean born. Pakistanis in Bradford and Bangladeshis in Tower Hamlets were rated as being the slowest to suburbanize however there is much evidence that this second group are redefining Asian London by moving to boroughs such as Redbridge in suburban East London. Sandhu (2003a) has observed that 'Brick Lane has always been a holding area, a temporary interzone for immigrants who have not yet fully settled in England . . . It's a slow and incomplete journey as far as many Bangladeshis are concerned. The canny ones, those with contacts or who strike lucky with property or businesses, move away, following the Central Line artery out to upscale areas such as Woodford and Loughton'. Bangladeshis have found homes in other East London boroughs including the distinctly outer-London Redbridge and neighbouring Newham which has campaigned to be reclassified as 'inner London' to receive increased government subsidy has also redefined east London's social composition and it is predicted that the Conservative-led government's restrictive cap on housing benefit claims will force populations requiring state assistance to live further and further away from central London. The journey from inner east London to suburban Redbridge undertaken by Bangladeshis is much like that which the Jewish made a century earlier as noted by Hall (2007) in the case of the Gants Hill neighbourhood and theorized at the level of Jewish migratory patterns at large (Waterman and Kosmin 1986). There are also examples of writing on Jewish suburban London, for example the Hendon-set novel *Disobedience* by Naomi Alderman (2006) about orthodox closed communities which garnered a review in *The Guardian* simply entitled 'this is Hendon', drawing attention to the incongruity between a location that is on the face of it unexceptional and the lives behind the closed Jewish orthodox communities described (Rabinovich 2006).

Around the time of New Labour's election associated cool Britannia rhetoric was invoked aiming to update traditional imagery of Britishness with more forward-thinking less hidebound conceptualizations, it seemed as if Asians had gone from invisibility to hyper-visibility. The journalist Sarfraz Manzoor (2008:257–8) refers to (i) Number One hit band Cornershop (ii) box office hit 1999 film *East is East* and (iii) Monica Ali's novel *Brick Lane* in the following observation:

> If someone had told me fourteen years earlier, when I had been watching Indian films with my family on our rented video player, that there would be a time when Asha Bhosle would feature in a number one hit single, I would have considered them insane. It was as insane as a group of British Asians becoming

pop stars. As unlikely as the thought of being Asian might be considered as being cool, that white people might pay to watch a film about a Pakistani family growing up in the seventies or read a book about a Bangladeshi woman or laugh at a comedy sketch where the joke was on them and not the Asians performing the skit.

As a Punjabi Sikh raised in the provincial town of Gloucester, Sukhdev Sandhu (2003b:236) has claimed, 'Anti-suburbanism has a special resonance for young Asians. Their parents have traditionally seen the suburbs as a promised land, light at the end of the industrial tunnel'. Yet many second-generation Asians: the children of suburbia have themselves actively chosen suburbia as their own residential location on becoming adults themselves. A suburban sensibility can be discerned in much of the work reflecting Asian youth culture. The weekly chat show *The Kumars at Number 42* starring cast members of *Goodness Gracious Me* Sanjeev Bhaskar and Meera Syal is set around the exploits of an extended British-Indian family living in a detached mock Tudor house in suburban Wembley, north-west London.

Suburbia can be a creative hub too – imagined and real, from the Kumar's studio to the long-standing cultural production at studios in such outposts as Pinewood, Elstree and Ealing which all housed film studios. The Kumar's fictional home is at a site not far off from some of north-west London suburbia's contemporary emblematic features such as the United Kingdom's first IKEA superstore and the gigantesque Neasden Hindu temple BAPS Shri Swaminarayan Mandir. As cultural constructs, both suburbs and Asians are in keeping with Benedict Anderson's (2006) notion of 'imagined communities', of which it is impossible to ever have contact with all of its members, or those who identify with them.

In *Simpsons* episode 'Insane Clown Poppy' from the year 2000 (season 12, episode 3), the characters watch a teen drama which parodies *Dawson's Creek* featuring Bumblebee Man as guest star included to exhibit inclusivity. Lisa remarks, 'I'm all for ethnic diversity, but this is just pandering'. The question of the presence of ethnic minorities on-screen to satisfy quotas is a perennial one. The producer of *Goodness Gracious Me* Anil Gupta has made the following claim regarding when he began his career at the BBC: 'At the time, minority programming had a genre of its own. It was only made for those audiences. Asian people being funny wasn't on the radar', (Hundal 2005). In the same interview, he voices suspicion at the positive action training schemes by the BBC and others designed to encourage under-represented groups into the media. Gupta deliberately did not work on *The Kumars at Number 42* for fear of ghettoizing or pigeonholing himself as an 'Asian' but instead became executive producer of *The Office*. It is only when Asian suburban popular culture representation moves from marginal status to the mainstream that the journey of its cultural practitioners will be complete, yet colour blindness is also a pitfall if recognition of all difference must be erased out in the process. In 2011, controversy erupted over the highly exportable ITV programme *Midsomer Murders* set in a country village when the producer had to tender his resignation after explaining that its success was due to its all-white cast. The implication was that the unsayable had been said and that on-screen television diversity should be now a given. Ten years earlier, the then BBC controller Greg Dyke had made headlines for slating the corporation as 'hideously white'. There are fraught debates around 'the burden of representation' (Huq 1996) that are probably unresolveable to everybody's satisfaction. *Goodness Gracious Me* (which originally began life as a radio series) took its title from Spike Milligan's catchphrase when impersonating Indians in blacked-up tones, the sort of television that would be deemed politically incorrect and entail sackings in the present age.

This chapter has shown then that enduring stereotypical images of suburbia as culturally uniform were always difficult to apply to London and at a time that official British statistics can be painfully slow in documenting social change, contemporary on-screen representation and literary fiction has played a decisive role in exposing these old notions as woefully outdated. By Summer 2012, the findings of the decennial data collection exercise that resulted in the 2011 UK census had only just begun to appear in dribs and drabs. For many years previously, social scientists had had to rely on figures from 2001 – which in many ways given our accelerated culture was a different age before flat-screen television, text messaging and Wi-Fi internet were common in the suburban household. One of the key headlines the data spawned was that only 45 per cent of the capital now self-identify as 'white British' as London becomes more mixed, particularly in its suburban boroughs (Huq 2013). Fictitious representations of Asian London have moved on from old post-colonial narratives of arrival and initial settlement told so movingly for example in the Wole Soyika poem 'Telephone Conversation', to the stories of everyday second-generation life in the metropolis and its suburbs. Once sociologists talked about Asians 'caught between two cultures' (Anwar 1978) but now hybridity and new ethnicities are a given. In any case with demographers predicting on the basis on the 2011 Census findings that 'mixed race' will soon become the biggest category of ethnic group such essentialism and presuppositions of racial binaries and mutually exclusive categories have little or no place in modern London. As old 'them' and 'us' boundaries dissolve, the same applies to the dangers of dichotomies when it comes to thinking about the inner city and the suburb.

Notes

1 http://news.bbc.co.uk/1/hi/uk_politics/vote_2005/frontpage/4496247.stm. Also a survey conducted by Ipsos Mori for the *Eastern Eye* newspaper before the 2001 General Election for Eastern Eye found that 90 per cent of British Asians were loyal to the United Kingdom in the war against terrorism (the figure among Muslims was 87 per cent).

2 A US version of this remade as the Ortegas (a Hispanic family) commissioned by the Fox networks was never aired due to scheduling difficulties.

3 For example in the *New York Times* exotic travelogue feature (Rappeport 2006): 'A Real Taste of South Asia? Take the Tube to Southall', oddly named so as there is no London underground line there.

4 Numerous articles on Kureishi have been penned. *Londonstani* was central to the thesis of Blake Brandes I examined at Kent University Autumn 2011.

5 http://www.bbc.co.uk/programmes/b01pw38v

6 www.bbc.co.uk/asiannetwork/features/desi_dna.shtml.

7 www.bfi.org.uk/live/video/561.

8 https://signup.netflix.com/Search?v1=Suburban%20Dysfunction.

Conclusion: Same As it Ever Was?

It's so bloody nice. . . . Felicity treacle Kendal and Richard sugar-flavoured snot Briers . . . they're nothing but a couple of reactionary stenotypes confirming a myth that everyone in Britain is a loveable middle-class eccentric and I hate them.

(Vyvian from the *Young Ones* on *The Good Life*, quoted in Bowes 1990:131)

This book has attempted to look at the framing and representation of suburbia by popular cultural texts including literary, onscreen and aural forms in order to draw some conclusions about suburbs from the multiplicity of depictions discussed. If suburbia has been the subject under the microscope then popular culture is the lens through which it has been viewed. Mass popular culture after all can be a catalyst for cultural incorporation and given that suburbia is a concept that eludes easy definition, its reproduction in popular culture has helped to shape the concept in the popular imagination. Uniting all of the phenomena discussed is an ostensible desire to entertain the masses. The book has attempted to come up to date from the imagery of the Gray Flannel Suit and Pooter. A fuller account than space allows for here would consider other cultural forms or broader structural factors of socio-political change in suburbia but for now it can be said that the popular cultures discussed need to be located in context (i) alongside other competing media and culture, for example news reporting which commands sometime separate and sometimes overlapping audiences and (ii) against the backdrop of wider societal trends. Some of the cultural forms dealt with have distinctive conventions of genre and common plot devices (e.g. the sitcom) whereas others less obviously have categorical logics to them (e.g. popular music which covers sonically different styles, e.g. grime and Britpop). Literalness is not the primary aim of the portrayals that have been discussed here; dramatization in music, novels and onscreen representations of suburbia are as much about fantasy and escapism as they are to inform and practice social realism. They reflect suburban life as well as shaping it. Academics may dissect their narrative rhetoric but behind their messages and meanings most of what the Kinks, Orwell, Mike Leigh, the drama writers and all their peers that have appeared in the previous chapters have done is fundamentally the age-old art of storytelling, informing our understandings of suburbia along the way. In this way with their competing stories they have all contributed to the ambiguity of this somewhat liminal space of inbetween-ness: is it prison or promised land?

In some ways then the story of this book has been about erosion of the boundary between the categories of 'urban' and 'suburban' and the way that what we consider to be a suburb changes over time as have popular cultural forms. Pooter's suburban Holloway, now distinctly inner city, serves as a classic example. Light (1991:54) describes how 'late Victorian villadom so hated in its day [was] celebrated fifty years on by a new insecure middle class who were too busy attacking another generation of suburbanites to see the irony'. Her comment recalls Betjeman but the cycle often repeats, for example anti-suburban prejudice was a motivation behind the actions of the inner-city gentrifiers of the 1980s who moved to what were Victorian suburbs (Islington, Peckham, etc.) and whose own parents had raised them in interwar-built suburbia. She lists the Edwardian writer Ivy Compton-Burnett's list of examples of the vulgarity of the masses . . . 'the "coloured", the "youth", but also cinema-goers, thriller readers, those who live in the suburbs like Hampstead, buy shop flowers or shop cakes, or put milk in the cup first' (Light 1991:57). This all sounds quaintly anachronistic given recent history when difficulties that have faced London suburbs include riots (Ealing and Croydon, see Huq 2013) or UK-wide the decline of the high street in the face of online transactions, out of town shopping and recession. Since the trend towards the suburban novel began with the daily life chronicles of *Pooter* in *Punch* columns we have come a long way via Orwell's critical reflections, Delderfield's historical sweep of documentary through to post-apocalyptic science fiction and new Asian writing examples of which were looked at in Chapter 7 all of which have sustained the suburban tendency in fiction. The book itself has changed in form to a digital product accessed on an e-reader just as the physical product of music has been overtaken by digital downloads. The thirst for celebrity is seen now that both popstars and authors alike can be followed on twitter and with big book festivals (Haye on Wye, etc.) and big money prizes (The Booker, The Orange) as a result of which contemporary writers are not reclusive, cloistered individuals anymore. The form of the book has shrunk from clunky hardback to portable paperback and now the discreet, lightweight e-reader. When the erotic bondage themed novel *Fifty Shades of Grey* by a first-time author E. L. James (2011) revealed in disdainful tones to be a suburban mother of two it seemed appropriate that the book (followed by two subsequent titles making up a trilogy) became the first title ever to shift more copies in digital download rather than as hard copy as it could be read during a commute to and from the suburbs (where most people do their reading) without fellow passengers knowing what was being read.

Politically and demographically there is far greater diversity at work in suburbia than detractors would acknowledge. It is far more than a territory of 'conformist squadrons of Barratt estates told apart only by the cars on the drives' (Dean 2009). There are multiple suburbias which have all experienced continuity and change: Victorian and Edwardian areas of well-appointed detached villas in wide streets for the carriage classes, railway workers cottages, Edwardian terraces built for commuting clerks, planned 1930s semi-detacheds laid out on a grid-plan and postwar new-builds, residential settlements bordering industrial estates to name but a few types in Britain. Tenure varies too: the building societies helped home ownership explode but the financial downturn has helped expose the dangers of building economic strategy on an asset bubble. Meanwhile proto municipal garden suburbs were realized in council cottage estates rented on assured tenancies from local government; although the supply of social housing dried up after Thatcher whose policy of 'right to buy' sold these away from local authority control. In the United States there are the villas of the well-to-do as seen in the sets of television shows such as *Desperate Housewives* or more recently *Suburgatory* wrapped round with white picket fences yet there are also Levittowns, aluminium-sided cracker-box homes and even the dwellings of 'trailer trash'. There are differing cultures of suburbia in all of these as well as common constraints felt in all of them.

Representations feed into one another. Many of the cultural products referred to take more than one form sometimes spanning book, film, television series with accompanying theme song/hit record for example. The 1956 film *Man in the Grey Flannel suit* was repackaged for its 2011 DVD release with graphics similar to that of opening titles and DVD boxed sets of the popular drama serial *Mad Men* picturing a monochromatic suited city gent in a wide-brimmed hat. Representations similarly never take place in a vacuum. Industrial strife hit both *People Like Us* an ITV series based on Delderfield's Avenue books and Leslie Thomas's *Tropic of Ruislip* adapted for television as *Tropic* from ATV, which were never fully screened due to the disruption of the ITV strike of 1979. In Summer 2012 a dispute between the voiceover artists and Fox News also put the *Simpsons* continuation in peril. In answering the question set at the beginning, 'is there a separate category of "suburban"? popular culture it is probably safest to say that the term 'suburban' conceals a multiplicity of experiences meaning that if used as a category marker it runs the risk of oversimplifying social processes and over-determining by geography when structuring structures like social class, educational attainment ethnicity and gender are also predictors of life chances and cultures of the suburbs. Suburban representations have changed over time. Any depictions of any social phenomena are relational and context-specific and must be read in the light of broader socio-economic circumstances. Oil and house prices have underpinned the Western economy since at least the latter part of the twentieth century (Long 2011). Notwithstanding this, even factoring in economic downturn, the cost of the homes and cars we associate with the suburban lifestyle, has made this ideal more distant for many: more of a struggle for some and out of reach for others. Technology is also a driver of audience participation.

The rewinding of archival history through YouTube, Amazon, on-demand television catch-up services and any number of other mediums makes those circumstances and accompanying global context less straightforward than ever before, reflecting the complexity of contemporary suburbia which requires multiple understandings and mappings. J. R. Hartley would not have to trawl through the shops for *Flyfishing* anymore as in the old Yellow Pages television advertisement. The book could be found in a few clicks of a mouse. The art of accessing cultural products by smart phones and other handheld devices now feels more like leisure than 'computing', particularly as the action is now conducted via svelte, highly portable objects of desire not fixed components of the workspace. In allowing users to comment websites and blogs also become sounding board as well as technological means of view: opening up debate making them platforms in the widest sense. Audiences are affected by the music they listen to, books that they read and television and film that they watch but Frankfurt school-style models of the public as an undifferentiated mass or as vessels to be filled with the messages of popular culture ignore that the public may have very different, wildly divergent predispositions to begin with. The reception of active audiences is easy to overlook in rushing to solemnly declare that popular culture's relationship of suburban social norms is both to reflect (holding up a mirror to them) or reinforce them (acting more like a screwdriver). Cultural pessimists would argue that broadcasting, the literary arena, film and music industries have bowed to commercialism by privileging entertainment over information, popularity over quality and emotional appeal over reason in the age-old dumbing down debate but we have a situation of a shifting relationship between the production of cultural texts and their production in complex inter-related processes. New formats demand new research methodologies and theoretical paradigms. Technologies change but often core questions remain: you can just as easily dissect music listened to on ipods in a search for meaning as you could with that on gramophone records, the same goes for books read via modern e-readers.

Is there a descriptor of 'suburban' that we can apply to describe specifically suburban popular culture wedded to a set of values designed to embody a suburban aesthetic and appeal to a particularly suburban public? The answer is that if there is, it is constantly in flux. Different depictions represent different versions of suburbia: if you take Ballard's (2006) *Kingdom Come* Brooklands emerges as an unremittingly bleak dystopian wasteland lacking spiritual or moral backbone where cut-throat consumer culture has triumphed. However earlier portrayals saw the suburbs as a veritable utopia. Suburbia is complex construction, it is more than a place on a map. It is a territory that, despite being portrayed as stifling straitjacket is flexible: constantly changing and displaying a seemingly limitless capacity to adapt to circumstances. Suburbia, as we have seen, can be socially constructed, literally constructed and culturally constructed. Popular culture's ever multiplying forms and varied versions of suburbia capture the transformations undergone by wider society. This can be heard in the music which has soundtracked suburbia, read on the page and seen on the large and small screens where suburbia has been reflected and refracted. The suburbs were conceived in optimism. When talking of the UK social housing variety envisaged as 'homes fit for heroes' for returning ex-servicemen, Bayliss (2002:376) for example describes 'low density, quasi rural estates complete with winding lanes, cottages, gardens, trees and greens'. Arguably some of these council cottage estates have not fared well and are exhibiting distinct signs of wear and tear around their centenary period. Alongside ideas of 'white flight' we can also now talk of 'brown flight' (for suburbanising black and Asian people) or perhaps even 'yellow flight' (to describe eg the South Korean Asians of New Malden), Huq (2013).

Suburbia has become a popular idiom for multiple cultural products from pop videos to lengthy novels and other forms that this book has not gone into such as advertising where the suburbs are often seen in print and onscreen, for example as home to the Oxo family whose round-the-dinner table talk appeared in the spaces in between programmes to British television viewers for generations. The resulting body of work offers us a view of suburbia from multiple perspectives and it can be concluded from it that, without us realizing it, suburbia has become a potent cultural signifier as seen in the title of the Grammy 2011 album of the year *The Suburbs*, a surprise win awarded to a long player from Canada's Arcade Fire.

The book has attempted to look at examples where the suburbs shape the end product rather than being the incidental backdrop as could be argued was the case with, for example the films *Donnie Darko* (a teenage misfit in a peripheral neighbourhood) and *Shaun of the Dead* (zombies rampage around mock-Tudor streets). Suburban values, themselves in a state of continual renewal and modification, are then often to be inferred rather than directly stated sometimes from cautionary tales of life on the perimeter. Even cartoons which are *prima facie* aimed at children have depicted the social structures of the suburbs with recent examples openly critical of the 'them' and 'us' binary logics that the privatized world of suburbia can connote. The 2011 CGI (computer-generated image) feature film *Gnomio and Juliet* put a suburban twist on Shakespeare's *Romeo and Juliet* in a twenty-first century update designed for children. The setting of a pair of semi-detached houses in Verona Drive was scene of an age-old raging feud between the Montague and Capulet families with visual cues of Red and the Blue painted households and gnomes in their adjoining front and back gardens. The stylistic vernacular is the territory of Dunroamin familiar to the British. Dreamworks' *Over the Hedge* (2006) also hinted at similar themes in poking fun at the futility of narrow-minded parochialism implied by the sense of exclusionary practices that suburbs conjure up with the wasting of food and disregard for the environment also criticized – all from the perspective (and at the eye level) of backyard animals. Even if the suburbs as we see them in popular culture are geographically idealized and in political-administrative terms they are territorially bounded, suburbia as a set of attitudes cannot be cordoned off from its wider global, national, regional and local networks.

Popular culture was seen by Frankfurt School sociologists as a means through which dominant values are reaffirmed. The function of representations was to reproduce cultural norms be this quintessential Englishness or the American dream. The old model of popular culture forcibly effecting a systematic reproduction and reaffirmation of stereotypes, if it ever held true in the first place, is increasingly difficult to sustain given the flowering of new interactive cultural forms. For many years it felt as though portrayals of suburbia appeared to have responded very little in the changes to suburbia's increasing demographic and economic diversity. Cultural constructions of suburbia accordingly seemed to have conformed to an ideal type with the comfortably off white nuclear family, headed by male breadwinner dad and doting housewife mother repeatedly portrayed in films, television and even pop music and the novel. However changes appear to be underway. Recent years are showing a new narrative of economic uncertainty pervade the images we receive of suburbia through the media: popular culture does not operate divorced from national and international contexts or the prevailing political context. Reality television has been fastest to capture this historical moment with a clutch of programmes reflecting the recessionary climate as seen in Chapter 5. There is now growing recognition on the part of television programme-makers as well as viewers that white suburbia no longer represents the only legitimate suburban form worthy of being beamed at the masses. After years of accusations of its television sitcoms being unreflective of changes in British society, in 2011 the BBC axed the programme *My Family* following an 11-year run. The official reason was that it was time to move comedy on following the leaving of the nest of all of the children in the show. Critics were keen to dance on the grave of the show which had been most notable for its narrowness of focus with a cloyingly smug white middle-class suburban nuclear unit at its core (Gee 2011). It seemed that the constituency that primetime suburban family sitcom is aimed at and depicts is fragmenting. Suburban television must constantly update itself: the *Sopranos* and *Desperate Housewives* may have ended in the US but their "dramedy" style live on in *Breaking Bad* and *Suburgatory*. Other public discourses saw opponents of depicting diversity marginalized: when the producer of ITV's *Midsomer Murders*, set in an English village declared that he believed that the programme had succeeded due to its all-white cast, an inevitably media-led debate on plausibility and racism ensued and his swift sacking followed. The programme was not (even) set in suburbia but the furore showed the unacceptability of such statements in 2011. Old media offered a minimal level of interaction but today's cultural consumers are not always voiceless and powerless, for example reality shows audience role is decisive. Now more than ever all cultural texts exhibit inter-textuality, where they are inter-related to other texts. With forums and blogs the product in itself is never complete, it is difficult to ever have the final word.

It is important to remember that the mass-produced popular culture that communicates the suburban condition to us today exists in the shadow of previous versions: both the suburbs and television, novels pop, and film all now have a legacy and archival history rich for postmodern plunder. It is for this reason that cultural products as diverse as Blur's *Modern Life is Rubbish* album, Malkani's *Londonstani*, the film *Far from Heaven* and *The Simpsons* contain liberal sprinklings of pastiche, parody and satire among their constituent elements. Suburban commuting clerks or pen-pushers of the Pooter variety of today will most likely have a lengthened journey into the city as suburbia has expanded in enormity and their work now would involve IT making them instead button-pressers. They need not however keep their diaries simply to themselves: a worldwide audience is beckoned by social media, tweeting and blogging if they should wish to bring their thoughts to wider attention. The small screen has become bigger in terms of display inches but flatter in depth. We no longer talk of demand on the UK national grid at big televisual spectacles as the system struggles to cope when people put on the kettle after, for example as with the shooting of JR on *Dallas* (1980) but even with the changed way in which we view television, some 25 million in the United Kingdom still watched 2011's Royal Wedding live. Formats also alter as appetites have changed. Canned laughter is now rare on television sitcom, indeed the sitcom in its old incarnation is itself rare having been replaced by newer forms such as the comedy drama (*Shameless Desperate Housewives*), improvisation-based comedy (*Outnumbered*) and other shows which are filmed in almost documentary style (*The Royle Family, The Office*). With time what is new and improved can also become familiar as was the case with alternative humour with its studied amateurism as seen in *The Young Ones*. While we may be frustrated at how the lives of suburb-dwellers onscreen appear to be ones of tranquil insularity, the fact that shooting schedules cannot forsee real time events in part explains this. In *Mad Men* historical events like the Kennedy assassination serve as a framing device for the drama but this is only possible as the show is being made decades after these occurrences and we see things though twenty-first-century filters of acceptability. In the same way as the film *Far from Heaven* does, the tv series *Mad Men* shows subversion of the narrow-minded attitudes of the past. In *A Single Man* (2009), a grieving gay male struggles to come to terms with being denied access to his dead partner's funeral as it has been restricted to 'close family only'. Legrain (2011:38) is among those who debunk the myth of a former golden age claiming that in the 1950s 'Britain, for instance, was a country riven by class, where women were second-class citizens and gays imprisoned'. It is erroneous to cling on to an imagined past that never was and the safe distance of these two examples representing and the 1950s/1960s era of their setting exposes the faults of these times.

The heterogeneity and capacity for reinvention/renewal of suburban pop music and indeed of suburban strains of all of the popular cultural forms discussed here expose as hollow the idea that popular culture is all about reproduction of traditional norms. Among television ratings successes of recent years was ITV's *Downton Abbey*, a portrayal of decadent toffs in a country house at the turn of the last century. The BBC followed suit with a dusting off of 1970s hit *Upstairs Downstairs* remade for the twentieth century as a highlight of the Christmas 2010 programming schedule. The 1980s recession spawned the popular *Brideshead Revisited* and various Victorian era-set nostalgia programmes (*Last Days of the Raj, Jewel in the Crown, Passage to India*). Perhaps when times are hard we retreat into nostalgia, costume drama and period pieces of when Britannia really did rule the waves. Elsewhere other offerings during the same festive 2010 season included re-runs of less lavish television suburban-set Christmas specials picturing humdrum 1970s suburbia: *Terry and June* (in which an empty nester middle-aged couple in Purley quiver at the thought of the boss Sir Denis popping in), the *Good Life* (domestic sustainability practiced by a couple whose male wage-earner turns his back on the rat race unlike the materialist couple next door) and *Butterflies* (an inept, i.e. bad-at-cooking housewife who daydreams about her love for a mysterious dark stranger which is unrequited). In an age of complexity the throwback to simpler times is striking. Seen from the standpoint of the new millennium viewers of these programmes will now regard them as historical artefact with added kitsch value.

We are fortunate to have the gains of feminism to take for granted: recognized rights which were once the hard-fought such as nursery entitlement, paternity and maternity leave, abortion, fertility treatment, contraception and equal pay – albeit with glass ceilings in place. The same point can be made about anti-discrimination legislation with reference to gays, ethnic and religious minorities who are all part of modern suburban population composition. Yet there is still a way to go to achieve true equality and the realization of 'having it all'. The modern woman in suburbia or society at large is much more likely than that of her mother's generation to be economically independent, better educated, earning a higher salary in a more professional position, better represented in politics and single/childless for longer. Yet as pointed out by Hilary Clinton on her last day of office as US Secretary of State achieving gender equality remains the unfinished business of the twentieth century. Unlike Marxist feminists we should recognize in the words of Bill Clinton, it is not just 'the economy stupid' but we should seek to change culture too to continue to combat injustice on the basis of gender, sexuality and ethnicity. In her autobiography Margaret Thatcher claimed that in her career as a woman in politics she needed to be better than the men around her to compensate for her gender; it seems wrong that women should only be able make it by apeing men and on masculine terms. Women's additional roles mean that they are frequently doing a "triple shift" of homemaker/work/childcare. It is equally important that one type of dependence (on men) or bondage (to the housework) is not substituted for another in enslavement by the working routine or to the vagaries of fashion, which McRobbie (2009) fears can be seen in reality/lifestyle programmes such as *What Not to Wear* and *Ten Years Younger* whereby old social hierarchies are re-established in the view presented of the ideal woman, often all the more pernicious as castigation of those 'who get it wrong' is by women. Just as Friedan noted in the 1960s women are still juggling multiple roles: in our ageing society being carer to elderly parents is also a modern responsibility. Additionally grandparenting now includes childcare responsibilities as lone parents and couples must work all the hours that god sends in an attempt to service a suburban lifestyle as housing and childcare costs rise.

Each chapter of this book has dealt with a separate aspect of popular culture in order to seek a better understanding of the suburbs. Just as suburbia means multiple things, popular cultural platforms and channels have diversified dramatically in recent history offering overlapping pleasures of its texts. The old order of cultural custodians has been challenged by new and social media. Transformation has been rapid. As an avid consumer of cultural products spanning five decades I can note that I was initially raised in a household with only one black and white television receiver. For much of my youth there were only three British television channels (pre-Channel 4 in 1982).[1] Now there are countless alternatives on offer to anyone looking to access popular culture in our modern multi-channel, multi-platform world. You need not even own a television set to watch television thanks to online catch-up services. The CD was once revolutionary succeeding the once revolutionary cassette. The latter inspired both the volumes of Du Gay et al. (1997) and Bull (2000) on personal stereo, that is magnetic tape player, but both this and the CD now are distinctly archaic as music has dematerialized in digital downloads making a solid disc look demoded. The multiplicity of ways that media can be received also is a factor for consideration. People may listen to music or watch television or films for a number of reasons: diversion and escape from everyday situations or concerns, to satisfy curiosity, to alleviate boredom or to identify with particular products or values (Huq 2006). These basic functions have been termed as a consideration of 'Uses and Gratifications' (McQuail 1972; McQuail et al. 1972). Watching television in early adverts for television sets was portrayed as a group activity with a box of delights centrally positioned in communal space acting as a bonding mechanism for the (implicitly white nuclear) family but in reality it may be a side or supplementary activity, the other things it is secondary to are multiplied with the availability of new media allowing people to be in front of the internet and television at once. While Hoggart wrote famously on the uses of literacy (1958) the uses of media and popular culture have multiplied and people do not just devote their attention to one form at a time. Many television programmes will now have a hash tag for a twitter feed given out regularly on the show inviting viewers to publically comment and share their instantaneous reactions with others while they watch. Part of the attraction of television as marketed to the suburb dweller was that it was a night out on the town without the risk of leaving your front door. In this way it was a cultural leveller. In theory Broadband too is just a preserve of the suburban as it is for the city dweller and country resident – although connection times can be frustratingly slow in some rural locations.

Cunningham (2004:424) refers to Victorian times in stating 'It is perhaps unsurprising, then, that suburbia should be recognized at least as much by attitude as by location. If it was not always easy to tell what or where a "suburb" was, it was always simple to define something as "suburban": the object becomes less nominal than adjectival, less a bounded entity than a conglomeration of attitudes'. The observation still holds true: the suburb is in many ways looked down on as the second-order city: of its margins and not really an integral part of it. Suburban popular culture often seems to mirror this condescension: taking place in comic context. Yet in the downturn, imagery of the suburbs as self-satisfied and (semi) detached from the harshness of city life is out of line with reality: hard times on the edge are upon us as I have written elsewhere (Huq 2011; 2013). The complexity of the outer city is just as pronounced as it is at the core of the metropolis. Insecurity breeds falling living standards in both. For years now it has been claimed that there is cultural convergence too between national cultures sped up by globalization and cultural imperialism. Taylor (2000:138) is not alone in arguing that we are witnessing 'the Americanization of British everyday life'. The US Right-wing Tea Party movement have led a nostalgic campaign for the America that their fathers and the founding fathers knew (Tea Party Patriots 2010). Among slogans used by the French student protestors both in late 2010 and earlier against proposed pension reforms has been 'We want what our parents had' (Dilday 2006). Popular culture can be a catalyst for cultural incorporation, validation and reproduction, for example as a barometer for the acceptability of ethnic communities or presenting suburbia as an ideal type category. Some of the examples looked at are whimsical others are more angry. Some are trashy and low-budget (the low-fi of punk, shoestring independent cinema, the British situation comedies where it almost looks like the plywood sets quiver at times). Others have had serious money spent on them and generated large receipts. Suburbia needs to be considered in a frame of reference away from the ever-looming shadow of *Terry and June*. Politically suburbia is slowly shifting centre-stage, in the UK for example, in talk of the 'squeezed middle' and the ring doughnut strategy pursued by Boris Johnson successfully when mayoral candidate for London. After years of neglect from policy-makers this can only be welcomed (Huq 2013).

In the episode of BBC2 anarchic student flat-sharing commentary *The Young Ones* that the quote at the top of this chapter is drawn, the hippie character Neil's parents who pay him a visit and his dad asks him despairingly 'Why can't you be in one of those decent situation comedies that your mother likes?' Some surreal banter follows before the opening titles of the *Good Life* with gentle woodwind melody strike up before the punk character Viviyan rips his way through the picture to declare 'We're not watching the bloody *Good Life*' before shouting a volley of 'bloody bloody' exclamations and making the statement above. Alternative comedy, to which stable *The Young Ones* belonged, was itself culturally significant in the 1980s when it emerged as it deliberately set out to be anti-racist and anti-sexist unlike the sitcoms and stand-up performers of old and appeal to a youth audience-share in the process. The point being made by Viviyan above that is that there is a mismatch between the suburban niceness we are invited to view on the *Good Life* and the harsher reality of modern Britain. The status quo that viewers are invited to uphold is being for once disrupted not perpetuated. Certainly many features that have become present now on the suburban landscape were long ignored by television, film, novels and to a lesser degree pop. In consequence the suburbia as seen in some of the best-known historic depictions is probably more of a symbolic landscape than a real place where lifeworlds are territorially bounded and geographically idealized as far from danger with women and children first and the male breadwinner working hard in the cut-throat city to provide them their privileged suburban life. Within this set-up the most obvious historic omissions include ethnic diversity and the working classes. At other times television has played on a mismatch principle where new *arrivistes* are transplanted to the suburbs particularly in comedy, for example *Birds of a Feather* with two east-end girls made-good moving to nouveau-riche suburban Chigwell in Essex. However in the second decade of the second millennium it is now impossible to imagine humour derived from a situation such as that in *Mixed Blessings* or *Love Thy Neighbour* or a character such as the stereotyped Japanese/Chinese neighbour played by Mickey Rooney in *Breakfast at Tiffanys*.

Portrayals produced retrospectively set in earlier time periods show that anxiety and tension have always been present in the suburbs even if contemporaneous depictions did not always cover this: for example, the multiple neuroses of Betty from *Mad Men* as compared to relatively carefree life of the character played by Doris Day in *Please Don't Eat the Daisies*. The climate seems to be ever-sunny in both and both women are housewives but Betty feels repressed and lacking satisfaction whereas Day's character throws herself into organizing the school-play. Doubtless many of the audiences of earlier onscreen depictions would have found difficulty recognizing their lives in the idyllic suburbia with all problems airbrushed away as seen in earlier eras which glossed over the negative features of suburbia. Today most would most likely have to be working mums to make ends meet. In an age of media literacy it seems less likely that audiences will unthinkingly swallow what is served up before them without programme-makers being aware of disapproval, which can be registered by tweeting or in the founding of a Facebook group in seconds. Mike's *Young Ones* rejoinder 'That's a highly articulate outburst there, Vyv. I only hope they're not watching', is less easy to hope for with i-player and YouTube archiving television history on a scale never seen before. Un-missable television and the songs you can't live without hearing have a new double-meaning as opportunities to access them expand rendering them unavoidable. Some time ago Iain Chambers (1986:196) talked of 'protected suburban livers [*sic*], distant from the inner-city zones of poverty and neglect'. In contemporary times this sounds hopelessly outmoded as the two categories are becoming ever-more similar in their characteristics. The move to the suburbs often signalled a relief for pent up city dwellers, an exhalation of air. By the late 1970s with rising oil prices and pressures on working wives an ITV suburban-set sitcom had appeared called *A Sharp Intake of Breath* with a title capturing the reverse. Anxious times on the edge are evermore present with the onset of the financial downturn. Nevertheless both suburbia and the popular culture that represent it are far more dynamic than has been assumed by their critics. As the chapters of this book have shown, in keeping with the 'vibrancy' marketing claim of suburban boroughs, the contemporary suburb has a vitality that cannot be overlooked due to its urban mix of ethnic, religious, age, cultural, land-use and racial diversity. In the US too public policy has responded to suburban happenings: in December 2012 a horrific school shooting at Newtown, Connecticut, long featured in US suburban depictions as at the edge of New York looked almost certain to usher in attempts at tightening American gun laws.

Future directions for the popular culture's representation of suburbia are likely to be shaped by technological advance. Moores (2004:23) has argued that the media settings of phenomena including the internet and mobile phones are overlaid with the physical location of the users and that 'electronically mediated communication transcends the boundaries of physical settings'. As we have seen throughout digital communications mean a dematerialization of some popular cultural form, for example book to e-book and CD to MP3 or i-tunes file and played through services like Lastfm or Spotify which serve as digital jukeboxes. Onscreen representations are accessed differently, for example streamed via digital catch up services, on YouTube or through on-demand services like Netflix or Lovefilm. Even the cinema has changed from suburban high street fleapit to exurban leisure park. New technology brings new forms of cultural spectacle. At a public lecture at the London School of Economics (LSE) Paul Gilroy (2012) termed a range of phenomena of electronically perpetuated racism 'digitalia'. This includes the rash of internet racism videos, for example the woman spouting racial abuse on the Croydon tram in 2011 that went viral, who he pointed out was a member of the white dispossessed working class from New Addington, a council estate in Croydon borough making it effectively a suburb of a suburb. These are accompanied by user commentary as occurs with all youtube content. Other examples where social media became the news itself included the Robin Hood airport tweeter who was likened to John Betjeman and the poem 'Slough' for his tweet: 'Crap! Robin Hood Airport is closed. You've got a week and a bit to get your sh** together, otherwise I'm blowing the airport sky high.' His claim that it was sent during a moment of frustration while the airport in England's midlands region was closed by snow was finally accepted when the initial verdict which saw him being fined for sending a 'menacing tweet' was overturned by appeal. He was flanked by comedians/prolific tweeters Al Murray and British 'national treasure', Stephen Fry, during his court appearance. Twitter in part has assumed such popularity as it allows the ordinary person in the suburbs feel connected to the celebrities that they follow and direct post to their newsfeed in instantaneous real time. Various public figures have come a cropper after hasty tweets which had to be hastily withdrawn as they had had no clearance from further up the chain, for example Labour's Diane Abbot MP for saying that whites like to play a game of divide and rule or Adian Burley the Conservative MP who tweeted that the widely praised London 2012 Olympic games opening ceremony staged by Danny Boyle, the director of *Trainspotting* and *Slumdog Millionaire* was 'lefty multicultural crap'. These interactions also show how the boundaries of public and private are blurring. You do not even have to be present to be an expert on suburban viral events, or even in the same country as their unfolding. Footage of rioting in suburban areas such as Ealing and Croydon shot on camera phones seeped out on YouTube in 2011 inspiring academic articles and blogposts aplenty (Huq 2013a). In 2012 I witnessed a presentation from a professor from Finland at a conference in Istanbul, Turkey, talking about racial abuse on a tram in New Addingdon (Dervin 2012).

As the global financial crisis took root Farrar (2008) claimed for CNN 'Devastated by the subprime mortgage crisis, hundreds of homes have been foreclosed and thousands of residents have been forced to move, leaving in their wake a not-so-pleasant path of empty houses, unkempt lawns, vacant strip malls, graffiti-sprayed desolate sidewalks and even increased crime.' The assumptions made by the *Young Ones* sketch of suburbia as unremittingly nice no longer hold and arguably never did. The office space in suburbs and number of people working from home who do not require offices to do so thanks to broadband for example belies them as simply dormitory towns to service a city-working population. The argument that suburbia needs to be treated on its own terms seems to be gaining ground just at the same moment that it is taking on more and more urban characteristics. After all what we think of as the suburbs changes over time. Put another way yesterday's suburbia is often the inner city of today. For Avila (2006) the suburbs meant 'the decentralization of urban life'. Manifold evidence exists of movement in both directions as the inner city and suburb gradually elide into one another. Inner-city gentrification by taking what were multi-occupancy dwellings (typically bedsits) into single-family ownership with their own gardens is actually upholding the suburban ideal that it was a reaction against, in effect suburbanizing the city. The gated community is nothing if not a modern twist on the suburban home where defensible space rules supreme. *Slate* magazine (Lemann 1997) declares that 'suburbia won'. While this might be overstating the case by implying that the suburb and inner city have been at war, the popular culture examples discussed vividly serve as evidence of the dynamic nature of the suburbs; these are not dead places but very much alive being both creative and a stimulus for creativity. From the Essex marshes of *Fishtank* to the slang-filled neon-lit streets of *Londonstani*'s Hounslow via multiple examples of suburbs in the US, Canada and Australia, representations of the suburbs are increasingly voluminous and diverse. As for the 'happy ending' that all good cultural products crave, it can be concluded that suburbia is a concept that is constantly in a state of renewal but importantly one for which it is far from the end of the road.

Note

1 Indeed the BBC had only one channel until ITV began broadcasting in 1955, although this is before my recollection.

Bibliography

Aaron, M. (ed.) (2004) *New Queer Cinema: A Critical Reader*. New Jersey: Rutgers University Press.

Ackroyd, P. (2000) *London: The Biography*. London: Vintage.

Akass, K. and McCabe, J. (eds) (2006) *Reading Desperate Housewives: Beyond the White Picket Fence*. London: IB Tauris.

Alam, M. and Husband, C. (2005) *British-Pakistani Men from Bradford: Linking Narratives to Policy*. New York: Joseph Rowntree Foundation.

Anderson, B. (2006) *Imagined Communities*. London: Verso.

Andrews, M. (1998) 'Butterflies and Caustic Asides: Housewives, Comedy and the Feminist Movement', in S. Wagg (ed.), *Because I Tell a Joke or Two: Comedy, Politics and Social Difference*. London: Routledge, pp. 50–64.

Ann Leslie/BBC (1991) *Think of England: Dumroamin*, screened BBC2, 5 November 1991.

Anwar, M. (1978) *Between Two Cultures: a Study of Relationships between Generations in the Asian Community in Britain*. London: Commission for Racial Equality.

Applebaum, S. (2010) 'Interview: Todd Solondz', *Jewish Chronicle*, 8 April, at: www.thejc. com/arts/arts-interviews/30191/interview-todd-solondz.

Avila, E. (2006) *Popular Culture in the Age of White Flight: Fear and Fantasy in Suburban Los Angeles*. Berkeley, CA: University of California Press.

Ballard, J. G. (1979) *The Unlimited Dream Company*. London: Paladin

— (1997) 'The Ultimate Departure Lounge' at: http://jgballard.com/airports.htm.

— (1998) *Running Wild*. London: Flamingo.

— (Spring 2001) '"Welcome to the virtual city"', in Urban myth', *Tate, The Art Magazine*, 24, p. 33.

— (2003) *Millennium People*. London: Harper Perennial.

— (2006) *Kingdom Come*. London: Fourth Estate.

— (2008) *Miracles of Life: An Autobiography Shanghai to Shepperton*. London: Harper Perennial.

Barker, P. (2009) *The Freedoms of Suburbia*. London: Frances Lincoln.

Bauman, Z. (2004) *Community: Seeking Safety in an Insecure World*. Cambridge: Polity.

Baxter, J. (ed.) (2008) *J. G. Ballard: Contemporary Critical Perspectives*. London: Continuum.

Bayliss, D. (2003) 'Building Better Communities: Social Life on London's Cottage Council Estates, 1919–1939', *Journal of Historical Geography*, 29(3), pp. 376–95.

Baym, B. (Fall 1984) 'Review of "*The Witches of Eastwick*"', *The Iowa Review*, 14(3), pp. 165–70.

BBC (2009a) 'Landmarks: The Norman Conquests', 13 April 2001, at: www.bbc.co.uk/ programmes/b00jlc1l.

— (2009b) 'Anger over ITV Duchess Programme', 18 September, at: http://news.bbc. co.uk/1/hi/8207003.stm.

— (2009c) www.bbc.co.uk/pressoffice/proginfo/radio/2009/wk15/mon.shtml.

Bennett (2000) *Music, Identity and Place*. Basingstoke: Palgrave Macmillan.

Betjeman, J. (2009) *Betjeman's England,* introduction by Stephen Games. London: John Murray.

Betti, J. (1995) 'Class Dismissed? Roseanne and the Changing Face of Working-Class Iconography', *Social Text*, 45(14), pp. 125–49.

Beuka, R. (2001) 'Just One Word . . . "Plastics": Suburban Malaise, Masculinity, and Oedipal Drive in *The Graduate*', *Journal of Popular Film and Television*, 28(1), pp. 12–21.

— (2004) S*uburbianation: Reading Suburban Landscape in Twentieth-Century American Fiction and Film*. New York: Palgrave Macmillan.

BFI (undated) 'Race and the Sitcom', at: www.screenonline.org.uk/tv/id/1108234/index. html.

Bhanot, K. (2010) *Too Asian Not Asian Enough*. Birmingham: Tindall Street.

Billen, A. (1994) 'The Billen Interview: Andrew Billen Visits Author J. G. Ballard in his Peeling Semi to Discuss Class, Feminism and the Material World', *The Observer*, Sunday, 7 August, at: www.guardian.co.uk/books/1994/aug/07/ sciencefictionfantasyandhorror.jgballard.

Bluemel, K. (Fall 2003) '"Suburbs are not so bad I think": Stevie Smith's Problem of Place in 1930s and '40s London', *Iowa Journal of Cultural Studies* at: www.uiowa.edu/~ijcs/ suburbia/bluemel.htm.

Boorman, J. (2003) *Adventures of a Suburban Boy*. London: Faber and Faber.

Borthwick, S. and Moy, R. (2004) *Popular Music Genres: An Introduction*. Edinburgh: Edinburgh University Press.

Bowes, M. (1990) 'Only When I Laugh', in A. Goodwin and G. Whannel (eds), *Understanding Television Studies*. London: Routledge, pp. 131–43.

Bracewell, M. (2002) *The Nineties: When Surface Was Depth*. London: Flamingo.

Bragg, B. (2006) *The Progressive Patriot*. London: Bantam Press.

Brah, A. (1 April 1999) 'The Scent of Memory: Strangers, Our Own, and Others', *Feminist Review*, 61(1), pp. 4–26.

Brewer, C. (2010) 'Theater in Chicago: Detroit at Steppenwolf Defines the New Reality', at Show Me Chicago site, 21 November, at: www.chicagonow.com/ show-me-chicago/2010/09/theater-in-chicago-detroit-at-steppenwolf- defines-the-new-reality/.

Brooker, C. (2011) 'Midsomer's Plain Daft. So Why Might Adding Brown Faces Make Viewers Suspend Disbelief?' in *The Guardian*, 21 March, at: www.guardian. co.uk/commentisfree/2011/mar/21/charlie-brooker-midsomer-murders?INTCMP =SRCH.

Brown, M. (2008) 'Hanif Kureishi: A Life Laid Bare', *Daily Telegraph*, 23 February, at:
   www.telegraph.co.uk/culture/books/3671392/Hanif-Kureishi-A-life-laid-bare.html.

Brunsdon, C. (1997) *The Feminist, the Housewife and the Soap Opera*. Oxford:
   Clarendon Press.

— (Summer 2004) 'The Poignancy of Place: London and the Cinema', *Visual Culture in
   Britain*, 5(1), pp. 59–73.

Bueka, R. (2004) *Suburbia Nation: Reading Suburban Landscape in Twentieth-Century
   American Fiction and Film*. New York: Palgrave Macmillan.

Bull, M. (2000) *Sounding Out the City – Personal Stereos and the Management of
   Everyday Life*. Oxford: Berg.

Burdsey, D. (2007) 'Role with the Punches: The Construction and Representation of
   Amir Khan as a Role Model for Multiethnic Britain', *Sociological Review*, 55(3),
   pp. 611–31.

Caesar, E. (2005) 'Hard-Fi: The Staines massive', *The Independent*, 27 February, at: www.
   independent.co.uk/arts-entertainment/music/features/hardfi-the-staines-massive-4
   99660.html.

Cain, J. (1941) *Mildred Pierce*. New York: Alfred Knopf.

Campbell, J. (2008) 'Strange Fiction: J. G. Ballard Talks to James Campbell',
   The Guardian, 14 June, at: www.guardian.co.uk/books/2008/jun/14/
   saturdayreviewsfeatres.guardianreview10.

Campbell, S. (1999) 'Beyond "Plastic Paddy": A Re-Examination of the
   Second-Generation Irish in England', *Immigrants and Minorities*, 18(2&3), pp. 266–88.

— (2004) '"What's the Story?": Rock Biography, Musical "Routes" and the
   Second-Generation Irish in England', *Irish Studies Review*, 12(1), pp. 63–75.

Carey, J. (1992) *The Intellectuals and the Masses: Pride and Prejudice among the Literary
   Intelligentsia 1800–1939*. London: Faber and Faber.

Carney, R. (2000) *The Films of Mike Leigh: Embracing the World*. Cambridge: Cambridge
   University Press.

Castronovo, D. (2004) *Beyond the Gray Flannel Suit: Books from the 1950s that Made
   American Culture*. London: Continuum.

Caterall, A. (1998) 'Guru in Seven', *Empire*, August, at: www.empireonline.com/reviews/
   reviewcomplete.asp?FID=1203.

Chambers, D. (2001) *Representing the Family*. London: Sage.

Chambers, I. (1986) *Popular Culture: The Metropolitan Experience*. London: Methuen.

Chambers, S. (2006) 'Desperately Straight: The Subversive Sexual Politics of Desperate
   Housewives', in K. Akass and J. McCabe (eds), *Reading Desperate Housewives: Beyond
   the White Picket Fence*. London: IB Tauris, pp. 31–41

Channel 4 (undated) *Desperate Housewives*, at: www.channel4.com/programmes/
   desperate-housewives.

Charlton, E. (2006) 'Houellebecq manqué: Eliza Charlton Reviews *Tourism* by Nirpal
   Singh Dhaliwal', *Daily Telegraph*, 11 April 2006 at: www.telegraph.co.uk/culture/
   books/3651478/Houellebecq-manque.html

Childs, P. (2000) 'Suburban Values and Ethni-Cities in Indo-Anglian Writing', in Webster, R. (ed.), *Expanding Suburbia: Reviewing Suburban Narratives*. Oxford and New York: Berghahn, pp. 91–107.

Clapson, M. (1998) *Invincible Green Suburbs, Brave New Towns: Social Change and Urban Dispersal in Postwar England*. Manchester: Manchester University Press.

— (2003) *Suburban Century: Social Change and Urban Growth in England and the USA*. Oxford: Berg.

Clarke, A. (1997) 'Tupperware: Suburbia, Sociality and Mass Consumption', in Silverstone (ed.), *Visions of Suburbia*. London: Routledge, pp. 132–60.

Clayton, E. (2008) 'Richard's Snapshot of Estate Life 25 Years', *Bradford Telegraph and Argus*, 22 May, at: www.thetelegraphandargus.co.uk/leisure/tatheatre/theatrefeatures/2288558.Richard___s_snapshot_of__Estate_life_25_years_on/.

Cleto, T. (1999) *Camp: Queer Aesthetics and the Performing Subject*. Michigan: University of Michigan Press.

Cloonan, M. (Summer 1997) 'State of the Nation: "Englishness", Pop and Politics in the Mid-1990's', *Popular Music and Society*, 21(2), pp. 47–70.

— (1999) 'Popular Music and the Nation-State: Towards a Theorisation', *Popular Music*, 18(2), pp. 193–207.

Colebrook, M. (2012) 'Have Conformity, Will Consume: Jonathan Franzen's *Freedom*' at Narratives of Suburbia, Colloquium, The University of Westminster, 15 June 2012.

Collins, A. (2004) *Where Did it All Go Right?: Growing Up Normal in the 70s*. London: Erbury.

Collins, R. (1982) 'From Subject to Object and Back Again: Individual Identity in John Cheever's Fiction', *Twentieth Century Literature*, 28(1), pp. 1–13.

Collins, W. (2008/1852) *Basil*. Oxford: Oxford University Press.

Coren, G. (2010) 'Giles Coren Lives the Good Life – But Not for Long', *Daily Mirror*, 10 November, at: www.mirror.co.uk/celebs/tv/news/2010/11/10/giles-coren-lives-the-good-life-but-not-for-long-115875-22705446/#ixzz1QUgg7ojv.

Cunningham, G. (2004) 'Houses in Between: Navigating Suburbia in Late Victorian Writing', *Victorian Literature and Culture*, 32(2), pp. 421–34.

— (2007) 'London Commuting: Suburb and City, the Quotidian Frontier', in G. Cunningham and S. Barber (eds), *London Eyes: Reflections in Text and Image*. New York and Oxford: Berghahn Books, pp. 7–25.

Cunningham, M. (1998) *The Hours*. London: Fourth Estate.

Daily Mail (2009) 'The Fergie Backlash (Part Two): Estate Erupts for a Second Time over TV Documentary', at: www.dailymail.co.uk/news/article-1207491/ITV-Duchess-programme-prompts-anger-Estate-erupts-second-time-TV-documentary.html#ixzz1IYDa0ZIX.

Daliwal, N. (2006) *Tourism*. London: Vintage Originals.

— (2007) 'Cameron Is Given a Black Eye by the Real Southall', *The Sunday Times*, 22 July.

Daniels, S. (2006) 'Suburban Pastoral: Strawberry Fields Forever and Sixties Memory', *Cultural Geographies*, 13(1), pp. 28–54.

Davies, J. (1995) 'All Bingo, Barbie and Barthes?' at: www.timeshighereducation.co.uk/
    story.asp?storyCode=97037&sectioncode=26.

De Stefano, G. (2007) *An Offer We Can't Refuse; The Mafia in the Mind of America*.
    London: Faber and Faber.

De Wilde, G. (2006) 'Put a Bit of Dub in Your Step', 14 October, at: www.telegraph.co.uk/
    culture/music/3655896/Put-a-bit-of-dub-in-your-step.html.

Dean, W. (2009) 'Hedgy Comedy', *The Guardian*, 28 March, at: www.guardian.co.uk/
    culture/2009/mar/27/comedy-television?INTCMP=ILCNETTXT3487.

Defino, D. (2002) 'Todd Solondz', in Y. Tasker (ed.), *Fifty Contemporary Filmmakers*.
    London and New York: Routledge, pp. 311–18.

Delderfield, R. F. (1958) *The Dreaming Suburb*. London: Hodder & Stoughton Ltd.

Dervin, F. (2012) 'Rants against Multiculturalism Caught on Camera in Britain: Racism
    Without Races?' in Steve Garner (ed.), *Debating Multiculturalism*. Dialogue Society
    at: www.dialoguesociety.org/publications/academia/768-debating-multiculturalism
    -2.html.

Devereux, E. (2006) Understanding the *Media*. London: Sage

Dickinson, G. (2006) 'The Pleasantville Effect: Nostalgia and the Visual Framing of
    (White) Suburbia', *Western Journal of Communication*, 70(3), pp. 212–33.

Dicks, B. (2004) *Culture on Display*. Buckinghamshire: Open University Press.

Dilday, K. (2006) 'A Question of Class, Race, and France Itself: Reply to Richard Wolin',
    3 May, at: www.opendemocracy.net/globalization-village/reply_wolin_3503.jsp.

Dines, M. (2009) *Gay Suburban Narratives in American and British Culture:
    Homecoming Queens*. Basingstoke: Palgrave Macmillan.

Ditum, S. (2010) 'Elisabeth Sladen's Sarah Jane: More than Just a Fantasy Mother',
    accessed on 22 October 2011at: www.guardian.co.uk/commentisfree/2011/apr/22/
    elisabeth-sladen-sarah-jane-doctor-who?INTCMP=ILCNETTXT3487.

Donaldson, S. (1969) *The Suburban Myth*. New York: Columbia University Press.

Donnell, A. (2007) 'Feeling Good? Look Again! Feel Good Movies and the Vanishing
    Points of Liberation in Deepa Mehta's *Fire* and Gurinder Chadha's *Bend It Like
    Beckham*', *Journal of Creative Communications*, 2(1–2), pp. 43–55.

Draper, D. (1997) *Blair's First Hundred Days*. London: Faber and Faber.

Du Gay, P., Hall, S., Janes, L., Mackay, H. and Negus, K. (1997) *Doing Cultural Studies*:
    The Story of the Sony Walkman. London and New York: Sage Publications.

English, R. (2009) '"You toffee-nosed git": How Duchess of Hoodies Fergie was Greeted
    on Shameless' Estate', 14 September, at: www.dailymail.co.uk/news/article-1205689/I
    TV-Duchess-programme-provokes-anger-How-Sarah-Ferguson-greeted-
    Shameless-estate.html#ixzz1IYFPuyfM.

Eugenides, G. (1994) *The Virgin Suicides*. London: Bloomsbury.

Farrar, L. (2008) 'Is America's Suburban Dream Collapsing into a
    Nightmare?' 16 June, at: http://articles.cnn.com/2008–06–16/tech/suburb.
    city_1_suburban-dream-cnn-yandell?_s=PM:TECH.

Fazackerley, A. (2006) 'Rumpled and Ready to Rumble', *Times Higher Education Supplement*, 27 January, at: www.timeshighereducation.co.uk/story.asp?storyCode=200976&sectioncode=26 (p. 7).

Feeney, M. (2005) 'The Voice of *Desperate Housewives:* It's Preachy and Banal. Just Like the Show', *Slate,* 23 May, at: www.slate.com/id/2119399/.

Ferguson, E. (2003) '300 Reasons Why We Love *The Simpsons*', *The Observer*, 20 April, at: www.guardian.co.uk/theobserver/2003/apr/20/features.review7.

Finnegan, R. (1989) *The Hidden Musicians: Making Music in an English Town.* Cambridge: Cambridge University Press.

Fisher, M. (7 July 1995) 'Indie Revolutionaries', *New Statesman and Society.*

Fornäs, J. and Lindberg, U. (1995) *In Garageland. Youth, Rock and Modernity*. London and New York: Routledge.

Franzen, J. (2010) *Freedom.* New York: Fourth Estate.

Freeman, N. (2010) 'Tony Blair's Memoir Vies with Franzen for Bad Sex in Lit Prize', *The New York Observer*, 18 October, at: http://observer.com/2010/10/tony-blairs-memoir-vies-with-franzen-for-bad-sex-in-lit-prize/.

Frey, W. (1979) 'Central City White Flight: Racial and Nonracial Causes', *American Sociological Review*, 44, pp. 425–48.

Friedan, B. (1963/2010) *The Feminine Mystique*. London and New York: Penguin Modern Classic.

Frith, S. (1997) 'The Suburban Sensibility in British Rock and Pop', in Silverstone, R. (ed.), *Visions of Suburbia*. London: Routledge, pp. 269–79.

Gabrielson, T. (2009) 'The End of New Beginnings: Nature and the American Dream in *the Sopranos, Weeds*, and *Lost*', *Theory & Event* [online], 12(2).

Gaines, D. (1991) *Teenage Wasteland: Suburbia's Dead End Kids*. New York: Pantheon Books.

Gammell, C. (2011) 'BBC to Introduce More Working Class Comedy', *Daily Telegraph*, 23 January, at: www.telegraph.co.uk/news/uknews/8277022/BBC-to-introduce-more-working-class-comedy.html.

Gardiner, J. (2010) *The Thirties: An Intimate History of Britain.* London: Harper Press.

Gardner, T. (2003) 'Beneath the Blue Suburban Skies', last modified 2007. *Turn Me On, Dead Man* blog at: www.turnemondeadman.org/Burb.

Garreau, J. (1991) *Edge City: Life on the New Frontier.* New York: Doubleday.

Gates, J. (2010) 'Looking Back: Sad Fate of Southall's "palace"', *Ealing Gazette*, 30 March, at: www.ealinggazette.co.uk/ealing-news/local-ealing-news/2010/03/30/looking-back-sad-fate-of-southall-s-palace-64767-26140654/.

Gee, C. (2011) '*My Family* should Have Been Axed Years Ago', *Daily Telegraph*, 25 March, at: www.telegraph.co.uk/culture/tvandradio/8407107/My-Family-should-have-been-axed-years-ago.html.

Gershuny, J. (2005) 'Busyness as a Badge of Honor for the New Superordinate Working Class', *Social Research*, 72(2), pp. 287–314.

Gett, S. (1984) *Success under Pressure*. New York: Cherry Lane Books.

Geyrhalter, T. (1996) 'Effeminacy, Camp and Sexual Subversion in Rock: The Cure and *Suede*', *Popular Music*, 15, pp. 217–24.

Gibson, W. (1984) *Neuromancer*. New York: Ace Science Fiction.

Gillespie, M. (1995) *Television, Ethnicity, and Cultural Change*. London: Routledge.

Gilroy, P. (2012) '"My Britain's Fuck All": *Zombie* Multiculturalism and the Race Politics of Citizenship', public lectured delivered at LSE on 30 May 2012.

Glancey, J. (2008) 'Osbert Lancaster: Savage Grace', *The Guardian*, 3 October, at: www.guardian.co.uk/artanddesign/2008/oct/03/osbert.lancaster.cartoon/print.

Goldsworthy, V. (2005) 'The Love that Dares Not Speak its Name: Englishness and Suburbia', in David Rogers and John MacLeod (eds), *Revisions of Englishness*. Manchester: Manchester University Press, pp. 95–106.

Govinden, N. (2007) *Graffiti My Soul*. Edinburgh: Canongate Books.

Green, N. (2005) 'Songs from the Wood and Sounds of the Suburbs: A Folk, Rock and Punk Portrait of England, 1968–1977', *Built Environment*, 31(3), pp. 255–70.

Grossmith, G. (1892/1997) *The Diary of a Nobody*. London: Penguin.

Grossmith, G. and Grossmith, W. (1892) *Diary of a Nobody*. London: Penguin.

Gunn, S. and Bell, R. (2003) *Middle Classes*. London: Cassell.

Hall, P. (2007) *London Lives: Tales from a Working Capital*. Bristol: Policy Press.

Hall, S. (1981) 'Notes on Deconstructing the "Popular"', in S. Samuel (ed.), *People's History and Socialist Socialist Theory*. London: Routledge and Kegan Paul, pp. 227–40.

Halper, T. and Muzzio, D. (2011) 'It's a Wonderful Life: Representations of the Small Town in American Movies', *European Journal of American Studies* [Online], Document 8, 30 December, at: http://ejas.revues.org/9398.

Harris, C. (1988) 'Images of Blacks in Britain, 1930–60', in S. Allen and M. Macey (eds), *Race and Social Policy*. London: ESRC, p. 53.

Harris, R. (2004) *Creeping Conformity: How Canada Became Suburban, 1900–1960*. Toronto: University of Toronto Press.

Harrison, J. (2010) 'Community Musical Hits Back at Estate's Negative Image', *Ealing Gazette*, 21 September, at: www.ealinggazette.co.uk/ealing-news/local-ealing-news/2010/09/21/community-musical-hits-back-at-estate-s-negative-image-64767–27311938/.

Hatten, C. (2007) 'Bad Mommies and Boy-Men: Postfeminism and Reactionary Masculinity in Tom Perrotta's *Little Children*', *Critique: Studies in Contemporary Fiction*, 48(3), pp. 230–49.

Held, D., McGrew, A., Goldblatt, D. and Perraton, J. (1999) *Global Transformations: Politics, Economics and Culture*. Stanford: Stanford University Press.

Helsby, W. (2005) *Understanding Representation* (Understanding the Moving Image). London: BFI.

Hinsliff, G. (2008) 'Ethnic Middle Classes Join the "White Flight"', *Observer*, 20 April, at: www.guardian.co.uk/world/2008/apr/20/race.communities.

Hoggart, R. (1958) *The Uses of Literacy*. London: Pelican Press.

Holland, P. (2000) *The Television Handbook*. London: Routledge.

Hornby, G. (2008) 'Life in the Fast Lane Will Soon be Over for "Top Gear" Blokes', *Telegraph*, 8 July, at: www.telegraph.co.uk/comment/personal-view/3560308/Life-in-the-fast-lane-will-soon-be-over-for-Top-Gear-blokes.html.

Hundal, S. (2005) 'How Television Still Suffers from Stereotyping', *The Independent*, 3 October.

Hunt, P. (2010) 'Introduction' to K. Grahame (2010 reissue), *The Wind in the Willows*. Oxford: Oxford University Press.

Hunt, T. (2004) *Building Jerusalem: The Rise and Fall of the Victorian City*. London: Weidenfield.

Huq, R. (2003) 'Urban Unrest in Northern England 2001: Rhetoric and Reality behind the "Race Riots"', in A. Lentin (ed.), *Learning from Violence: The Youth Dimension*. Strasbourg: Council of Europe, pp. 42–52.

— (2006) *Beyond Subculture: Youth, Pop and Identity in a Post-Colonial World*. Oxford: Routledge.

— (2007) 'The Sound of the Suburbs', *Soundings: A Journal of Politics and Culture*, 37, pp. 35–44.

— (2008a) 'Don't Sneer at Suburbia', *Public Policy Research*, 15(3), pp. 148–52.

— (2008b) 'The Sound of the Suburbs: The Re-Shaping of Englishness and the Socio-Cultural Landscape after New Labour', in Mark Perryman (ed.), *Imagined Nation: England after Britain*. London: Lawrence and Wishart, pp. 49–62.

— (2011) 'Rethinking Suburbia in an Age of Insecurity: Hard Times on the Edge', in *Exploring the Cultural Challenges to Social Democracy*. London: Policy Network, pp. 77–81.

— (2013a) *On the Edge: The Contested Cultures of English Suburbia*. London: Lawrence and Wishar.

Hussain, Y. and Bagguley, P. (July 2005) 'Citizenship, Ethnicity and Identity: British Pakistanis after the 2001 "Riots"', *Sociology*, 39(3), pp. 407–25.

ITV (2009) 'The Duchess on the Estate: Press Release', ITV Press Centre, 18 August, at: www.itv.com/presscentre/theduchessontheestate/ep1wk34/default.html.

Jack, I. (2008) 'We Are All Suburban Now', *The Guardian*, 20 December, at: www.guardian.co.uk/commentisfree/2008/dec/20/suburbia-revolutionary-road-comment?INTCMP=SRCH.

Jackson, K. (1985) *Crabgrass Frontier: The Suburbanization of the United States*. New York and Oxford: Oxford University Press.

Jahn, M. (1982) 'Suburban Development in Outer West London, 1850–1900', in Thompson, F. (ed.), *The Rise of Suburbia*. Leicester: Leicester University Press, pp. 93–156.

James, E. L. (2012) *Fifty Shades of Grey*. London: Arrow Books.

Jones, O. (2011) *Chavs: The Demonization of the Working Class*. London: Verso.

Jones, R. (2011) http://channelhopping.onthebox.com/2011/04/01/us-version-of-the-inbetweeners/.

Jorgensen, D. (2009) 'Middle America, the Moon, the Sublime and the Uncanny', in David Bell and Martin Parker (eds), *Sociological Review Special Issue: Sociological Review Monograph Series: Space Travel & Culture: From Apollo to Space Tourism*.

pp. 178–99, at: http://onlinelibrary.wiley.com/doi/10.1111/sore.2009.57.issue-s1/ issuetoc.

Jurca, C. (1999) 'The Sanctimonious Suburbanite: Sloan Wilson's *The Man in the Gray Flannel Suit*', *American Literary History*, 11(1), pp. 82–106.

Kaufer, E. (2009) 'Ally McBeal to Desperate Housewives: A Brief History of the Postfeminist Heroine', *Perspectives on Political Science*, 38(2), pp. 87–98.

Kaufman, S. (1967/2002) *Diary of a Mad Housewife*, new edn. London: Serpent's Tail.

Kibble-White, G. (2002) *20 Years of 'Brookside'* with an Introduction by Phil Redmond. London: Carlton Books Ltd.

Kidd, A. and Nicholls, D. (1999) *Gender, Civic Culture and Consumerism: Middle Class Identity in Britain 1800 to 1940: The British Middle Classes, 1795–1939*. Manchester: Manchester University Press.

Knapp, K. (2011) 'Richard Ford's Frank Bascombe Trilogy and the Post-9/11 Suburban Novel', *American Literary History*, 23(3), pp. 500–28.

Kureishi, H. (1990) *The Buddha of Suburbia*. London: Faber and Faber.

— (1995) *The Black Album*. London: Faber and Faber.

Kutnowski, M. (2008) 'Trope and Irony in *The Simpsons*' Overture', *Popular Music and Society*, 31(5), pp. 599–616.

Lang, R. (1997) '*My Own Private Idaho* and the New Queer Road Movies', in S. Cohan and I. Hark (eds), *The Road Movie Book*. London and New York: Routledge, pp. 330–48.

Latham, R. (1995) 'Subterranean Suburbia: Underneath the Smalltown Myth in the Two Versions of *Invaders from Mars*', *Science-Fiction Studies*, 22(2), pp. 198–208.

Legrain, P. (2011) 'Progressives should Embrace Diversity', in *Exploring the Cultural Challenges to Social Democracy*. London: Policy Network, pp. 37–45, at: http:// policy-network.net/uploads/media/160/7377.pdf.

Lemann, M. (1997) 'The Suburbs Have Won: But in New York, you wouldn't know it' in *Slate magazine*, 7 February, at: www.slate.com/articles/briefing/articles/1997/02/ the_suburbs_have_won.html.

Letts, Q. (2009) 'First night review: Alan Ayckbourn's Season's Greetings', at: www. dailymail.co.uk/tvshowbiz/reviews/article-1337055/First-night-review-Alan-Ayckbo urns-Seasons-Greetings.html#ixzz1IIaAKBQc.

Light, A. (2004) 'Outside History? Stevie Smith, Women Poets and the National Voice', *English*, 43(177), pp. 237–59.

Lippert, B. (1997) 'Goddess at Large', *New York Magazine*, 19 May, pp. 22–3.

Long, C. (2011) 'Running Out of Gas: The Energy Crisis in 1970s Suburban Narratives', *Canadian Review of American Studies*, 41(3), pp. 342–69.

Lott, T. (1996) *The Scent of Dried Roses*. London: Penguin.

— (2004) *The Love Secrets of Don Juan*. London: Penguin.

— (undated) 'Interview with Tim Lott', at: http://readers.penguin.co.uk/nf/shared/ WebDisplay/0,,213768_1_10,00.html.

Loukides, P. and Fuller, L. (1991) *Beyond the Stars: Plot Conventions in American Popular Film*. Ohio: Bowling Green University Popular Press.

Luckett, M. (1999) 'A Moral Crisis in Prime Time: *Peyton Place* and the Rise of the Single Girl', in M. Haralovich and L. Rabinovitz (eds), *Television History and American Culture: Feminist Critical Essays*. Carolina: Duke University Press, pp. 75–97.

Lynn, K. (1995) *Hemingway: His Life and Work*. Cambridge, MA: Harvard University Press.

MacDonald, C. (2010) *Rush, Rock Music and the Middle Class: Dreaming in Middletown*. Bloomington, IN: Indiana University Press.

Madelid, L. (2007) *Roadrunner: Rock Tours in 60s*. London: Premium Publishing.

Malik, S. (2002) *Representing Black Britain: Black and Asian Images on Television*. London: Sage.

— (2007) '"UK is Finished; India's too Corrupt; Anyone Can Become Amrikan": Interrogating Itineraries of Power in *Bend It Like Beckham* and *Bride and Prejudice*', *Journal of Creative Communications*, 2(1&2), pp. 79–100.

Malkani, G. (2006) *Londonstani*. London: Fourth Estate.

Manzoor, S. (2008) *Greetings from Bury Park*. London: Bloomsbury.

Massey, D. (2006) 'London Inside-Out', *Soundings*, (32), pp. 62–71.

Maxey, R. (September 2006) '"Life in the Diaspora is Often Held in a Strange Suspension": First-Generation Self-Fashioning in Hanif Kureishi's Narratives of Home and Return', *The Journal of Commonwealth Literature*, 41(3), pp. 5–25.

McAuley, I. (1993) *Guide to Ethnic London*, 2nd edn. London: Immel.

McCarthy, C. (1998) 'Educating the American Popular: Suburban Resentment and the Representation of the Inner City in Contemporary Film and Television', *Race, Ethnicity and Education*, 1(1), pp. 31–48.

McDonald, C. (2010) *Rush, Rock Music, and the Middle Class: Dreaming in Middletown*. Indiana: Indiana University Press.

McQuail, D. (1972) *Sociology of Mass Communications*. Harmondsworth: Penguin.

McQuail, D., Blumler, J. and Brown, R. (1972) 'The Television Audience: A Revised Perspective', in D. McQuail (ed.), *Sociology of Mass Communication*. London: Longman, pp. 135–65.

McRobbie, A. (2004) 'Post-Feminism and Popular Culture', *Feminist Media Studies*, 4(3), pp. 255–64.

— (2008) 'Postfeminist Passions', *The Guardian*, 25 March, at: www.guardian.co.uk/commentisfree/2008/mar/25/gender.

McRobbie, M. (2009) *The Aftermath of Feminism: Gender, Culture, and Social Change*. London: Sage Publications.

Medved (1992) *Hollywood vs. America: Popular Culture and the War on Traditional Values*. New York: HarperCollins.

Meline, G. (2010) 'The Suburbs' review, 2 August, at: www.metroactive.com/music-clubs/arcade-fire-suburbs.html.

Melly, G. (1970) *Revolt into Style: The Pop Arts in the 50s and 60s*. Oxford: Oxford University Press.

Melville, C. (2004) 'Beats, Rhymes and Grime', *New Humanist*, 119(6), at: http://newhumanist.org.uk/822/beats-rhymes-and-grime.

Merskin, D. (2007) 'Three Faces of Eva: Perpetuation of the Hot-Latina Stereotype in *Desperate Housewives*', *Howard Journal of Communications*, 18(2), pp. 133–51.

Mills, B. (2005) *Television Sitcom*. London: British Film Institute.

Minzesheimer, B. (2009) 'John Updike: His Novels Were "a time capsule" of His Era', *USA Today*, 28 January, at: www.usatoday.com/life/books/news/2009-01-27-updike-obit_N.htm.

Monaco, J. (2000) *How to Read a Film*. Oxford: Oxford University Press.

Moody, R. (1994) *The Ice Storm*. New York: Little Brown & Co.

Moores, S. (2004) 'The Doubling of Place: Electronic Media, Time-Space Arrangements and Social Relationships', in N. Couldry and McCarthy (eds), *Media Space: Place, Scale and Culture in a Media Age*. London: Routledge, pp. 21–37.

Morley, D. (1998) '"So-called Cultural Studies: Dead Ends and Reinvented Wheels"', in Ted Striphas (ed.), *The Institutionalization of Cultural Studies*', *Cultural Studies*, 12(4), pp. 476–97.

Morrison, B. (2012) 'Writing Britain: The Nation and the Landscape', in *The Guardian*, 4 May, at: www.guardian.co.uk/books/2012/may/04/writing-britain-blake-morrison.

Mugan, C. (2006) 'Dubstep: Straight outta Croydon', at: www.independent.co.uk/arts-entertainment/music/features/dubstep-straight-outta-croydon-409487.html.

Mumford, L. (1961/91) *The City in History: Its Origins, its Transformations, and its Prospects*. London: Penguin.

Muzzio, D. and Halper, T. (2002) 'Pleasantville? The Suburb and its Representation in American Movies', *Urban Affairs Review*, 37, pp. 543–74.

Nash, R. (1963) 'Max Shulman and the Changing Image of Suburbia', *Midcontinent American Studies Journal*, 4(1), pp. 27–38.

Nasser, N. (2003) 'The Space of Displacement: The Making of Muslim South Asian Places in Britain', *Traditional Dwellings and Settlements Review* 15(2), pp. 7–21.

— (2004) 'Southall's Kaleido-Scape: A Study in the Changing Morphology of a West London Suburb', *Built Environment*, 3(1), pp. 76–103.

— (2006) 'Metropolitan Borderlands: The Formation of BrAsian Landscapes', in N. Ali, V. Kalra and S. Sayyid (eds), *A Postcolonial People: South Asians in Britain*. London: Hirst, pp. 374–91.

Nasta, S. (2002) *Home Truths: Fictions of the South Asian Diaspora in Britain*. Basingstoke: Palgrave (esp. chapter 5).

Naylor, S. (2002) 'The Mosque in the Suburbs: Negotiating Religion and Ethnicity in South London', *Social & Cultural Geography*, 3(1), pp. 39–59.

New Malden People (2011) Discussion Forum Post by BeckyCreative at: www.newmaldenpeople.co.uk/discussions/New-Malden-lived-shadow-Kingston-Town-Centre-long/discussion-13462934-detail/discussion.html.

Newman, J. (1988) *John Updike*. London: Macmillan.

Newman, K. (1992) 'Wild West', *Empire* at: www.empireonline.com/reviews/
reviewcomplete.asp?FID=16894.

Nieves, E. (1997) 'OUT THERE; Heart of Suburban Darkness? Here? Uh-uh',
30 November, at: www.nytimes.com/1997/11/30/style/out-there-heart-of-suburban-
darkness-here-uh-uh.html.

Norman, P. (2002) *Symphony for the Devil: The Rolling Stones Story*. London: Pan.

— (2004) *Shout! The True Story of the Beatles*. London: Pan.

O'Connell, S. (2006) 'Dubstep', 4 October, at: www.timeout.com/london/music/
features/2083/1.html.

O'Day, M. (2002) 'David Lynch', in Y. Tasker (ed.), *Fifty Contemporary Filmmakers*.
London and New York: Routledge, pp. 244–52.

Oates, J. (2002) *Southall and Hanwell: History & Guide*. Stroud: Tempus.

Offord, P. (2007) 'The Blockheads Return – with a New Kid in tow', *Echo*, 16 November,
at: www.echo-news.co.uk/news/1839165.the_blockheads_return_with_a_new_kid_
in_tow/.

OK (2011) 'US version of *The Inbetweeners* to be made by MTV!', 3 April, at: www.ok.co.
uk/celebrity-news/view/33975/US-version-of-The-Inbetweeners-to-be-made-by-
MTV-/.

Orwell, G. (1935/69) *A Clergyman's Daughter*. Harmondsworth: Penguin.

— (1936/2000) *Keep the Aspidistra Flying*. London: Penguin.

— (1939/75) *Coming Up for Air*. London: Penguin.

— (1941) 'The Lion and the Unicorn', in S. Orwell (ed.), *Collected Essays: My Country
Right or Left (1968)*. London: Secker and Warburg.

Oswell, D. (2000) 'Suburban Tales: Television, Masculinity and Textual Geographies',
in David Bell and Azzedine Haddour (eds), *City Visions*. Harlow: Longman Press,
pp. 73–90.

Panayiotou, A. (2012) 'Deconstructing the Manager: Discourses of Power and
Resistance in Popular Cinema', *Equality, Diversity and Inclusion: An International
Journal,* 31(1), pp. 10–26.

Parekh, B. (2000) *The Future of Multi-Ethnic Britain*. London: Runnymede Trust with
Profile Books.

Parkinson, D. (1998) 'My Son The Fanatic', *Empire*, June, at: www.empireonline.com/
reviews/reviewcomplete.asp?FID=1977.

Parsons, T. (1998) *Bigmouth Strikes Again*. London: André Deutsch Ltd.

Paterson, R. (1987) 'Restyling Masculinity: the Impact of Boys from the Blackstuff', in
Curran, J., Smith, A. and Wingate, P. (eds), *Impacts and Influences: Essays on Media
Power in the Twentieth Century*. London: Routledge, pp. 218–30

Peach, C. (1996) 'Does Britain Have Ghettos?' *Transactions of the Institute of British
Geographers*, 22(1), pp. 216–35.

Peach, C., Brown, J. and Foot, R. (eds) (1994) *Palgrave Migration: The Asian Experience*.
Basingstoke: MacMillan.

Pearson, G. (1976) '"Paki-Bashing" in a North-East Lancashire Cotton Town: A Case Study in Its History', in G. Mungham and G. Pearson (eds), *Working Class Youth Culture*. London: Routledge & Kegan Paul, pp. 48–81.

Penny, L. (2010) 'FarmVille: They Reap What You Sow', *The Guardian*, 19 November, at: www.guardian.co.uk/commentisfree/2010/nov/19/farmville-they-reap-what-you-sow?INTCMP=SRCH.

Perera, S. (1999) *Haven't Stopped Dancing Yet*. London: Spectre.

— (2000) *Bitter Sweet Symphony*. London: Spectre.

— (2002) *Do the Right Thing*. London: Spectre.

Perkins, A. (2007) *A Very British Strike: 3 May–12 May 1926*. London: PanMacmillan.

Perkins, T. (1979) 'Rethinking Stereotypes', in M. Barrett et al. (eds), *Ideology and Cultural Production*. New York: Croom Helm, pp. 139–59.

Perotta, T. (2004) *Little Children*. New York: St Martin's Press.

Pfeil, F. (1995) *White Guys: Studies in Postmodern Domination and Difference*. London and New York: Verso books

Pile, S., Brook, C. and Mooney, C. (eds) (2000) *Unruly Cities: Order/Disorder*. London and New York: Routledge.

Poniewozik, J. (2009) 'How the Simpsons Animate Us', *Time*, 18 June, at: www.time.com/time/specials/packages/article/0,28804,1902809_1902810_1905181,00.html#ixzz20j37hnwo.

— (2011) 'TV Tonight: Suburgatory', *Time*, 28 September, at: http://entertainment.time.com/2011/09/28/tv-tonight-suburgatory/#ixzz2267Nd92d.

Popoff, M. (2004) *Under Pressure: 30 Years of Rush at Home and Away*. Toronto: ECW Press.

Porter, P. (1998) *London: A Social History*. London: Hamish Hamilton.

Potter, C. (2002) *I Love You but . . . Romance, Comedy and the Movies*. London: Methuen.

Priestley, J. B. (1934) *English Journey*. London: Heinemann in association with Gollancz.

Quin, R. (2004) 'Mothers, Molls, and Misogynists: Resisting Italian American Womanhood in *The Sopranos*', *The Journal of American Culture*, 27(2), pp. 166–74.

Rabinovich, D. (2006) 'This is Hendon', *The Guardian* at: www.guardian.co.uk/books/2006/mar/04/featuresreviews.guardianreview20?INTCMP=SRCH.

Rankin, R. (1984) *East of Ealing*. London: Victor Gollancz.

— (1988) *The Sprouts of Wrath*. London: Victor Gollancz.

— (1997) *The Brentford Chainstore Massacre*. London: Victor Gollancz.

— (2003) *The Witches of Chiswick*. London: Victor Gollancz.

— (2009) *Retromancer*. London: Victor Gollancz.

Raphael, A. (2007) 'The Party that has Lasted for 30 Years', *Observer*, 14 October 2010, at: www.guardian.co.uk/media/2007/oct/14/television.bbc.

Rappeport, A. (2006) 'A Real Taste of South Asia? Take the Tube to Southall' in New York Times 29 January 2006, at: http://travel.nytimes.com/2006/01/29/travel/29dayout.html?pagewanted=all&_r=0..

Raynor, J. (1969) *The Middle Class*. Harlow: Longmans.

Redfern, P. (2003) 'A New Look at Gentrification: Gentrification and Domestic Technologies', in D. Clarke, M. Doel and K. Housiaux (eds), *The Consumption Reader*. London: Routledge, pp. 122–6.

Redhead, S. (1990) *The End of the Century Party*. Manchester: Manchester University Press.

Reeves, R. (2007) 'Middle England: They're Nicer than You Think', *New Statesman*, 25 October, at: www.newstatesman.com/politics/2007/10/middle-england-class-social.

Reynolds, S. (1990) *Blissed Out: The Raptures of Rock*. London: Serpent's Tail.

— (2005) *Rip it Up and Start Again: Post Punk 1978–1984*. London: Faber and Faber.

Rhys Jones G. (2006) *Semi-Detached*. London: Michael Joseph.

Richards, K. (2010) *Life*. London: Phoenix.

Riesman, D. (1950/2001) *The Lonely Crowd: A Study of the Changing American Character*, abridged and rev. edn, with a foreword by Todd Gitlin. New York: Yale University Press.

— (1958) 'The Suburban Sadness', in W. Dobriner (ed.), *The Suburban Community*. New York: G.P. Putnam's Sons, pp. 375–408.

Ritzer, G. (1993) *The McDonaldization of Society*. London and New York: Sage.

— (2004) *The Globalization of Nothing*. Thousand Oaks, CA: Sage.

— (2005) 'The Weberian Theory of Rationalization and the McDonaldization of Contemporary Society', in P. Kivisto (ed.), *Illuminating Social Life: Classical and Contemporary Theory Revisited*. Thousand Oaks and Delhi: Pine Forge Press, pp. 38–58.

Robins, D. (1992) *Tarnished Vision: Crime and Conflict in the Inner City*. Oxford: Oxford University Press.

Rogers, R. and Power, A. (2001) *Cities for a Small Country*. London: Faber and Faber.

Rojek, C. (2007) *Brit-Myth: Who Do the British Think They Are?* London: Reaktion.

Román, E. (2000–1) 'Who Exactly is Living "La Vida Loca"?: The Legal and Political Consequences of Latino-Latina Ethnic and Racial Stereotypes in Film and Other Media', *Gender, Race and Justice*, 4, p. 37.

Rowe, K. (1990) 'Roseanne: Unruly Woman as Domestic Goddess', *Screen*, 31, pp. 408–19.

Roy Rosenzweig Center for History and New Media (n.d.) 'Who Was Betty Crocker?', at: http://chnm.gmu.edu/sidelights/who-was-betty-crocker/.

Royle, T. (1982) *Death before Dishonour: The True Story of Fighting*. London: Mainstream.

Royston, J. (2010) 'EDL Cancel Harrow Protest over Halal School Menus Due to "Tommy's Court Case"', at: www.harrowtimes.co.uk/news/8711461.EDL_cancel_Halal_protest_due_to_court_case/.

Russell, B. (1953) *Satan in the Suburbs: And Other Stories*. New York: Simon and Schuster.

Russo, V. (1987) *The Celluloid Closet: Homosexuality in the Movies*. New York: Harper and Row.

Saha, A. (2006) '"Londonstani" by Gautam Malkani; "Tourism" by Nirpal Singh Dahliwal', *darkmatterjournal*, 14 June, at: www.darkmatter101.org/site/2007/06/14/londonstani-by-gautam-malkani-tourism-by-nirpal-singh-dahliwal/.

Sandall, R. (2007) 'The Modfather Returns', *The Sunday Times*, 2 September, at: http://entertainment.timesonline.co.uk/tol/arts_and_Entertainment/music/article2347958.ece.

Sandhu, S. (1999) 'Paradise Syndrome' *London Review of Books*, November, Review of Midnight All Day by Hanif Kureishi at: www.lrb.co.uk/v22/n10/sukhdev-sandhu/paradise-syndrome.

— (2000) 'Paradise Syndrome', *London Review of Books*, 18 May, at: www.lrb.co.uk/v22/n10/sukhdev-sandhu/paradise-syndrome.

— (2003a) 'Come Hungry, Leave Edgy', *London Review of Books*, 9 October, at: www.lrb.co.uk/v25/n19/sukhdev-sandhu/come-hungry-leave-edgy.

— (2003b) *London Calling: How Black and Asian Writers Imagined a City*. London: HarperCollins.

Sanghera, S. (2009) 'Sorry, but Breakfast at Tiffany's is Simply Racist', *Time*, 6 October, at: www.timesonline.co.uk/tol/comment/article6861895.ece.

Sardar, Z. (2008) *Balti Britain: A Provocative Journey through Asian Britain*. London: Granta Books.

Savage, J. (1991) *England's Dreaming: Sex Pistols and Punk Rock*. London: Faber and Faber.

— (1996) *Time Travel from the Sex Pistols to Nirvana: Pop, Media and Sexuality, 1977–96*. London: Chatto and Windus.

Schoene, B (1998) 'Herald of Hybridity: The Emancipation of Difference in Hanif Kureishi's *The Buddha of Suburbia*', *International Journal of Cultural Studies*, 1(1), pp. 111–30.

Scott, J. and Marshall, G. (2005) *A Dictionary of Sociology*. Oxford: Oxford University Press.

Scruton, R. (1998) *An Intelligent Person's Guide to Modern Culture*. Illinois: St Augustine's Press.

Sharp, S. (2006) 'Disciplining the Housewife in and Domestic Reality Television' in K. Akass and J. McCabe (eds), *Reading Desperate Housewives: Beyond the White Picket Fence*. London: IBTauris.

Shriver, L. (2010) 'Beautiful Betty: A Warning from Home-Making History', 10 March, at: www.guardian.co.uk/commentisfree/2010/mar/10/betty-mad-men-feminine-mystique.

Shuker, R. (2003) *Popular Music: The Key Concepts*. London and New York: Routledge.

Shukla, N. (2010) *Coconut Unlimited*. London: Quartet Books.

Shulman, M. (1958) *Rally Round the Flag, Boys!* New York City: Bantam Books.

Silverstone, R. (ed.) (1997) *Visions of Suburbia*. London: Routledge.

Simon, D. (2004) *Tony Soprano's America: The Criminal Side of the American Dream*. New York: Basic Books.

Skegg, M., Hodgkinson, W., Raeside, J. and Dean, W. (2010) 'Watch This', *The Guardian*, 3 February, at: www.guardian.co.uk/tv-and-radio/2010/feb/03/natural-world-horizon-desperate-housewives-mad-men.

Spector, B. (2008) 'The Man in the Gray Flannel Suit in the Executive Suite: American Corporate Movies in the 1950s', *Journal of Management History*, 14(1), pp. 87–104.

Spencer, C. (2012) 'Detroit, National Theatre, Review', 16 May, at: www.telegraph.co.uk/culture/theatre/theatre-reviews/9270776/Detroit-National-Theatre-review.html.

Spigel, L. (2001a) *Welcome to the Dreamhouse: Popular Media and Postwar Suburbs.* California: Duke University Press.

— (2001b) 'Media Homes: Then and Now', *International Journal of Cultural Studies*, 4(4), pp. 385–411.

Stasi, L. (2011) 'Burb's the Word: New Comedy that Finally Understands City Kids' in New York Post 28 September 2011, at: http://www.nypost.com/p/entertainment/tv/burb_the_word_qhWAogkSxiulS3HQ80HMpI.

Stratton, J. and Ang, I. (1994) 'Sylvania Waters and the Spectacular Exploding Family', *Screen*, 35(1), pp. 1–21.

Strickland, C. (1996) 'Can Sitcom Make It with L.I. Setting?' *New York Times*, 1 December, at: www.nytimes.com/1996/12/01/nyregion/can-sitcom-make-it-with-li-setting.html?pagewanted=all&src=pm.

Sugg-Ryan, D. (1997) *The Ideal Home through the 20th Century: Daily Mail Ideal Home Exhibition.* London: Hazar.

— (2000) '"All the world and her husband": The *Daily Mail* Ideal Home Exhibition, 1908–39', in M. Andrews and M. M. Talbot (eds), *All the World and Her Husband: Women in Twentieth-Century Consumer Culture.* London: Cassell, pp. 10–22.

Syal, M. (1996) *Anita and Me.* London: Flamingo.

— (1999) *Life Isn't All Ha Ha Hee Hee.* London: Flamingo.

Tanner, T. (1987) 'A Compromised Environment', in H. Bloom (ed.), *John Updike.* New York: Chelsea House Publishers, pp. 36–56.

Tasker, Y. (ed.) (2002) 'Tim Burton', in *Fifty Contemporary Filmmakers.* London and New York: Routledge, pp. 73–81.

Taylor, P. (2000) 'Which Britain? Which England? Which North?' in D. Morely and K. Robins (eds), *British Cultural Studies.* Oxford: Oxford University Press, pp. 127–44.

Taylor, S. (1938) 'The Suburban Neurosis', *Lancet*, 1, pp. 759–61.

— (1958) 'Suburban Neurosis Up to Date' [leading article], *Lancet*, 1, pp. 146–7.

Tea Party Patriots (2010) 'Blog: "What would our founding fathers think of America today?"' 29 June, at: www.teapartypatriots.org/BlogPostView.aspx?id=507970c7–2346–42f6-adf0-ac85d0469ffe.

Tew, P. (2008) 'Situating the Violence of J. G. Ballard's Postmillennial Fiction: The Possibilities of Sacrifice, the Certainties of Trauma', in J. Baxter (ed.), *J. G. Ballard: Contemporary Critical Perspectives.* London: Continuum, pp. 107–19.

Thomas, L. (1974) *Tropic of Ruislip.* London: Coronet Books.

— (2008) 'Downshifting Narratives in Contemporary Lifestyle Television', *Cultural Studies*, 22(5), pp. 680–99.

Thompson, F. M. L. (1982) *The Rise of Suburbia*. Leicester: Leicester University Press.

Thorns, D. (1973) *Suburbia*. London: Paladin.

Times Online (2007) 'Morrissey Complains that Immigration Has Led to the Loss of Britain's Identity', *Times*, 29 November, at: www.timesonline.co.uk/tol/news/uk/article2967758.ece.

Tinniswood, A. (1999) *Arts and Crafts House*. London: Mitchell Beazley Art & Design.

Updike, J. (1960) *Rabbit, Run*, London: Penguin.

— (1968) *Couples*. London: Penguin.

— (1984) *The Witches of Eastwick*. London and New York: Penguin.

— (1990) *Rabbit at Rest*. London: Penguin.

— (2008) *The Widows of Eastwick*. London and New York: Penguin.

Wagg, S. (1998) *Because I Tell a Joke or Two: Comedy, Politics, and Social Difference*. London: Routledge.

Waldie, D. J. (2004) *Where We Are Now: Notes from Los Angeles*. Santa Monica, CA: Angel City Press.

— (2005) *Holy Land: A Suburban Memoir*. New York and London: Norton.

Waltonen, K. and Du Vernay (2010) *The Simpsons in the Classroom: Embiggening the Learning Experience with the Wisdom of Springfield*. North Carolina: McFarland.

Washburn, K. and Thornton, J. (eds) (1996) *Dumbing Down: Essays on the Strip Mining of American Culture*. New York: Norton.

Waterman, S. and Kosmin, B. (1986) 'Mapping an Unenumerated Population: Jews in London' in *Ethnic and Racial Studies* vol. 9, pp. 484–501

Wazir, B. (1999) 'Champagne is Uncorked as Noel Moves Out of Supernova Heights', *Observer*, 28 November, at: www.guardian.co.uk/uk/1999/nov/28/burhanwazir.theobserver.

Webb, R. (2009) 'Story of the Song: Hong Kong Garden, Siouxsie and the Banshees' (1978), *Independent*, 21 August, at: www.independent.co.uk/arts-entertainment/music/features/story-of-the-song-hong-kong-garden-siouxsie-and-the-banshees-1978-1775005.html.

Webster, R. (ed.) (2001) *Expanding Suburbia: Reviewing Suburban Narratives*. Oxford: Berghahn Books.

Weightman, G. and Humphries, S. (1983) *The Making of Modern London, 1815–1914*. London: Sidgwick & Jackson.

Weller, P. (2007) *Suburban 100*. London: Random House.

Wells, H. G. (1911) *The New Machiavelli*. London: John Lane.

Whelehan, I. (2005) *The Feminist Bestseller: From Sex and the Single Girl to Sex and the City*. Basingstoke: Palgrave Macmillan.

Whyte, W. (1956/2002) *The Organization Man*. London and New York: Simon & Schuster.

Williams, N. (1990) *The Wimbledon Poisoner*. London: Faber and Faber.

Williams, R. (1971) *Orwell*. London: Fontana.

— (1976) *Keywords: A Vocabulary of Culture and Society*. London: Fontana.

— (1977) *Marxism and Literature*. Oxford: Oxford University Press.

Willis, P. (1977) *Learning to Labour: How Working Class Kids Get Working Class Jobs*. Farnborough: Saxon House.

Willmott, P. (1963) *The Evolution of a Community: A study of Dagenham after forty years*. London: Routledge & Kegan Paul.

Willmott, P. and Young, M. (1957) *Family and Kinship in East London*. London: Pelican.

— (1960) *Family and Class in a London Suburb*. London: Routledge and Kegan Paul.

Wilson, S. (1955/2008) *The Man in the Gray Flannel Suit*. London: Penguin.

Winters, J. (2008) 'Inside Out: ASME Celebrates its 125 Years', *Mechanical Engineering: The Magazine of ASME*, at: http://memagazine.asme.org/articles/2005/August/Celebrating_125th_Anniversary.cfm.

Wood, J. (2010) 'The Kids are Alright', *Saturday Guardian*, 30 May 2009.

Wood, Robert C. (March 1958) 'Metropolitan Government, 1975: An Extrapolation of Trends the New Metropolis: Green Belts, Grass Roots or Gargantua?' *The American Political Science Review*, 52(1), pp. 108–22.

Woolaston, S. (2006) 'Keeping Up with Liz Jones', *The Guardian*, 25 March, at: www.guardian.co.uk/books/2006/mar/25/fiction.features.

Wynn, N. (2004) 'Counselling the Mafia: *The Sopranos*', *Journal of American Studies*, 38, pp. 127–32.

Yates, R. (1961) *Revolutionary Road*. New York: Vintage Books.

Young, H. (2008) 'Hugo Young: 1938–2003: "Inside Track"', *The Guardian,* 15 November, at: www.guardian.co.uk/books/2008/nov/15/politics-the-hugo-young-papers.

Your Local Guardian series (2010) 'Croydon Rite of Passage for Malcolm McLaren', 14 April, at: www.yourlocalguardian.co.uk/news/8097586.Croydon_rite_of_passage_for_Malcolm_McLaren/.

Zuberi, N. (2001) *Sounds English: Transnational Popular Music*. Urbana, IL: University of Illinois Press.

Index